THE MILITANT VEGAN

FOR THE TOTAL DESTRUCTION OF ALL ANIMAL ABUSE INDUSTRIES

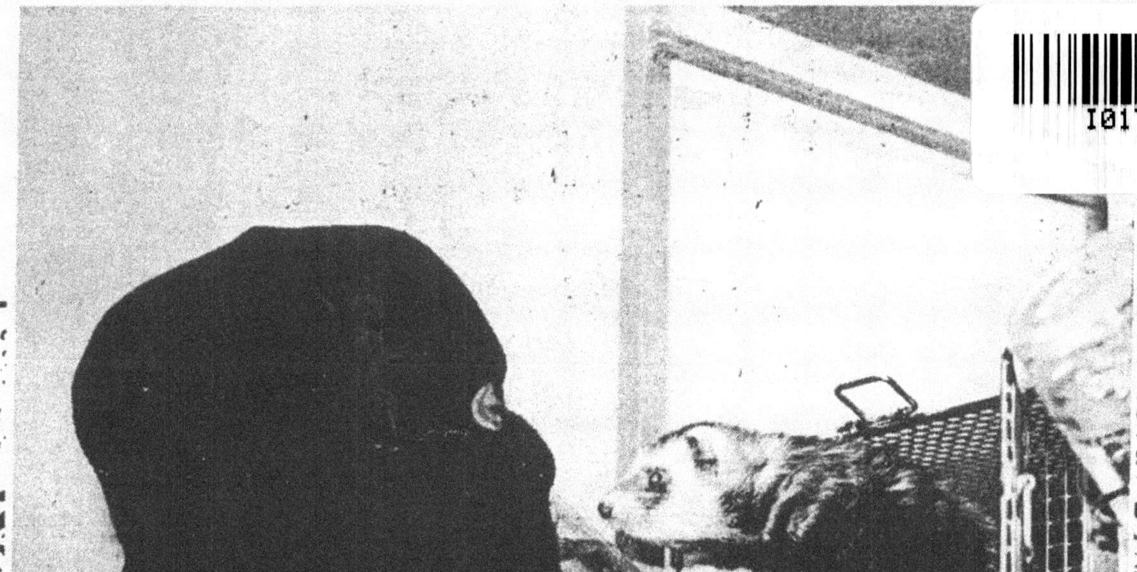

IN THIS ISSUE:

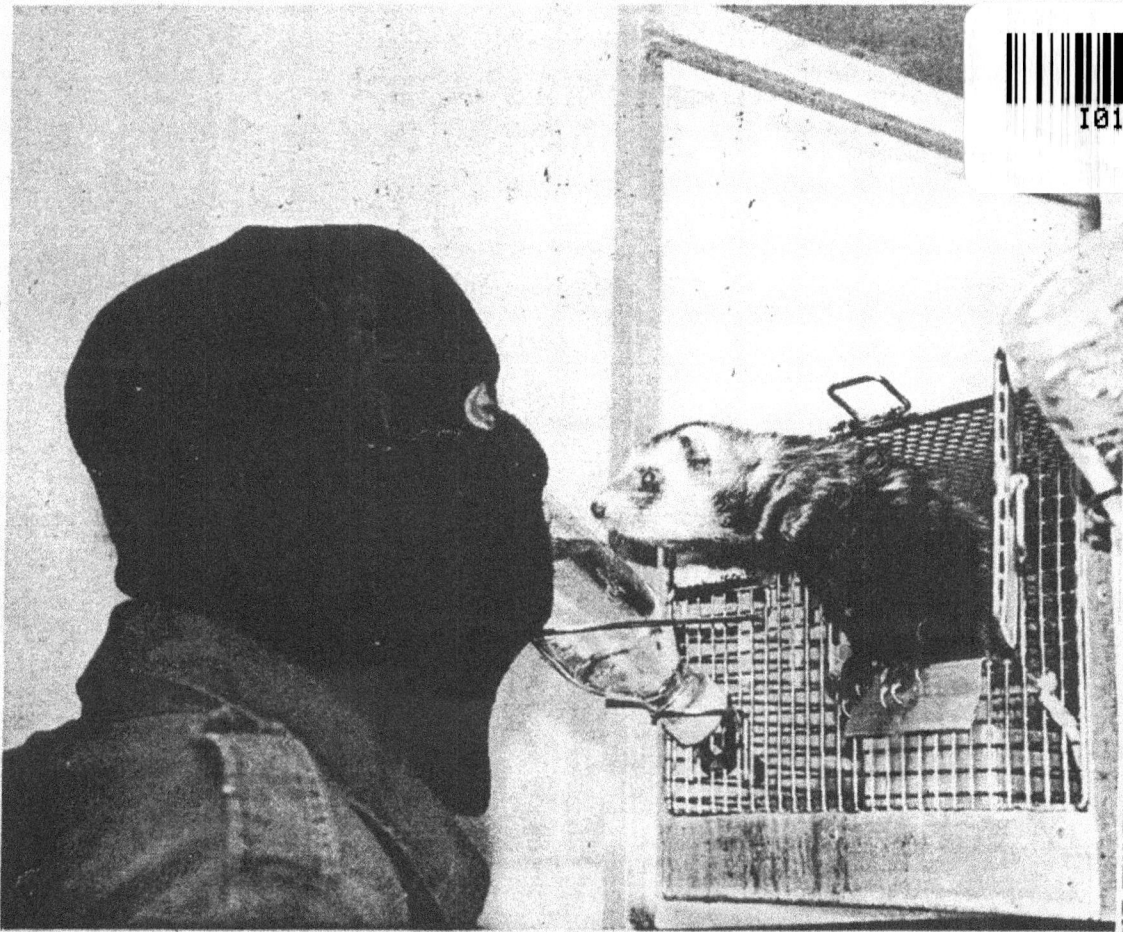

- LATEST ALF RAIDS!
- EXCERPTS FROM "THE ALF PRIMER" AND "WITHOUT A TRACE!"
- AND MORE!

THE MILITANT VEGAN-1993 #1

The Militant Vegan is being released because there has been a media blackout in the U.S. on direct action on behalf of enslaved animals. We hope to spread the news of recent ALF activities and to increase support for the vegan prisoners in North America.

In addition, we are including most of The ALF Primer and Without A Trace, along with a page from Ecodefense.

Please notice the articles on Johnathan Paul and Darren Thurston, and do what you can to support them!

IMPORTANT! The Militant Vegan is not a "Hardline" zine, and we stand in total opposition to their patriarchal and heterosexist politics.

Addresses: Mail news clippings of ALF attacks to: Profane Existence/ Box 8722/Minneapolis, MN 55408 and Earth First! Journal/ Box 5176/ Missoula, MT 59806
The only ALF Support Group in North America is at Box 75029, Ritchie Stn./Edmonton, Alberta/ T6E 6K1 Canada.

If you are new to the ideas of veganism, write PETA at Box 42516/ Washington, DC 20015 for recipes, nutrition and other information. Two helpful books are Animal Liberation by Peter Singer, and Diet for a New America by John Robbins.

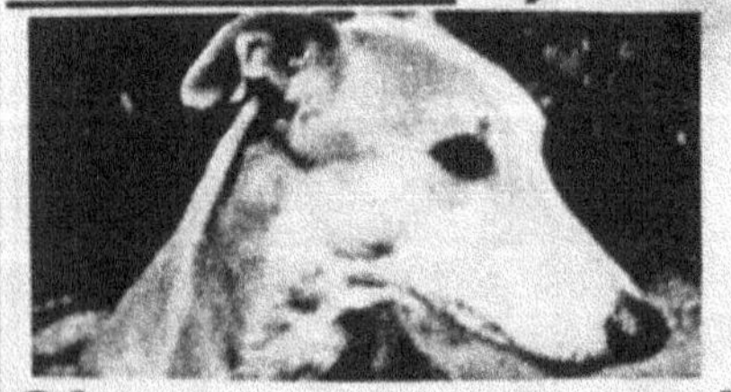

Since we are not printing an address, we encourage and beg you to reproduce this magazine! Let's get this information distributed to vegans across North America!

The Animal Liberation Front consists of small autonomous groups of people all over the world who carry out direct action according to the ALF guidelines. You cannot become a member of - or an ALF activists - by joining or writing to any ALF Support Group, which are completely separate organizations.

Any group of people who are vegetarians or vegans and who carry our actions according to ALF guidelines have the right to regard themselves as part of the ALF.

Disclaimer: This publication is produced for informational purposes only! We do not intend to encourage crime!

The Militant Vegan

All Eight Issues
1993-1995

The Militant Vegan was a low-production-value, limited-circulation, photocopied publication that never enjoyed much of an audience outside the vegan straight edge Hardcore scene of the mid-1990s (although music scene references were entirely absent, its origins and target demographic were clear). While I expect few will see the historical value of this collection, I have a reverance for *The Militant Vegan* as my early window into the world of direct action and the ALF.

Try to imagine the historical context from which *The Militant Vegan* arose: The Animal Liberation Front had carried out its most strategic campaign to date, targeting weak points in the fur industry in a multi-state liberation and arson spree called Operation Bite Back. The media was nearly silent. There was no internet, so activists outside the small media markets where these raids happened were unaware this campaign was underway, and some of the raids weren't reported by the media at all. The Animal Liberation Front (again, pre-internet) had little-to-no platforms to which they could disseminate their communiques, rally the movement to join them in taking action, or let the world know of their victories.

It was from this void *The Militant Vegan* emerged. To quote issue #1, *"The Militant Vegan is being released because there has been a media blackout on direct action on behalf of enslaved animals."*

Before the internet, animal liberation news could only be spread through photocopied documents like *The Militant Vegan*, distributed person-to-person, and seen by few. Reading *The Militant Vegan* was like a window to a secret history you watched unfold in its pages.

I sent for my first copy after a review in *Maximum Rock N Roll* (the long-running punk fanzine). Some time later, *The Militant Vegan #5* arrived in the mail. I approached it as a curious and supportive voyeur (I wouldn't become vegan until several months later, or carry out any direct action for another year beyond that).

In the summer of 1994, while I had yet to throw myself into the frontlines of the animal liberation movement, I remember reading issue #5 and having the sense that the vegan revolution was actually underway.

Issue #1 was published just as Operation Bite Back ended, and as the net was closing in on one of its architects, Rod Coronado. Among other ALF activity, these issues document the unfolding of that investigation and Rod Coronado's flight (and eventual arrest).

While dominated by re-purposed material (such as ALF primers and newspaper clippings), there is some notable content, ALF history, and other direct-action themed rarities contained in these pages. Some of it I have never seen elsewhere. *The Militant Vegan* published some of the first publicized fur farm addresses - several of which would go on to be raided by activists. A communiqué for the Malecky Mink Farm arson (also part of Operation Bite Back) is a rare piece of ALF history. And even the grainy newspaper article reprints can't be downplayed, in a time when to not live in an area where an ALF action had occurred was to never know it happened at all - were it not for *The Militant Vegan.*

Word of ALF actions were almost impossible to come by in this period, and *The Militant Vegan* offered impact just in revealing the work of these anonymous activists (even news of a broken window offered inspiration to this 17 year old, who had yet to meet another vegan).

Appropriately, the final issue concludes with the closing of one chapter in the story that *The Militant Vegan* opened with: the arrest of Rod Coronado, and a letter from him written in jail.

To the anonymous editors—whoever you are—you had an impact. And this book preserves the history that may have been lost had *The Militant Vegan* never existed.

-Peter Young

This compilation first published in the United States in 2020.

ISBN 978-1-7327096-7-6

Also published by Warcry:

Flaming Arrows: Collected Writings of Animal Liberation Front Activist Rod Coronado (Rod Coronado)

From Dusk 'til Dawn: An Insider's View of the Growth of the Animal Liberation Movement (Keith Mann)

Underground. The Animal Liberation Front in the 1990s

Liberate: Stories & Lessons On Animal Liberation Above The Law (Peter Young)

DIARY OF ACTIONS

EVERY DAY OF THE YEAR, WOMEN AND MEN OF THE ANIMAL LIBERATION FRONT DIRECTLY INTERVENE TO STOP ANIMAL SUFFERING, AT THE RISK OF LOSING THEIR OWN FREEDOM. ACTIONS OCCUR ACROSS THE WORLD FROM ITALY TO AUSTRIA TO CANADA TO SWEDEN. BELOW ARE SOME ACCOUNTS OF RECENT ACTIONS:

CANADA

1991

Mar. -Edmonton AB; J. Rose a store that sells furs has their mural and wall painted, locks glued and windows smashed.
-Edmonton AB; Darek's Furs had their windows smashed.

Feb. - Edmonton AB; The ALF paid a visit to the house of a vivisector from the University of Alberta who has been killing dogs for over 11 years. They painted his house and two cars, slashed all the tires, and smashed two front windows of his house.

June -Edmonton AB; Derose Bros. Meats had their shop painted with slogans and two trucks were spray painted, daubed with paint stripper, and had their windshields sprayed with etching fluid $2000 damage.

Aug.20 -Edmonton AB; Two trucks belonging to DeRose Bros. Meats were spray painted and one set on fire. $17,000 damage.

Sept. -Edmonton AB; Paris Furs had SCUM daubed on their front window with etching fluid. They have since installed a video security camera monitering their front window.

Nov. -Edmonton AB; Queen City Meats spraypainted with slogans, a Kentucky Fried Chicken had their locks glued.
-Edmonton AB; Hurtig Furs shop in Edmonton Centre shopping mall had 4 windows daubed with etching fluid.
-Darek's Furs had windows daubed with etching fluid.

Dec. -Edmonton AB; Three Fur Council of Canada billboards, were paint bombed.

Dec.14 -Edmonton AB; Three delivery trucks of Billingsgate Fish Company were spraypainted, had their tires slashed and set ablaze . The building was also painted with slogans and a sign damaged with paint bombs. A fourth device failed to ignite in another truck. $100,000 damage

Dec.30 -Edmonton AB; Activists set ablaze a truck belonging to Hook Advertising and spraypainted others with slogans, $10,000 damage. Hook signs carried ads from the Fur Council of Canada earlier this month.

UNITED STATES

91

. 1 -Chicago IL; Cook County Hospital's Hektoen Laboratory was raided. Liberating 11 rabbits and 10 guinea pigs. They also gave 20 baboons dried fruit and banana's.

ne 10 -Corvallis OR; Oregon State University's Experimental Fur Farm was broken into, where activists destroyed equipment and data base, and set fire to a storage shed. $62,000 damage.

e 15 -Edmonds WA; the ALF planted incendiary devices in Northwest Fur Foods Cooperative. The cooperative is a major supplier of foods for Northwestern fur farms including OSU Experimintal Fur Farm. The resulting fire caused $800,000 damage.

g. 13 -WA; Seven coyotes released, 6 mink and 10 mice liberated and $50,000 in damage done to two laboratories. (no more details available at press time)

c.21 -Yamhill OR; An incendiary device was set that destroyed the processing plant at the Malecky Mink Ranch.

92

n.1 -Edmonton AB; Ouellette Packing Plant was spraypainted and had paint bombs thrown at it. Their van was spraypainted, tires slashed, and set ablaze.

n.3 -AB; Animal Rights Militia claims to have poisoned 87 Canadian Cold Buster Chocolate bars in Calgary and Edmonton because of the University of Alberta vivisector Larry Wang's 16 years of animal experiments that led to the invention of the bar.

.4-7 -Calgary AB;Saks Furs had windows smashed, Rupps Meats had windows smashed and spraypainted, 3 Kentucky Fried Chicken shops spraypainted, 1 fur shop on 17th ave. had windows etched, 1 fur shop on 4th st. had windows etched, one fish shop had windows etched and spraypainted, 1 fur shop had windows smashed, and a butcher on McLeod Trail spraypainted.

Jan.8 -Edmonton AB; A delivery truck of Ouellette Packers had it's tires slashed.

Jan.9 -Edmonton AB; Billingsgate Fish had all three of their replacement delivery trucks spraypainted and tires slashed (18 tires).

Feb. 7 -Calgary AB; Fur stores were damaged

June 1 Edmonton AB-29 cats liberated from the University of Alberta. Research documents taken and equipment destroyed.

U.S. 1992-Known Actions
January 13-Walnut Creek, CA-"Corrosive chemical " thrown on the windows of a fur store.

February 28-Lansing, Michigan-$100,000 damage done to Michigan State's mink research program. Documents were taken, and vivisectors' offices were burned.

June-Memphis, Tennessee-fur stores were attacked with painted slogans and smashed windows.

South Carolina-"A new group called the Vegan Front trashed a fur store."

July 7-Chicago, IL-An attempt was made to burn fur billboards with molotov cocktails. One sign was partially burned.

August 9-Memphis, TN-3 "hardliners" arrested while vandalizing a fur store.

October-Minneapolis, MN-Swanson's meats had windows of delivery trucks smashed and slogans were painted.

October 24-Milville, Utah-Animal Damage Control lab burned and 29 coyotes freed.
-Logan, UT-Documents taken and a vivisector's office was burned. Total damage: $100,000.

November 8-Minneapolis, MN-5 trucks at Swanson's Meats were burned and the locks to the building were glued. Damage estimated at $100,000.

"RESEARCHER" UNDER ATTACK...

AND FOR GOOD REASON

SUPPORT NEEDED FOR ANIMAL LIB ACTIVIST

In the early morning hours of June 1, 1992, twenty-nine cats were rescued from a fate filled with pain - neurological experiments. The cats were liberated from a kennel belonging to the University of Alberta in Edmonton. The Animal Liberation Front claimed responsibility for the action, which caused over $50,000 in damages to offices and labs.

In the late evening hours of June 19, armed men raided the home of Darren Thurston and arrested him for break, enter, ... theft over $1000, and mischief over $1000. Confiscated were all his clothes, books, files, computer and computer disks. Several days later RCMP pulled Grant Horwood off a bus and charged him in the same incident. Grant was given bail at $4000 cash, ordered to live with his mother in Calgary, and not to associate with anyone involved in animal rights. Darren has been denied bail three times now. Police have also issued a Canada-wide warrant for the arrest of another "suspect" - an activist living in BC.

Among Darren's files taken by police were all those relating to the ALF Support Group and its publication COMBAT. In a move similar to the arrest of ALF members in Toronto in 1987, the police have charged Darren with almost every ALF action that took place in Edmonton over the past year. His files contained press releases and communiques mailed to the Support Group from ALF cells claiming responsibility for various actions. It seems that, to the police, possession of these documents warrants charges.

To date, Darren has been charged with the following (in addition to the three U of A charges): Arson, in connection with a firebombing of three trucks belonging to Billingsgate Fish Co.; Mischief over $1000, in connection to another attack on Billingsgate where 18 tires were slashed; Three counts of mischief over $1000, in connection to the paint-bombing of Fur Council of Canada billboards; Break, enter, and arson, in connection with an incident where a Hook Outdoor Advertising boom truck was burned, and; Attempted arson and mischief, in connection to an attempt to burn an Ouellette (egg) Packers van.

It is typical of police to lay on the charges in the beginning so as to have an advantage in plea bargaining. At this point we are unaware of any physical evidence in regard to any of the charges Darren and Grant face. The only clue comes from an Edmonton Journal article (June 23) which states, "A picture sent to the Journal - showing two people holding cats - led police to a local hotel room and, eventually, to the suspects."

When the Preliminary Hearing comes up Oct. 26, Darren will have been in jail for more than four months. He is surviving off of overcooked and nutritionless vegetables, a vegan diet being just a fantasy in jail. With the ALF Support Group no longer functioning, there is virtually no support or community in Edmonton to support him. What is needed now most are letters of support, which would surely brighten up his day.

Subpoenaed by the feds

- Ingrid Newkirk, a founder of People for the Ethical Treatment of Animals and recent author of "Free the Animals" a controversial book on the founder of the U.S. arm of the ALF.
- Alex Pacheco, co-founder of People for the Ethical Treatment of Animals. The organization often speaks for the ALF following raids.
- Amy Bertsch and Steven Simmons, public relations officials with PETA.
- Gary Beverstock, a sanctuary manager for PETA.
- Deb Stout, a Montana environmentalist who writes appeals of federal predator control efforts. Stout's parents and brother have also been summoned to appear before the Michigan grand jury.
- Patricia Halleran, a single mother in Oregon who was an organizer with the Oregon Hunt Saboteurs. The Hunt Saboteurs shared a post office box with the Coalition Against Fur Farms. The coalition was founded in part by Rod Coronado, key suspect in the ALF raids.
- Mark Dey, also of the Oregon Hunt Saboteurs.
- About a half-dozen other people who have asked not to be named or who could not be contacted. Some say they have

WHAT YOU CAN DO TO HELP:

1. **Send letters of support to:**
   Jonathan Paul
   Spokane County Jail
   1100 W. Mallon
   Spokane, WA 99260
2. **Send letters to the judge:**
   Judge Nielsen
   US District Court
   920 W. Riverside
   Spokane, WA 99201
3. **Send letters to the editor:**
   Moscow-Pullman Daily News
   107 S. Grand
   Pullman, WA 99163

   The Spokesman-Review
   W. 999 Riverside
   Spokane, WA 99201
4. **Send money to help cover expenses**
   (make checks payable to
   Activist Support Group/OTF):
   Activist Support Group
   P.O. Box 13765
   Portland, OR 97213
5. **Don't cooperate**
   with the F.B.I. or federal investigations
6. **Send letters of support**
   to a Canadian activist in jail facing many charges relating to ALF activities:
   Darren Thurston
   Edmonton Remand Centre
   9660 - 104 Ave.
   Edmonton, Alberta,
   T5H 4B5 Canada

More information about Darren is available from:
ALF Support Group Canada
P.O.Box 75029, Ritchie Stn.
Edmonton, Alberta
T6E 6K1 Canada

STOP GRAND JURY WITCH HUNTS!

FREE JONATHAN PAUL!

FOR IMMEDIATE RELEASE
NOV. 21, 1992

[redacted]

SUPPORT NEEDED FOR JAILED ENVIRONMENTAL/ ANIMAL LIBERATION ACTIVIST

Dear friends,

On Nov. 3, 1992 Jonathan Paul was jailed by a federal judge for refusing to testify at a secretive grand jury in Spokane, Wash. The grand jury is "investigating" the successful activities of the Animal Liberation Front and is one of several which has been subpoenaing witnesses in Washington, Oregon, and Michigan states.

Jonathan Paul, an environmental/animal liberation activist, invoked his Fifth Amendment rights when he was asked questions about other activists at the hearing. A federal judge then granted him immunity from self-incrimination - a tactic to "encourage" witnesses to talk. When Jonathan maintained his right to remain silent he was cited for contempt of court and jailed. He will remain in jail until the judge decides to release him, or until this particular grand jury is over in Dec. of 1993.

Before being led away Jonathan stated, "I will not feed information to this government that wants to destroy political movements."

The grand jury process has been used extensively by the U.S. government since at least the 1960's to harass and impede political movements it disagrees with. The targets in the 60's were the civil rights and anti-war movements and the Black Panthers; in the 70's it was the feminist, Puerto Rican independence, and the American Indian movements; in the 80's it was the Central American Sanctuary movement; and this decade it's the radical environmental and animal liberation movements.

Government disruption has ranged from overt violence to covert disruption and disinformation to legal harassment. Grand juries specifically have been employed to force activists to spend time, money, and energy defending themselves. These investigations have also served to create divisions between those who will "cooperate" and those who won't, as well as to spread fear and intimidation.

Jonathan Paul, one of the founders of the Hunt Saboteurs in California, is not unfamiliar with government harassment over ALF activities. Several years ago he was charged along with two others in connection with the University of Oregon lab raid in 1986. Charges were eventually dropped when the government could not produce evidence to proceed to trial, but only after thousands of dollars were spent on lawyers fees and time and energy was wasted dealing with the legal system.

-

The fact that you can be sent to jail for refusing to testify at a grand jury for as long as 18 months is an incredible abuse of the judicial system. The grand jury is nothing more than a huge fishing expedition which the government uses when it has little or no evidence to pin a "crime" on.

We must demand, ultimately, the abolishment of the grand jury process, and immediately, we must demand that Jonathan Paul be set free, for he is guilty of nothing more than sticking to his constitutional rights. On December 1, 1992 the grand jury reconvenes in Spokane, and Jonathan will be called back to court to be asked again to testify. We can voice our demand to have Jonathan freed by demonstrating in front of the courthouse on that day. Join us there or protest outside a federal building in your own city.

Animal liberation group trashes kennel, takes cats

No arrests made

andals claiming to be from the nal Liberation Front trashed a versity of Alberta kennel for and cats used in medical re- ch Monday and stole 29 cats.

he 4 a.m. break-in appeared to been carefully planned by le who were familiar with the ted facility, says Dr. David director of the Health Sci- s Laboratory Services section h operates the kennel.

ere was no sign of forcible at the site on 127th Street of Ellerslie Road, he said.

employee sleeping in a house metres away heard nothing. ugh the kennel holds about 50 which usually bark and howl angers.

ick red paint was splashed on and windows, drug vials were hed, equipment was wrecked, lay in pools of water from taps urned on and bags of animal ing were ripped open and ered.

gans such as "ALF" and edom" were spray-painted on walls, and "Happy Environ- Week" was sprayed on the of the trashed main office.

ey wreaked (a) considerable nt of vandalism. That's an act rrorism, it's not an act of ing," said Neil.

s calculated to try and strike nto the research community at they will move away from e of animals."

nage was estimated at up to 0.

cab and box of a truck used nsport animals were blistered paint thinner, while an nity was sprayed-painted on erior wall.

envelope later left in an *Ed- n Journal* mail slot contained ss release headed "Animal ation Front Celebrates onment Week With Cat Lib- n."

that was enclosed included of two masked people each g a cat.

press release was printed on ery taken from Laboratory l Services and claims the ere to be involved in "useless inful experiments."

day's liberation and econom- age are part of our on-going gn against all animal tortur- uch will end only when the imal is free and the last lab ed to the ground."

one of the researchers who with the cats says they are d for a variety of purposes, ng neurological experiments.

ng these experiments, the s are anesthetized so they eel pain, says the researcher, sked not to be named to arassment.

n the experiment is finished, s are killed with an overdose thetic, the researcher said.

cats apparently too wild to were left in the community om which the others were said Neil. None of the 50 the kennel was taken.

stickers have previously lastered in university labs. s is the first time that facili- e been damaged, Neil said.

U of A recently opened a re- animal care centre on the ampus with improved hold- ilities and tight security, in- video cameras, motion sen- d special locks, he said.

rity at the Ellerslie kennel inimal. Neither the main or the kennel gate was and employees found two of entrance doors unlocked. people have keys for the g.

als had decided additional ions would be too difficult stly, says Neil. That will now nsidered.

"I regret to say that I was once a researcher myself.

"I know how these animals are treated and I don't think the life of a human being is worth that.

"I find the idea of experimenting on animals so a few drug companies can make more money absolutely repugnant."

"DAMN RIGHT!"

Staff relied on the dogs in the kennel to bark and wake them in a nearby house if strangers approached. But they were unaware of the Monday incident until three hours after it happened.

"THE DOGS COOPERATED!"

"I don't know the circumstances of this particular situation, but if the animals were being used in biomedical research then direct action may certainly have been called for," said Roger Mugford of the Animal Behavior Centre in London, England.

"YEP"

The break-in by people claiming to be Animal Liberation Front members has shaken the university community, said another professor who did not want to be named because of fear of being victimized.

"This isn't new. We've always been nervous about it and now they've started at a different level.

"We just don't want it to escalate."

Although the group is supposedly relatively harmless, "we've had death threats against people and we've had people move on that basis.

"The RCMP has all of that," he said.

A rock was hurled through the window of another professor's home and the slogan "ALF" was spray-painted on his garage.

"ALF TACTICS WORK!"

Security at the kennel on 127th Street north of Ellerslie Road will be improved, said Dr. David Neil, director of Health Sciences Laboratory Animal Services.

An alarm system, better locks and more secure doors may be installed.

"WATCH OUT!"

The militant animal rights group is on the FBI's list of the 10 most dangerous domestic terrorist organizations, says a recent report by the U.S. Congress on worldwide terrorism.

The ALF was responsible for 44 bombings and 422 violent incidents in the United Kingdom in 1989, and it also has operations in Canada and the U.S., says a recent article in the scientific journal Science.

"THE FBI HAS A RIGHT TO BE SCARED!"

"They took some of the cats in an arbitrary way and then they wreaked a considerable amount of vandalism," he said. "That's an act of terrorism, it's not an act of rescuing. It's calculated to try to strike fear into the research community so that they will move away from the use of animals."

"CORRECT!"

Health Sciences Laboratory Animal Services
University of Alberta
Edmonton

ANIMAL LIBERATION
HUMAN LIBERATION

Most experiments 'immoral'

NEWS RELEASE
June 1, 1992
For Immediate Release

ANIMAL LIBERATION FRONT CELEBRATES ENVIRONMENT WEEK WITH CAT LIBERATION

The Animal Liberation Front claims responsibility for a raid early this morning at the University of Alberta's Ellerslie Research Station, 127 St. and 9 Ave. SW. We have liberated a total of 29 cats from this animal prison farm, removed research documents, and destroyed research equipment and records.

The cats were to be used in useless and painful experiments in research labs throughout the U. of A. The ALF believes that humans do not have any rights to inflict pain and suffering on any other species. The cats, most of whom were former pets, have been given veterinary examinations and will be placed in homes of caring people. We are saddened to have left behind hundreds of animals including more cats, many dogs, goats, sheep, mice, rats, deer, pigs, and elk.

Documents show that approx. 80,000 animals are vivisected each year by the U. of A. Experiments university researchers inflict on animals include sensory deprivation, sleep deprivation, exposure to disease, toxic substances and radiation, among the endless horrors.

The black and white film we've sent to the Edmonton Sun and the Edmonton Journal shows the actual liberation in progress. It also shows, along with the video we sent to the CBC and CTV affiliate, the cats safely in the arms of their liberators.

All animals have an inherent right to live their lives free from human interference. Today's liberation and economic damage are part of our ongoing campaign against all animal torturers which will end only when the last animal is free and the last lab is burnt to the ground.

The Animal Liberation Front urges everyone to join us in celebrating Environment Week by liberating our four-legged brothers and sisters from their wretched prisons.

Animal Liberation Front

Chicago

Firebombs removed from rail overpass

Twenty-one "improvised Molotov cocktails" were found hanging Wednesday morning from a railroad overpass at Foster Avenue, police said.

Police speculated they were the work of animal-rights activists who objected to advertisements on the overpass for a nearby fur store.

Police had to block traffic on Foster and Ravenswood Avenues near the overpass as well as trains on the Chicago & North Western North line for more than an hour while the devices were removed and rendered harmless, said Cmdr. Joseph Grubisic of the bomb and arson unit.

He said only one of the devices, all made from peanut butter jars, had completely ignited, and it caused minor damage to a sign for Keim Fur Shop, 1820 W. Foster Ave.

"I think they were looking to destroy the signs, but it was very dangerous," Grubisic said. "What if somebody walks by and burning gasoline falls on them? What if a woman is walking by with a baby in a stroller?"

Chicago Tribune, 7-8-92

Sixteen years of so-called "research" on animals by the University of Alberta's Dr. Larry Wang led to the developement of the Canadian Cold Buster Chocolate Bar, A candy snack that, supposedly, prevents hypothermia. One letter from the Animal Rights Militia nearly led to it's demise.

The poisoning hoax launched by the ARM against the Cold Buster bar would have come straight out the text book, if there were one.

On Jan. 2nd several major Albertan newspapers and TV stations received a communique from the ARM, claiming they had contaminated 87 Cold Buster bars with oven cleaning fluid and returned them to store shelves for public consumption. Included with the communiques were samples of the contaminated bars.

ALF BACK ON THE ATTACK

On November 8 five trucks owned by a Minneapolis meatpacker were firebombed and spraypainted with slogans like "Meat is Murder" and "ALF". The meatpacking buildings' locks were also glued. The owner of Swanson Meats (2700 26th Ave. S. Mann) estimated the total damage at about $100,000.

A month earlier, the windshields of all of Swanson's trucks were smashed and painted with animal liberation slogans. The owner had the trucks moved to to a site closer to 26th Avenue after that, where a cab driver reported them burning at about 3:30 that Sunday morning.

Fortunately, the pigs have no leads on the case as of our going to press. The response from the media and liberal animal rights groups such as ARC (Animal Rights Coalition) has been typical: complete condemnation of the act and labelling it "terrorist." If they're going react predictably, then let us be typical in our response, also: We say "right on!" to anyone who sabotages the property of capitalists who brutally oppress other beings, whether those beings are exploited workers or cows and pigs. Support the ALF, and turn the volume up!

— shamelessly lifted from the Strib

WALNUT CREEK

Vandals hit fur shop

Vandals threw a corrosive chemical on the windows of a fur shop over the weekend, which the shop owner contends is the latest in a string of attacks by animal rights activists.

"I don't see it as a coincidence that this happened just after their benefit," said owner Wayne Meyers, referring to Friday night's fundraising event for the Contra Costa Animal Rescue Foundation.

Meyers, who sells mink, fox and rabbit fur coats, said animal rights activists have threatened him numerous times and picketed his store. Vandals have stuck burning cherry bombs to the store windows, causing an undetermined amount of damage, he said. Police said the fur store has experienced more than its share of vandalism, but had no evidence linking the incident to animal rights groups.

By Tribune staff and news services

Food product yanked after poisoning threat

Stores in the Alberta cities of Edmonton and Calgary pulled a new energy bar from their shelves Friday after a previously unknown animal rights group claimed it had injected the product with liquid oven cleaner. Edmonton police spokesman Kelly Gordon said it was too early to say if the claim was true. But police were advising people not to eat the product, Canadian Cold Buster, which has been on the market about a month. In a letter received Friday by the Canadian Press news agency and the Edmonton Journal, the Animal Rights Militia claimed it had injected 87 bars in stores in Edmonton and Calgary with one-fifth of a teaspoon of liquid oven cleaner.

In the early morning of Sunday, December 15/91, ALF activists descended on the premise's of Billingsgate Fish Market in Edmonton, Alberta. The team quickly went to work spraypainting the building and throwing paint bombs at it, slashing tires of the four trucks and spraypainting them. They then placed timed incendiary device's in each of the trucks. Some time later the devices ignighted engulfing three of the trucks in flames, destroying them completely ($100,000 damage). The last device in the fourth and largest truck failed to ignite.

Billingsgate

Bryan Fairbank, owner of Billingsgate Fish Company, and his wife Zlably survey the fire damage to three of the company's trucks Sunday

Bruce Edwards, The Journal

ANIMAL LIBERATION FRONT GUIDELINES:

The Animal Liberation Front carries out direct action against animal abuse in the form of rescuing animals and causing financial loss to animal exploiter's, usually through the damage and destruction of property. Their short term aim is to save as many animals as possible and directly disrupt the practice of animal abuse. Their long term aim is to end all animal suffering by forcing animal abuse companies and individuals out of buisiness. It is a non-violent campaign, activists taking precautions not to harm any animal(human or otherwise). Because ALF actions are against the law activists work anonymously, either in small groups or individually, and do not have a central contact address or any centralised organization or coordination.

ALF RAIDS MINK LAB

The following is a statement from the **Animal Liberation Front (ALF)**: "Early on the morning of February 28, 1992, the Great Lakes Unit of the Animal Liberation Front (ALF) struck Michigan State University's experimental fur farm in East Lansing. Minks were in cramped cages, and foxes and otters were seen on the premises, held in equally poor condition. Gas chambers used to kill minks at the poultry research were damaged. The office of head researcher Richard Aulerich at Anthony Hall was also raided, and records detailing abuse against experimental subjects were confiscated. Key chains made from the minks' severed paws were found in the office of the mink research department.

"This action is in retaliation against the torture and slaughter of native Michigan wildlife by Aulerich and his associates. Minks are born to be wild, not to be research tools in ten-inch cages. Over the past seven years, the minks of Michigan have been held captive and subjected to attempted domestication to provide fur. [See photo below.]

"As a pioneer in the field of mink research, Aulerich has helped fur farmers in America exploit and execute millions of animals with regard to neither their ecological importance or their psychological well-being. He has served as the fur farm industry's problem-solver when it comes to tragedies resulting from the intensive confinement of free-roaming predators.

"It is obvious that MSU is being used by this special interest group as a research center that satisfies the monetary greed for people who exploit wildlife for fur. As a recipient of tens of thousands of dollars from the Mink Farmers Research Foundation and the USDA, Aulerich uses the facilities of MSU to further his own career status and the financial well-being of a socially unacceptable industry. (Now as the American fur farm industry declines—600 farms, USDA figures, 1991—Aulerich must search for new industries to support his dirty work, His very career depends on it.) But the animals aren't the only victims. The taxpayers and students are pawns in the game of industry-supported institutions and institution-supported industry.

"In research papers taken, Aulerich states that wild minks, as predators high on the food-chain, are highly susceptible to environmental toxins. He therefore contends that they are ideal and promising candidates for experimentation. Yet the effects of fungicides and herbicides, such as PCBs, have already been well documented. Aulerich is simply exploiting the public's concern over environmental pollution. In his own words, minks suffered from "wasting syndrome," bloody stools, 40 percent loss of body weight, stomach ulcerations, high kit mortality, anorexia, and "hyperexcitability." If these farcical attempts at solving environmental degradation continue, so will ALF's attacks against mink research at MSU.

"In regard to the research of human-induced deafness in minks, Aulerich need not create more victims of this unfortunate handicap. Deaf minks produce no data that can be accurately extrapolated to humans. Rather than spend precious research dollars on non-human models, Aulerich should work with deaf humans who can communicate their trauma, and with it, create concrete findings to benefit other deaf individuals. Such clinical work is the only acceptable alternative to animal research.

"ALF envisions a human-animal relationship that respects the ecological integrity of fur animals in their native environment. ALF seeks not to place animals on a higher ethical platform than humans but simply to ask fur animal researchers such as Aulerich to return all hostages to their homelands. If ALF is considered terrorist due to our prioritizing of life over profit and property, then we accept that label with pride. But ALF sees terrorism as the forced ingestion of toxic substances into innocent victims, gas chambers operated for vanity, and the continued environmental destruction by chemical companies ready to poison the earth and its inhabitants for money.

"If the war on the mink nations continues, so shall ALF's campaign—until the last mink cage is empty, and its prisoners running free. WE HAVE JUST BEGUN TO FIGHT!

"For the foxes, otters and minks at MSU's fur animal concentration camp,

"[signed] Animal Liberation Front, Great Lakes Unit"

Officials from Michigan State University said years of records were lost and $100,000 damage was done. Key chains made from minks' feet were found in drawers in the facility. The Animals' Voice Magazine fully supports and commends the ALF for its actions.

FP41
FP124
FP108

ALF TORCHES OREGON MINK PLANT

Ed. Note: This missive arrived anonymously, attached to a copy of a December 22 Salem Statesman Journal *article which reported the blaze but raised doubts about the cause of the fire. A telephone call to Oregon State Police Lt. Richard Hein confirmed that the fire was indeed arson and that as of 1-2-92 there were no suspects.*

December 21, 1991— Western Wildlife Cell members of the Animal Liberation Front (ALF) raided Malecky Mink Ranch in Yamhill, Oregon, and set an incendiary device that destroyed the processing plant of this fur farm near Salem.

Intelligence sources revealed that the fur farm was to be sold, with intentions to continue exploitation of fur animals. Malecky Mink Ranch was a recipient of information from Oregon State University's Experimental Fur Farm, and had developed innovative methods of commercial exploitation of mink for the fur trade.

No mink or humans were injured in the ALF's fourth action against the United States Fur Farm industry. Fleshing machines, drying drums, skinning racks, feed mixers, freezers, and a workshop were all effectively destroyed in this economic attack against the tools of death and destruction.

This action was taken to avenge the lives of mink murdered on the ranch in the past and to prevent the further imprisonment of native wildlife in the future. 750,000 mink are slaughtered every winter in the Northwest for the fur trade, and over four million nation-wide on over six-hundred fur farms.

The Animal Liberation Front also announces a new campaign against the fur trade, one that directly targets the insensitive humans who wear fur garments. We will fight the fur-wearers in the streets. No longer shall the ecological arrogance of the public supporters of the fur trade go unchallenged. ALF members shall arm themselves with battery acid and dye, and will inflict damage on the furs worn by humans. Fur is for four-leggeds, not two. The lives of fur animals will be avenged.

The fur industry is responsible for the demise of not only native North American wildlife, but the destruction of native peoples' cultures as well. Over the last four-hundred years this barbaric industry has waged a genocidal war against animals and humans. Through the introduction of social and physical disease, the fur trade has forced native people to participate in their bloody practice, or perish like so many animals in traps and cages.

It is time to eliminate this anthropocentric profit-centered beast before the last howl is heard. ALF calls on all peoples to join in the battle against this ecologically destructive regime, and to defend the defenseless from the oppression of our own species. We must destroy that which destroys the animals, earth, and ourselves.

On behalf of the mink, fox, bobcat, lynx, and coyote nations, ALF shall wage non-violent war against the fur trade. *Until the last fur farm is burnt to the ground.*

—Animal Liberation Front, Western Wildlife Cell

Government Crackdown on the Animal Liberation Movement

Over the past few months, the FBI and federal prosecutors have called Grand Juries in Montana, Michigan, Washington, and Oregon to try to gain information on 'Operation Bite Back,' the Animal Liberation Front (ALF) clandestine campaign against the declining fur industry. The people called up to testify in Montana refused to answer questions and were released. Members of People for the Ethical Treatment of Animals are being called to testify in Michigan. Even more seriously, longtime activist Rod Coronado of the Coalition Against Fur Farms was forced to go underground when the FBI issued a warrant for his arrest. He is accused of being part of an ALF unit that has rescued a number of animals and caused over a million dollars in arson damage in a series of attacks since last summer. A SWAT team with machine guns landed in a helicopter at his home, but to this date, Coronado has not been caught.

Known ALF actions over the past few months includes the February 28 arson attack on the Michigan State University mink torture program, which resulted in over $100,000 in damage; a raid on the University of Alberta on June 1 in which 29 cats were liberated and records destroyed; a molotov cocktail attack on fur billboards in Chicago on July 8; and attacks on fur stores in Memphis, Tennessee. Also, a new group called the Vegan Front trashed a fur store in South Carolina. A hunting magazine reports that the National Trappers Association was forced to move its offices after an ALF article in the Earth First! Journal listed it as a potential target.

On the night of August 9, three activists, two women and a man, were arrested while vandalizing a fur store in Memphis. Apparently, the police had staked out local fur stores in hopes of making arrests.

An ocean-based direct action group, the Sea Shepherds, came under FBI scrutiny in August after the Japanese government filed a complaint against them. The Sea Shepherds were ramming Japanese fishing boats using illegal drift nets. In actions this year, from the

Gulf of California to the sea off the Aleutian Islands, the group has defended ocean life by slashing nets, ramming ships, and splattering them with red paint and buturic acid.

The ALF fights animal exploitation by rescuing animals from laboratories, fur farms, and factory farms, and by engaging in sabotage against all animal abuse industries. Actions can be as simple as super-gluing locks, and occur in cities across the U.S. For more info on the ALF, write the ALF Legal Support Group at Box 42/ 10024-82nd Ave./ Edmonton, Alberta/ TGE 1Z3/ Canada. For info on a group that is defending radical activists, call the National Foundation for Animal Law at (916)-454-6150.

EARTH FIRST! HOTLINE: (415) 949-0575

ALF BITES BACK........

#1: Corvallis, Oregon, June 10, 1991

Oregon State University's Experimental Fur Farm is raided by the ALF. Damage was estimated at $150,000. However, the greatest blow to the researcher was the loss of records, logbooks and data. Immunization records detailing the genetic history of the mink were removed, leaving researchers with little evidence to continue experimentation. At the completion of these experiments the mink are gassed. Their pelts are then sold through the Seattle Fur Exchange with proceeds going back into further experimentation.

In a press release issued after the raid, the ALF stated, "This action is in direct response to the exploitation and environmental terrorism committed daily by the fur industry. As long as the electrocution, gassing and enslavement of animals continues, similar actions by the ALF will continue, until the last fur farm is burnt to the ground. Expect to hear from us...."

#2: Edmonds, Washington, June 15, 1991

Using information obtained form the OSU break-in, the ALF strikes the Northwest Fur-Breeders Cooperative, igniting a three-alarm fire that destroys one quarter of the facility and causes $800,000 in damages. The facility acts as a distribution center for newly developed mink diets that have proven cost effective. By striking the Cooperative, the ALF interfered with the most crucial element of mink and fox farming — diet.

3: Pullman, Wahington, August 12, 1991

THE ALF claims responsibility for a multi-building break-in at Washington State University. Twenty-three mink, coyotes and mice are rescued from the USDA's Fur Animal Research Facility, where experiments are being conducted on native wildlife. WSU serves the industry as a fur animal disease research unit. Documents, including photographs and experimental records, are seized, computers smashed and sulfuric acid is sprayed over the entire data base, causing serious damage.

An ALF communique issued to the press after the raid states, "We believe that coyotes, mink, beaver, otter, marten and fisher have the right to live unmolested in their native habitat without the fear of exploitation by the fur and livestock industries. Until coyotes and other animals live free from the tortuous hand of humankind, no industry or individual is safe from fur animal liberation. The ALF has just begun to fight."

Reforming the Fur Industry, ALF-Style

BY THE ANIMAL LIBERATION FRONT

The entire fur and trapping industry can be eliminated within three years. Two years ago we stated that it could be done in five, and so far it is going according to schedule.

Although there seems to be renewed interest in trapping and fur farming, 40% of all fur farms *have gone out of business and trapping license sales have fallen as much as 75% in some states.* Fur stores are closing left and right and it seems that most department stores are dropping fur-related items. They are on the run, but they're preparing for a last-gasp comeback and the pressure must be increased.

Of course, education tactics are *very* important, but the Animal Liberation Front focuses on direct action. First, let's address the trapping issue. Get a copy of a magazine called *The Trapper and Predator Caller*. If you can't find a copy, call them at 1-800-258-0929 and ask them who sells their publication in your town. (Note: Do *not* ask them to send you a copy. If you do, they'll have your name and address. *Never* use a private phone when you use an 800 number. The caller's number may automatically be recorded by the company being called. If your state permits the phone company to sell caller-identification services, make all local telephone calls from a pay phone. And make *all* toll calls from a pay phone to avoid their being listed on your phone bill.) The magazine lists trapping supply companies, and the state trapper associations along with the officer's names and addresses. Call these people and act interested in trapping. If possible, find out where they are setting their traps. Consider the possibility of having a quiet little party in the trapper's fur shed where they keep their traps, pelts, and assorted equipment. Trapping is a business and if you destroy their means for doing business, they just may go out of their murderous business, if not their moronic minds.

Now for some heavier anti-trapping fun! There are four big trap manufacturers left in North America for steel jaw legholds, soft catch legholds, and body grip traps. They are Woodstream (the biggest which makes Victors and Conibears) in Lititz, PA; BMI in Willoughby Hills, OH; Duke Traps in West Point, MS; and Bridger in Ogden, UT. Just for the record, a turd named Harry Winter in Willits, CA is manufacturing a trap called the Dog Proof Coon Trap.

Shut these places down and we would cripple the wild fur industry severely. Remember they doubtless have security guards. Every hit makes them tighten security so be cautious and make it count! Group security is *absolutely essential* so don't tell *anyone*.

Be warned that trappers and fur farmers are likely to be strong and armed and woods wise. **Their livelihood (deadlihood) involves intimacy with blood, guts, and murder. They are not likely to be finicky when dealing with anybody they believe is** mucking about with their income.

Other important targets are the publications of the fur trade. The National Trappers Association (major anti-animal rights group and publisher of *American Trapper Magazine*) has offices in Bloomington, IL. *Fur-Fish-Game*, the other of the three major trapping magazines, is in Columbus, OH.

VANITY
HURTS!

The Trapper and Predator Caller is published by Krause Publication, Iola, WI. There are two trade journals catering to the retail fur industry: *Fur Age Weekly* in Glenwood Landing, NY, and *Fur World* in New York City. Destroy these means of communication within the industry *and* their traps, and the whole industry will be hurting.

In 1990 there were 660 fur farms left. Chances are there is one within a two to three hour drive of where you live. Contact the murderers listed in the back of *The Trapper and Predator Caller* and tell them you'd like to visit a fur farm because you may want to start your own. They might tell you where one is located. Unless the farmer lives right there, this should be an easy hit. If you visit them during the day, consider what to do about your appearance, vehicle, and license plate.

On mink farms, there are usually a number of mink 3-4 years old used as breeding stock. The rest are less than a year old. **Releasing the breeding stock and other adult-sized mink into the compound not only disrupts the whole process, but severely** handicaps the farmer in differentiating breeding stock from the sale animals. Such mischief can ruin the next year's breeding plans. When this happened to one mink farm two years in a row, it shut down.

Spraying the animals with non-toxic dye, the way Greenpeace and Sea Shepherd spray seal pups, ruins the commercial value of the pelts. There are various colors of sheep dye that are non-toxic. Be careful not to spray the animals' eyes and ears.

Other sites that need a heavy dose of justice are distribution centers of the processed furs: Seattle Fur Exchange, Seattle, WA; D. Cohn Fur Processors, Greenville, SC; National Superior Fu[r] Dressing, Chicago, IL; Russ Carme[n] Lures, New Milford, PA; Hudson Ba[y] Co. Fur Sales, Corstadt, NJ; Crown [of] MN Inc. Minneapolis, MN; Klubertan Equipment Co., Ederton, WI. To loca[te] them, let your fingers do the walkin[g]. Your local phone directories are goo[d] for something besides creating prof[its] for clearcutters.

Retail fur stores, listed under "fur" [in] your yellow pages, are the easiest hi[ts]. Glue the locks, spray paint the me[r]chandise, etch the windows. Be cr[e]ative and go for maximum impact.

This guide is a waste if action is n[ot] taken. This is war in defense of the innoce[nt]. The risk we take is nothing compared to t[he] suffering caused by the fur industry. P[ut] these words into action. There's no time [to] waste. Good luck and total secrecy.

Note: If companies conduct busin[ess] through a post office box, the Post Office w[ill] readily provide the street address of [the] company.

Fugitive talks of life in hiding

BY KEN OLSEN

He's twenty something and charismatic, with an easy smile, intense drive and a $35,000 price on his head.

The fur industry loathes him for posing as a mink farmer and making a videotape that later aired on the TV news program "60 Minutes."

His friends call him committed; the FBI calls him a "person of interest," probably a euphemism for "suspect."

He's Rodney Adam Coronado, a spokesman for the Animal Liberation Front who continues to elude law enforcement 16 months after the group started lighting fires and setting research animals free in the Pacific Northwest and Midwest. Its activities include a raid at Washington State University in August 1991.

At least three grand juries and two dozen witnesses have been assembled, in part to try and find Coronado and link him to several ALF raids.

He says he dodged two arrest attempts — though federal agents say there is no warrant out for him — and that he intends to remain free.

"I'm a self-proclaimed warrior," Coronado said in one of several exclusive telephone interviews with the *Moscow-Pullman Daily News*. "I want to continue to be recognized as a representative of animal nations and the environment and if the government chooses to see me as a criminal, when destruction of the environment is legal, I'll take that with being a part of the solution."

Coronado's friends are afraid of what that may mean.

"I think if they got him they would make him the Leonard Peltier of the animal rights movement," said Jonathan Paul, a friend of Coronado's who was recently subpoenaed to a grand jury hearing. Peltier, a leader in the American Indian Movement, is in federal prison after a controversial conviction in the death of two FBI agents in the 1970s. Sympathizers consider him a scapegoat.

"I think they definitely want to get someone" in connection with the recent ALF raids, Paul said. "I seriously have fears for (Rod's) life."

Paul says he thinks federal agents are pressing hardest for Coronado because he's a minority.

"The police suspect me," Coronado says, "and the fur industry flat-out knows I provided the video that caused them so much damage."

Federal law officers say they want to talk to Coronado about the

[r]aids — which have caused [m]ore $2 million in damage — [b]efore someone gets hurt or [k]illed in one of the fires.

Oct. 31– Nov. 1, 1992

In the spring of 1990, Coronado and other members of the radical environmental group Earth First! started documenting animal abuses on fur ranches, he says. With the support of Friends of Animals, Coronado took the name of Jim Perez and posed as someone interested in learning the mink-raising trade.

He visited trade shows. Fur ranchers took him under their wing.

A Montanan even demonstrated mink-killing techniques on camera, and that contributed five famous seconds to a "60 Minutes" broadcast on fur farming in December 1991, according to Priscilla Feral, president of Friends of Animals.

"I'd heard he'd be very reliable," Feral says of her decision to hire Coronado to get the footage, part of the "Faces of Fur" video the group now sells. "He was."

The fur industry said the film was staged. But the National Board of Fur Farm Organizations circulated a wanted poster of Coronado and a female companion that warned fur ranchers to be careful who they hired, according to a National Board memo.

Two animal activists, posing as future furriers, "videotaped several unflattering scenes which we believe have formed the basis for a new 'undercover' video being widely distributed to national media outlets by Friends of Animals," a board memo said. The same activists are suspects in ALF raids and arsons in Oregon and Washington, the basis for a National Board reward of $35,000, it said.

The film project prompted Coronado to buy out a retiring fur farmer, "rehabilitate" 40 mink, four bobcats and two lynx, and set them free. In the course of doing research for his rehabilitation project, Coronado landed in Pullman in August 1991.

While he was here, the Animal Liberation Front made its third hit of the summer, vandalizing two USDA research offices housed at WSU and setting coyote, mink and mice free. Coronado acknowledges faxing a press release about the WSU raid to the Associated Press in Spokane, but denies taking part in the raid.

"I circulated articles I had about WSU, sort of blatantly hoping someone would do something," Coronado said. "I'd like to think one or two of the ALF actions were as a result of information I was able to get out."

There's more to come at WSU, he hints.

"I think people in the ALF definitely know WSU has acquired more bears and continue to work on native wildlife," he said. "It's not a question of if the ALF will strike WSU, but when."

Despite this information, "spokesman" is as specific as Coronado gets about his role with the ALF.

"I will never publicly elaborate on my relationship with the ALF, other than to not deny open support for their actions," he said.

Coronado and a compa[nion] surfaced in Michigan in [Feb]ruary, weeks before an [ALF] raid at Michigan State Un[iver]sity. He says he was [far] away when the raid went d[own].

He wintered in southern [Ore]gon and departed days b[efore] the FBI and Bureau of Alc[ohol,] Tobacco & Firearms came [call]ing, he says. In June, a[gents] again went looking for him[, this] time on ships belonging t[o] Sea Shepherd.

Capt. Paul Watson con[firms] that, saying his ships [were] searched by U.S. officia[ls in] San Francisco and Seattl[e and] by Canadian officials near [Van]couver Island.

All of this has forced [Coro]nado underground, he a[dds]. Gone are the days of tele[vision] appearances, like one in [Port]land last year, where h[e de]cried the plight of caged [mink] and other animals on fur f[arms].

Now he lives off co[ntribu]tions from other activist[s and] sympathetic people and t[ries to] stay out of sight. His [name] surfaces occasionally i[n the] *Earth First! Journal* whe[re he] encourages others to ta[ke up] the cause.

"My very existence [is a] threat to the U.S. govern[ment]," Coronado said. "They hav[e def]initely identified me [as] working within the confi[nes of] the system.

"I see it as being one [of the] requirements of being a [warrior] of the earth, not a person[al sac]rifice."

ALF suspect in Utah State raid

BY KEN OLSEN
Staff Writer

Federal investigators are puzzled by a raid at Utah State University last Saturday that has almost all the trappings of the Animal Liberation Front.

The problem: No one has claimed credit for the raid. The FBI, Bureau of Alcohol, Tobacco & Firearms and other agencies are asking the press to keep an eye out for any press release from the perpetrators, according to the Associated Press.

The ALF typically sends a press release and photographs to a newspaper or wire service within hours of a raid. Or the group sends a video tape to a nearby television station depicting animals being freed.

Someone set two fires in the early hours of Saturday morning that damaged the Logan, Utah office of a U.S. Department of Agriculture predator researcher. His field office in nearby Millville was destroyed by fire.

In both cases, clocks were supposedly connected to the devices that started the fires early Saturday morning. At the field office, accelerants were allegedly used to spread the fire.

If those allegations are true, it means the fires fit the pattern of other recent Animal Liberation Front raids around the Pacific Northwest and in Michigan.

Valuable research records at Utah were destroyed. Holes were cut in 27 pens housing more than 56 coyotes. A dozen escaped and most have been recaptured.

Once again, all of the signs of an ALF raid. But the ALF normally leaves graffiti at the site of its raids with blood-red spray paint, including the trademark acronym "ALF."

Building panels with graffiti in Utah were removed before reporters were able to look at them. One had a red spiral painted on it with four feathers dangling from it.

The fact that no media has been contacted about the most recent raid raises the possibility that it's a copycat crime or that the ALF is being more cautious about contacting the press.

Three grand juries, investigating a series of ALF raids including one at Washington State University last year, have put pressure on some two dozen people who are at least acquainted with suspected ALF members. Rod Coronado, who last spring told this newspaper he faxed a press release to the Associated Press in Spokane following the WSU raid, is being hunted by the FBI and Bureau of Alcohol Tobacco and Firearms.

To date, however, there have been no arrests in connection with the rash of incidents.

An ALF timeline

This is a chronology of the most recent incidents the Animal Liberation Front has taken credit for or is suspected in perpetrating:

- **June 10, 1991:** Arsonists torch a barn and offices used with the mink research program at Oregon State University in Corvallis. Damage estimated at $125,00.
- **June 15, 1991:** Arsonists torch a warehouse at the Northwest Food Farm Cooperative in Edmonds, Wash., an operation supplying feed to mink farmers. Damage estimated at $800,000.
- **Aug. 13, 1991:** Raiders vandalize two WSU research offices and liberate seven coyotes, six mink and 10 mice from USDA research facilities. Damage is estimated at $50,000 to $100,000.
- **Dec. 21, 1991:** Arsonists torch buildings at the inactive Malecky Mink Ranch near Yamhill, Ore. Damage is estimated at $125,000.
- **Feb. 28, 1992:** Arsonists torch two research offices and vandalize a mink farm at Michigan State University. Two mink are liberated.
- **Oct. 24, 1992:** Arsonists torch two USDA research offices connected to a Utah State University predator research center. About a dozen coyotes were liberated. Damage is estimated at $100,000.

#4: Yamhill, Oregon, December 21, 1991

A blaze rips through a mink processing plant at Malecky Mink Ranch. The farm, when in full operation, killed from 4-5,000 mink annually before processing their skins to sell to a New York company. The building that owner Hyneck Malecky describes as the heart of his operation, containing a pelt drying room, feed mixing equipment, skinning racks, drying drums, fleshing machines, freezers and a workshop, is destroyed. There were no injuries. An anonymous caller to KGW-TV, Portland, says the ALF accepts responsibility for the destruction

#5: East Lansing, Michigan, February 27, 1992

In the first action of its kind in Michigan ,the ALF raids Michigan State University's Experimental Fur Farm and breaks into the office of head researcher Richard Aulerich. Two mink are rescued and later released. An incendiary device ignites the offices of the Fur Animal Research Unit. Over thirty-two years of research data compiled for the fur farm industry, some yet to be published, is lost in the blaze, causing $125,000 in damage.

The ALF distributed a press release condemning fur animal research. "If ALF is considered terrorists due to our prioritizing of life over profit and property, then we accept that label with pride. But ALF sees terrorism as the forced ingestion of toxic substances into innocent victims, gas chambers operated for vanity and the continued environmental destruction by chemical companies ready to poison the earth and its inhabitants for money.... We have just begun to fight!"

By targeting the main recipients of mink industry funding, the ALF not only destroyed valuable data, but also created a media wave that resulted in public exposure of the fur farm issue. It is now up to the rest of us to follow the call of the wild and fight back against animal exploitation.

ALF Attacks ADC in Utah

In its sixth raid since June, 1991, the Animal Liberation Front (ALF) has claimed responsibility for the recent attacks on Animal Damage Control (ADC) facilities in Utah. On October 24, 1992 at the USDA Animal Damage Control Predator Research Facility (PRF) in Milville, Utah, and at ADC Project Leader Fredrick F. Knowlton's office at Utah State University's federally funded coyote research facility in Logan, ALF activists released coyotes and started fires resulting in over $100,000 in damage.

The US Department of Agriculture (USDA) facility held more than 100 coyotes used in behavioral research studies for the Animal Damage Control program. ALF cut holes in pens, releasing 29 coyotes, and started a fire in the lab which destroyed a third of the facility, causing serious damage to the rest of the vivisection laboratory. ALF was alerted to the presence of the coyotes by USU students. The USDA claims it studies coyote behavior to help sheep and cattle growers.

Over the last 70 years, the ADC has maintained a relentless and ruthless war against native predators. On behalf of sheep and cattle producers, the ADC has designed and developed predator control tactics such as snares, leg-hold traps, bait, and sterilization. To prevent financial loss to livestock interests who graze public lands, ADC has slaughtered millions of coyotes, wolves, bobcats, foxes, and cougars in a massive poisoning and gunning campaign across the West.

After setting fire to the PRC, ALF moved on to the Utah State University campus where Knowlton's office is located. Just fifty yards from the police station, raiders entered his office and began confiscating records detailing the illegal dumping of over two tons of radioactive coyote bodies, losses of radioactive- collared goats in field experiments, and tests where coyotes were left in leg-hold traps and snares for over eighteen hours. The documents detailed the force feeding of toxic poisons and records of aerial shootings of research coyotes. ALF then set a fire in the office which resulted in an estimated $10,000 in damage and destroyed much of his research.

This latest raid comes in the middle of three grand jury investigations into previous ALF attacks. Grand juries were convened in Michigan, Oregon and Washington in early spring and will run until next winter. Dozens of individuals have been questioned and subpoenaed and one activist, Jonathan Paul, was jailed for contempt on November 3 for refusing to testify before the grand jury in Spokane.

Grand juries are investigating the following incidents : a fire at Oregon State University's mink research facility in Corvallis (June, 1991); a fire at the Northwest Food Farm Cooperative in Edmonds, Washington (June, 1991); a raid at the USDA's Washington State University research facility (August, 1991); a fire at the Malecky Mink Ranch in Yamhill, Oregon (December, 1991); a fire at offices and research facilities at Michigan State University (February, 1992); and the recent fires at USU. Combined damage estimates of the raids total over $1,500,000.

The USU incident is being investigated by a task force composed of representatives from the FBI, the Bureau of Alcohol, Tobacco and Firearms, the Utah Fire Marshal's Office, the USU Police Department and the county sheriff's and attorney's offices. No arrests have been made.

"BATTLING THE ANIMAL LIBERATION FRONT"

9 THE PIG'S POINT OF VIEW

ne below article i discovered while looking through police magazines for any pictures. it is, essentially, the pigs point of view of the animal eration front. you should take it as such. i was both angry at their ndemnation of ALF (but, hey, everyone's entitled to their point of view, ...) and humoured at their treatment of ALF tactics, especially the label errorists". since reading it i have gained new insight on the ALF and it has lped me to see how police conduct "terrorist" investigations, and i believe if yone considers doing an ALF action, should definitely read up on the emy's theories!]

On April 3, 1989, between 0000 and 0500 hours, the Animal Liberation Front ALF) destroyed two research laboratories and burned a penthouse research nter and an off-campus office at the University of Arizona. The attack used $300,000 in damages, and led the university to divert $1 million into imal research protection.

ALF represents one of the newest terrorist groups confronting law forcement in the United States today. In this article, we will examine a brief story of ALF, the tactics it employs, the way the University of Arizona Police epartment (UAPD) reacted to the incident, the community's reaction, the isting intelligence about ALF, the media response and the anticipated impact n law enforcement in the future.

What Happened

On April 2-3, 1989, between 11:30 p.m. and 4:30 a.m., ALF systematically tacked four university buildings using two or three terrorist teams. In the io-West building, ALF members broke into a ground-floor door, took an evator to the sixth-floor research area and took 965 animals before stroying the labratories. While this attack was in progress, another team ok off an air vent cover approximately 12 feet off the ground, entered an air aft, then broke into a ground-floor research labratory in the Shantz uilding. Once these attacks were completed, one team broke into a ground-vel door in the Micro/Pharmacy building, entered an elevator and went to e penthouse, where team members took additional animals, destroyed a boratory and an autopsy room, then burned the entire area by pouring asoline on the walls and floor. As this team left the area, the other team went the office of the director of animal research, located in a house off campus. here, team members pried off a plywood subfloor covering, placed several harcoal briquettes under the wood floor and lit the briquettes. The ubsequent fire destroyed the house and all of its contents, and damaged the nimal research data located in the area.

Forty-five minutes after the last fire was extinguished, ALF distributed a o-page press release to Tucson's two newspapers and three major television ations. Twenty-four hours later, ALF released a videotape of the destruction, med by its own crew, to one local TV station, Channel 9. Transmitted via tellite from the headquarters of People for the Ethical Treatment of Animals ETA) in Washington, D.C., to Channel 9, the tape was shown on the three ajor television stations as the lead story on their evening news reports the y after the attack.

UAPD's Response

Recovering from this systematic vandalism, burglaries and two arson fires as a complicated task for all UAPD officers. Within 45 minutes of the first e, UAPD had discovered the other two destroyed research laboratories and egun its crime scene investigation. The various crime scenes indicated ALF d thoroughly prepared for this attack.

UAPD found little or no evidence left behind at any of the four crime enes, which is characteristic of an ALF attack. An examination of ALF's story indicates that the organization places personnel inside the planned rget, prepares extensively for its strikes, leaves little or no trace of physical idence for police purposes and operates at peak efficiency. UAPD estimated at ALF's attack on the university took approximately 90 minutes.

One of the biggest factors confronting UAPD in investigating this crime as its significance for the university community. The academic community bulated the cost: 1,100 mice, four rats, 11 frogs and 16 guinea pigs. Not all of ese were being used in medical research; 60 mice were being used in heat udies. It is hard to determine the monetary value assigned to the loss of vernment grants and the devastation suffered by each researcher. Despite e six weeks of intensive investigation, the running down of 150 leads and e extensive networking between UAPD and California police departments, ere have been no arrests and no suspects identified to date.

Community Reaction

The university community was quick to react. Four hours after the attack as discovered, the university held a press conference featuring the niversity president, the vice president of research, the director of animal search, the vice president of public relations and the police. the media were given statements on what types of research these stolen animals were being used in, how this would affect future medical research and what the future held in dealing with additional attacks by ALF.

Once the crime scenes were processed, the university authorized UAPD to immediately fund the hiring of off-duty police and security officers to guar all of the animal research areas on campus. As a result, all police agencies within Pima County were contacted by UAPD's payroll coordinator and a massive scheduling task began. By 1700 hours on April 3, 1989, 11 research sites had 24-hour police or security coverage.

This intensive coverage continued for six weeks following the attack.

To facilitate the security effort, the vice president of research ordered th immediate centralization of all animal research, from 11 locations down to three locations. Once the animals were moved, police administration and th vice presidents of research and administration began an ongoing review of

the police coverage that lasted for months and resulted in continuous modifications to the coverage. Complications occurred immediately as a res of the centralization of all animals. At first, professors could not and would move their animals experiments; then it took eight weeks after the attack to complete the centralization process. The shifts of police officers guarding these facilities were constantly modified in the summer of 1989, with the fi result being police coverage at all locations from sunset to sunrise.

As the hours were reduced, the cost associated with guarding these areas decreased from $40,000 per week to $10,000 per week.

Amoung the long-term direct results of the ALF attack were:

- the hiring of six additional full-time police officers assigned to patrol the university farms five to seven miles from the main campus; and
- the purchase of a campus-wide security system capable of meeting all levels of security needs to protect research areas on campus.

Like the university reaction to the attack, the public's reaction was quic and to the point: the Tucson community was outraged and, to date, its feelin remain unchanged.

[ed. note: every political, police or military force uses the "public's support" legitimacy - and it seems like the "public" always agrees with them. ask yourself: who in the "public" do they specifically ask for their opinions these things? do they even ask anyone?]

Media Attention

With the ALF statement in each Tucson paper and on each television and radio station, the media response to the university was immediate. Film crew and reporters toured the damaged laboratories, the burned penthouse and t director's office. The media were assisted by the university's director of pu relations to ensure that all affected areas of the university were covered. Dean's, directors, graduate and undergraduate students, and employees were interviewed. The overall reaction was outrage.

Available Intelligence

A terrorist arm associated with the animal rights movement, ALF has be associated with 85 break-ins within the United States since 1977, including $3.8 million destruction of an animal research facility at the University of California at Davis. the organization, founded in England, has developed a very closed membership; consequently, there is little know intelligence on ALF. Everything known about ALF is gathered from magazine or newspape articles, *[ed. note: i hope you caught that one! when writing about the ALF being anonymous. rmember: loose lips sink ships.]* such as the article described below.

Following the university attack, a local newspaper reporter, Carla McCla sought an audience with an ALF member in an attempt to understand why ALF had attacked the University of Arizona. Some excerpts from that interview follow:

McClain: The UA raid made a lot of people angry and frightened. You fires, you
damaged and stole public property. You didn't just liberate--a few animal People
see this as a crime, violence, even terrorism. How do you justify that?

ALF member: Unfortunately, right now there is no other way to rescu animals
to prevent their torture. I don't like to risk going to jail. This was not o on a
whim.

McClain: Who are you? Why did you decide to take such risks for this cause?

ALF member: I am a pretty normal person - I have a job, a house, a mortgage.
I got into the animal movement years ago, during my first year in med school. I dropped out in my first semester because of the dog lab. I couldn't handle cutting
open live dogs and killing them for that purpose. I'm embarrassed to sa now i did
nothing about it at the time except to leave school . . . Before you can jo

ALF, you are checked out thoroughly - for your sincerity, your commitment, years of action in the movement, a willingness to go to jail if you have to. It is not easy to get into ALF. To be honest, I'd really rather have a normal life. But now that I know what goes on in the labs, on the factory farms, I can't ignore it. I feel a sense of personal responsibility about what society does to animals. It is as if I were living in Nazi Germany and in my town there was a Buchenwald and I knew it and did nothing. People who tried to stop those horrors got killed for it. At least I won't be killed for this.

Historical Data

In 1962, Ronnie Lee and Cliff Goodman founded the Hunt Saboteurs Association, one of England's earliest animal rights organizations. At the time, Lee stated in a magazine article that he had founded the group following the principles of the Irish Republican Army. The group changed its name to Band of Mercy in 1972, and five years later it took its first actions in the United States, stealing two dolphins at the University of Hawaii.

ALF developed as a terrorist arm of the Band of Mercy, blowing up an animal research facility in Bristol, England, in the mid-1970's. Other documented incidents of violence include the following:

- On September 5, 1984, there was a bomb threat at the California Primate Center, and a bomb threat and vandalism at the home of the center's director.
- On December 22, 1984, death threats were received by researchers at the University of California at San Diego.
- On April 16, 1987, at the University of California at Davis, a research lab was burned down - causing $3.8 million worth of damage - and 18 campus vehicles were vandalized.
- In December of 1988, four individuals were killed while building pipe bombs at the Brazilian Consulate in New York City. One of those killed had been a student leader in the animal rights movement at the University of Calfornia at Berkeley.

At this writing, bombings continue in England and France.

ALF Tactics

There is limited reliable information regarding ALF's tactics, most of it garnered from magazine and newspaper articles based on interviews with ALF members.

ALF members are not always residents of the communities under attack. In fact, intelligence indicates there is a core of ALF members living in California, and it is possible that additional members have been flown in from England or other European countries.

ALF's typical modus operandi is as follows:

- Plant an individual inside the research structure or organization targeted by ALF.
- Through the Public Information Act, obtain any building blueprint information or government grant funding information associated with the facility.
- Obtain the names of the individuals associated with animal research and begin to systematically disrupt their personal lives.
- Perform several surveillance raids, including taking pictures of the facility, filming inside the lab research areas if possible and photographing the type of alarm systems used at the facility.
- Plan to defeat the alarm system or stage a police call away from the attack area.
- Conduct numerous dress rehearsals on how the attack will start, what parts each attack team will play (including all specific tasks), how to react to police involvement, how to deal with any type of interruptions by research personnel, how to avoid leaving physical evidence at the scene, and where to safely place the stolen animals.
- Obtain police scanners to monitor police activity in the area prior to and during the attack. Establish prearranged signals to announce police presence if diversion tactics fail and police stumble into an attack in progress. (To date, no police agency has apprehended and ALF member in the act of destroying a research facility.)
- Probe existing security measures surrounding animal research sites to ascertain how electronic security will monitor intrusions and how local security or police will respond to suspected intrusions on the attack site.
- Videotape the actual attack and prepare to send it to PETA headquarters for possible transmittal to a local television station following the attack.
- Prepare a detailed press release claiming responsibility for the attack, explaining exactly what the group did and how effective the attack was in deterring medical research in the area by releasing these animals. Have the press release distributed at all media facilities 45 minutes after the attack is complete.
- Pose as reporters and contact local police to ascertain any plans for extra security at animal research sites - particulary during Animal Liberation Month - as well as police reactions to animal rights attacks.

Following an ALF attack, these types of slogans will appear on the walls and/or floors of the destroyed laboratories: "Nazi Torture", "Animals Liberate Now", "No More Torture", "Scum", "Nowhere is Safe", "We Shall Return", "You Can't Hide from ALF", and "Animals are Not Research Tools". These slogans are sprayed and hand-painted in red enamel and red latex paint. All of these actions are characteristic of this groups activity reported to police in California, Arizona, Missouri, and Illinois.

As threatened, ALF returned to the University of Arizona approximately one year later, joining forces with Tucson's local Voice of Animals (VOA) group in March and April 1990. The president and treasurer of the Tucson chapter of VOA were arrested after being caught inside one of the new animal research construction sites at 2 a.m. on Easter Sunday. On April 21, 21 demonstrators out of 100 were arrested when they chained themselves to a construction fence at an animal research construction site, entered a construction site posing as architects, and took over an administration office in the Micro/Pharmacy building. During the next two weeks, UAPD arrested 20 additional persons associated with the VOA for probing our security, trespassing in animal research areas and assaulting one of our police officers *[ed. note: what this little sentence is supposed to do is to frighten you into not doing any actions with fear of arrest. true, they may have arrested 20 people, but did they say how many were actually charged? how many were released on false or circumstancial evidence?]*

In addition to these incidents, UAPD officers noticed a large number of California vehicles in and around our animal centers, many of them equipped with police monitors and portable radios. Many of these vehicles were found to be directly associated with the local VOA group attempting to probe our animal security.

What the Future Holds

Based upon statements of numerous ALF members, I believe we in law enforcement can expect the violence to continue. The question is, what can we do about it?

By effectively utilizing existing technology and taking full advantage of our professional network, we can successfully deal with ALF. *[ed. note: in plain english that means "we can use illegal shit such as bugs and taps to spy on 'em." technology indeed!]* Any police department that has any type of animal research in its jurisdiction is subject to an ALF attack. None of us is (sic) exempt, and we must work closely to track the acts of civil disobedience, criminal damage, animal theft, and arson committed by ALF across the country and around the world.

Local efforts could be strengthened by enacting federal legislation to make any attack on an animal research facility a felony, and by involving the FBI in investigating and gathering intelligence on this organization that is not just national but international in scope.

I believe the FBI should maintain a hotline to handle the intelligence information generated from all agencies involved in ALF arrests, actions and anticipated problems.

There should also be a coordinated effort with the FBI and local police when investigating any ALF attack. ALF has had very few of its members arrested, and no agency has successfully planted an undercover agent in this organization. Thus, the only hope for maximizing the available information is to maintain a highly efficient, closely linked network with other agencies.

Prevention of an ALF attack is complicated, but the best overall strategy is education. Although there are limited resource materials of any real value to law enforcement, the books listed below can provide background information on ALF and its related groups - PETA, VOA and True Friends:

- *The Mini-Manual of the Urban Guerrilla* by Carlos Marighella
- *Action for Animals*, a handbook designed specifically for ALF members
- *Ecodefense - A Field Guide to Monkeywrenching* by David Forman

There is also a bi-monthly magazine published by Prescription Press in Washington, D.C. - *The Animal Rights Reporter* - that will provide you with international and national information on the animal rights movement."

Scenting fresh air for the first time, a mink is released into the wild after animal liberators rescued and rehabilitated it—along with other animals—from an Oregon fur farm.

An Animal LIBERATION Primer

second edition

Compiled and edited by:
@nu

Foreword

This booklet has been produced to be a tool, a tool to empower the average person to make a difference in this world. It has been compiled from numerous sources, into a condensed volume of animal liberation tactics. Read this booklet once and then twice and then again. Make sure you know it inside out, before setting out to do anything.

Who are the ALF?

Members of the Animal Liberation Front are activists who directly intervene to stop animal suffering. At the risk of losing their own freedom, while following ALF guidelines:

ANIMAL LIBERATION FRONT GUIDELINES

- To liberate animals from places of abuse, i.e. fur farms, laboratories, factory farms, etc. and place them in good homes where they may live out their natural lives free from suffering.

- To inflict economic damage to those who profit from the misery and exploitation of animals; and

- To reveal the horror and atrocities committed against animals behind locked doors by performing non-violent direct actions and liberations.

When will we say NO to tyranny?

are routinely mutilated to accom-
odate the factory farm system.

The ALF and Direct Action.

As part of their personal campaign against animal abuse, ALF activists do not eat animal flesh, and many of them use no animal products at all. They come from all social classes, age groups, professions, races, religious and political persuasions, and all are prepared to go to jail, if that is what it takes to end animal suffering. They are committed to doing all that it takes to end animal abuse, short of harming any living being.

Direct action for animals began in England in the early 1960s when a group called the Hunt Saboteurs Association was formed. Hunt "Sabs" physically disrupt hunts by laying false scents, blowing hunting horns to send hounds off in the wrong direction, and chasing animals away to safety. The Hunt Saboteurs have effectively ended many traditional hunting events all over England.

In 1972 a group of Hunt Saboteurs decided that more militant action on behalf of animals was necessary and thus the Band of Mercy began. the Band of Mercy, named after a group of animal rights campaigners in the nineteenth century, smashed guns used on bird hunts and sabotaged hunters' vehicles by slashing tires and breaking windows. The group also began fighting other forms of animal abuse, setting fire to pharmaceutical laboratories and burning boats used for hunting seals.

In 1975 two members of the Band of Mercy, Ronnie Lee and Cliff Goodman, were caught trying to break into a laboratory and were sent to prison. After the arrest, support for direct action grew, and in 1976, the Animal Liberation Front was set up. Since that time, tens of thousands of animals have been rescued and millions of dollars worth of damage has been caused. It has been reported that ALF actions occur at the rate of 75 per week in Britain, ranging from raids on research laboratories to smashing the windows of fur shops. Today there are animal liberation groups in Britain, the USA, Australia, Italy, France, Germany, Canada, New Zealand, Austria, Denmark, Ireland, Japan, Netherlands, Spain and Sweden. While there are no formal communications between the groups, they all share the same goal: to save animals from suffering HERE and NOW.

ALF - The way we were.

This article discusses ideas that could be adopted by a local animal liberation group, it is based on personal experience of several ALF groups operating in the south of England between 1982 and 1984. We did for a while perfect a system where we could move from seeing to raiding an animal abuse centre in a matter of 48 hours; the number of animals we rescued ran into several thousands - with a record of 250 on one night from a vivisection dealer. We raided everything from schools which bred animals for dissection, up to major laboratories where there was 24-hour security and intricate alarm systems, although the majority of our actions were against factory farms and vivisection breeders.

We started out as a group of four people with one car. At our height there were as many as 50 active members split into several sub-groups, some of these sub-groups are still active, although the majority of our members have now ceased to be active--the pressure of living under the continuous threat of possible arrest taking its toll on many of the more active members.

Finding people to work with is the hardest of all your tasks. At the moment we see a spate of people who have become involved in groups, who, when arrested make statements incriminating themselves (let me mention here that *no one has ever got off by making a statement*); worse than this is the disturbing development of people making statements naming other activists and giving details of raids they have been involved with (in the criminal world this is known as "grassing" or "snitching").

In the prison cells some people make a belated and somewhat pathetic attempt to save their own skin by telling the police what they want to hear. But despite the police promises, snitching has never saved anyone's skin and when it comes to avoiding a beating in the cells, the police in general only use violence in interviews when they think it will get results. When people have been hit, and they begin to talk, the police are encouraged, while if they stay quiet "Mr. Nasty", is shepherded out of the interview room and "Mr. Nice" apologizes and appeals to you personally. People who believe in what they are doing and recognize the personal risks they are taking in advance of their of their arrest will not snitch. Those *people who snitch cannot really believe in what they are doing,* otherwise they would have the confidence and the peace of mind to recognize that in a direct action campaign some arrests are inevitable, and although they are unlucky to be arrested at that particular time, the struggle will go on. Their role once arrested is to say or do nothing to impair the struggle.

It is very important that the calibre of people is high and that you never work on a job you are not happy about. In a group you need some solid un-shakeable characters, young people without much insight are not a good idea. Look for commonsense, people not prone to showing off, no big egos and no one who boasts about what they've done or are about to do. The *longer you know people the better* and try never to ask someone to get involved unless you are confident that they are interested.

Finding a target: Your local animal rights group probably has a very good idea where the local labs, breeders, fur farms and battery units are, although unless you are already involved it is probably best to keep well clear of the local animal rights group; it is after all the *first place the police will come looking for information* on likely activists. Always study the location on the map and learn to recognize where you are in relation to roads, streams, footpaths, etc.

The first visit to a target should be during the day. Park well out of the way and approach the target on foot. Try to get as close as possible, look for ways in and ways out (not necessarily the same). Begin to develop your plan--where will you park? Which buildings will you enter? Which route will you take in? Where will your look-out be? Where will your break in point be? (seldom the front door). Where is anybody likely to disturb you? Once you are back in the car, try and sketch a map immediately so that you remember everything.

After seeing the place close up it is a good idea to retire to a distance and study your road map. Look for some ideal parking spots: in rural areas these will have to be off little-used country lanes, in the town it may well be in a housing estate. You may also decide that there are some convenient footpaths running around the back of the site, walk the length of these, but don't stay around the immediate area of the site for long enough to arouse suspicion.

Once you have seen all that you can during daylight, clear off and make a draft plan. Next, return at night, try out your route and find its weaknesses. Get as close to your target building as possible, ideally right up to the break-in point. Check the locks, doors and window fittings, look for signs of alarms, and general security.

Having surveyed the target area, make sure that your route in and out is *as simple as possible*, stick to hedges, count field boundaries, note the number of gates etc., anything that will make the route nice and easy. Try not to use wide open spaces as part of your route, hedges make you invisible in the dark. It is vital that you walk the route once at night before the job, as darkness is disorienting and places can look very different.

A good time to do a job is at new moon; if you live in the city you'd be surprised how much light is given out by the moon. Winter is ideal with its early dusks, late dawns, and cold, rainy, windy nights--no farmer is going to want to get out of bed at two in the morning just because he has heard a noise that could so easily have been the wind.

Once you are sure of the route, go there at the time and day of the week that you are planning to do the job, and do a complete walk-through. Park where you will be parking, walk the exact route and stay at the break-in point for as long as you need to there on the night. If everything works out then you are onto the next stage.

It cannot be stated enough that unless there are clear and obvious advantages *you should not take ALF actions during the day*. Darkness, and knowledge of the area around the target will ensure your escape, on foot, however many police units arrive. In 1981, an ALF group was stranded in the fields surrounding a beagle breeders' at Ross-on-Wye, the police had swooped on their transport and arrested their back-up driver. The group, with beagles, were at one time just the other side of a hedge from parked police vehicles; the group escaped and got the beagles away by traveling as fast as possible, on foot, across country, eventually contacting a supporter who arranged transport for them to be picked up.

However wrong things go on the night, don't give up--a clear head, good planning and determination should give you an edge on the police.

Once your group has got off the ground you should develop a core of people responsible for tools, planning raids, the initial break-in, the look-outs, and the organization of people and vehicles on the night. This group should enter the target area first, set up look-outs, check the area over, and when they are satisfied, break in and locate the animals. Only then should "the carriers" be brought in; their job is to bag or box the animals quickly and quietly and then leave. If the target has no alarms and no one on site the advance group could conceivably go in hours in advance and prepare everything so that the carriers and their vehicles are there for as short a time as possible.

One person should be responsible for collating all information on homes, so that when you find homes for fifty hens you do a battery unit, when it's thirty rabbits or ten dogs you do a breeder. In many ways the homing network needs to be bigger than the ALF group, ideally with 4 or 5 people who can take and disperse animals,

PROTEST FOR ANIMAL RIGHTS

UC Davis Primate Center

re-homing them *outside of the animal rights movement*. It is this ability to disperse animals so that your homes are never used up that will permit you to become an efficient animal liberation group. In general those people involved in the homing network *should not be in the ALF group* as it would be a very damaging blow should those people be arrested. Only members of the core group of activists should have contact with the homing network.

Tools are a vital consideration. You will need two pairs of bolt-cutters and two crowbars (large and small) a pair of diamond-tipped glass cutters, walkie-talkies and a rope. Have a proper tool-bag to carry them in, never touch them without wearing gloves, even when buying them, and always clean them between jobs. The blades on your bolt-cutters should be changed regularly--always after a lab job, and run a file over the end of your crowbars as they leave distinctive imprints on whatever they have jimmied open. The tools should *always be kept at a safe house* in between jobs. A safe house belongs to someone who *is not in your group* and not going to come to the attention of the police.

When you plan a job, it is advisable to have a plan "B" if things go wrong. Work out what you are going to do if you come across a guard or if the police arrive, which could be when you are going in, in the middle of the job, or on the way out with animals. Whatever happens don't panic, it only wastes time. You should have worked out which way to run, and who should be with you. You should know what could go wrong with your plan and have an easy solution to it when it arises. When it comes to running away it is probably best to all leave the site together heading in the same direction to a pre-arranged rendezvous point 3 or 4 fields away; from then on it may be better if you split up and travel in groups of three or four in different directions.

When doing a job you must have confidence in those who you are working with. When you appoint one or more lookouts you must be sure that they know what they are doing, that they are not frightened, and that should anything go wrong they will be able to notify you of what is happening. Once you are inside a place, you should just get on with your job, looking over your shoulder only wastes time. Do not panic if the animals begin to make a lot of noise, this is not unusual. Chickens and rabbits make a lot of noise but beagles are notorious and can be heard for miles; always remember that you have a lookout so get on with your job and the sooner you get out of the sheds the sooner the animals will quieten down.

If disturbed you should collect people and leave quickly, most people who discover you will be quite happy to frighten you off their property and then call the police. Unless you are confronted by a farmer who is literally shooting at you with his shotgun, you should not abandon anyone. Security guards are easier to deal with as the property is not theirs. Their job is not to be a hero but to phone the police, although any sign of weakness on your part may encourage them to grab hold of a tailender, so the rule is--don't panic, leave together, and leave quickly.

Parking a lot of vehicles for a raid can look suspicious, one way around this is to go out several hours earlier and park the carriers' cars in different streets in a nearby town or village. The whole of the carrying group can then be brought in by the vehicle which will leave with the animals, alternatively the carriers can come in, from different directions to a rendezvous point near the animal abuse centre and the animal transport only arriving when the group has got its hands on the animals--either arriving at a specific time, or being called up with a radio when the job is complete.

Whatever the plan always make sure that the animal van is the first away and has the safest route out of the area. It is important that if you decide to rescue animals *you are prepared to face a prison sentence*--the animals must be protected and if that means a choice between you going to prison or the animals being taken back, then you will be released, for the animals there is only one way out.

Although it is good to do jobs on home territory, you should consider travelling out of your area on occasions, the further you travel, the less chance of the police guessing that it was your group. It is important *not to get into a routine* of doing jobs on the same night of the week in the same police district. It is only when the police recognize a pattern of jobs that they will have the opportunity to start fishing for you.

Clothing is a very important consideration as police forensic science is now very advanced and can identify clothing, hairs, foot-prints, tools, paint, etc. In one criminal case forensic scientists proved that a discarded shoe was responsible for a foot print at the scene of the crime, they then managed to identify fibres inside the shoe as consistent with the fibre of thirteen different pairs of the defendant's socks. The police have access to highly sophisticated techniques, in practice these will only be used once they are convinced that you are the culprit, and they then can justify the enormous expenditure which is not acceptable for routine testing.

Wearing boiler suits can be a good idea as they cover your clothes, you can wear your party clothes underneath; when you reach your transport on your way home you can strip off the boiler suits,

xit from
north c
the labs
mento)
MEAT is murder

straighten your hair and look very presentable should you be stopped by the police. This works even better if you have a mixture of girls and boys in the car, then if you are randomly stopped by the police you can have a story to bluff them with, you could have been to a party, a wedding, etc. It is a good idea to have rehearsed false names, although this is complicated for your drivers if the vehicle is registered in their own name. It is a good idea to wear socks over your shoes, this prevents tell-tale footprints being left in the soft soil, and ensures that when you get back to your car your shoes won't be covered in mud. Always wear gloves, and never believe that a quick wipe with a damp cloth will remove your fingerprints.

Within a direct action campaign arrests are ultimately inevitable, either through bad luck, bad planning, good police work, a frame-up or an act of "god". The fact that you have been arrested does not necessarily mean that they have enough evidence to charge you, and if you are charged you will have the opportunity in court to give your defence. In the police station there is only one rule, "Never Make A Statement". In the war soldiers were instructed that should they be taken prisoner they should tell their captors their name, rank and serial number; in the animal rights movement it is name, address and date of birth, beyond that you should reply "no comment". Other interrogation techniques involve asking you what you had for breakfast, how long you have been a vegetarian, who do you live with, where did you meet and who planned the raid. Refuse to answer all questions, and NEVER MAKE A STATEMENT.

Other more interesting police tactics are when the police bring an item of evidence into the cell and tell you to pick it up with the obvious result that your fingerprint will be left on it, (it is particularly important to be wary of handling match boxes if you are being interviewed for arson). It has happened in the past that the police have walked into a cell with a quantity of cannabis and explained how easy it would be to plant it on the accused - so demonstrating their ability to frame you.

Sooner or later the police will inevitably try to frighten you, with their forecast of a long prison sentence if you don't help them, and eventually there will be the threat of physical attack. The physical assault rarely amounts to more than a bit of pushing around. It is designed to show you that they are loosing their patience and demonstrate that they can do what they like to you. It is very unwise to attempt to retaliate against your attacker. If you are more seriously beaten in a police cell you should roll into a ball with your back to a corner and your head tucked well down into your chest. NEVER MAKE A STATEMENT.

When and if you use the press it is worth considering your policy towards claiming actions. It is *not a good idea* to claim all your actions under a distinctive name, or to organize your press releases in a way which identifies the actions with one group of activists, this merely helps the police to put those actions together and start drawing a pattern about the way the group works. In general the national press are overwhelmingly hostile to animal liberation groups and so it is often a waste of time dealing with them.

If you phone through a press release to a paper they may well record it, if you send a letter they may well give the letter to the police so always be brief. You should explain why the target of the raid was chosen, how many animals they use, what they use them for and if possible provide a photo of the conditions inside. If you do supply a photo then remember it will be sent to the police as soon as the papers have finished with it. Unless you have a member of the group who is prepared to train themselves in the use of a video camera there is little point in attempting to use them on a raid. They are cumbersome and unless you know what you are doing the results will be unusable.

It is probably unwise to build up a trusting relationship with the local press, or with a particular reporter, second-rate reporters would claim to support anyone to get a story. You should always consider the implications should this "trusted" reporter tell the police all they knew.

What you have read in this article is a summary of the ideas used by our group, they illustrate the way in which we worked. If nothing else we proved that with hard work, commonsense, a passion for animal rights and the initial advantage of being unknown to the police, it is possible for a relatively small group of people to launch a campaign as we did which not only saves hundreds - and if you are lucky thousands - of lives, but can cause serious disruption to sections of the animal abuse industries.

Interviews with Animal Liberation Front Activists.

How did you become members of the ALF?
We are not members of the ALF, in fact the ALF has not one single member. We are ALF activists by virtue of the fact that we carry out actions, whether on an occasional or frequent basis. Immediately after superglue has been squirted into a fur shop lock the person/s involved becomes an activist. This is exactly how we became involved in direct action four years ago.

How do you go about carrying out actions?
There are a number of aspects that one has to take into consideration.

First and foremost it's important to have a look around the region at all the targets, laboratories, as many of the factory farms as one can find, hunt kennels, fur shops, slaughterhouses, etc. If actions have taken place already in your home area then it may be a good idea to go for the most straightforward, squirting paintstripper from a lemon juice squeezy, or a washing-up liquid squeezy bottle over the van(s) of an animal exploiter, gluing up fur shop locks to start with, then progress to factory farms which generally are not alarmed (there is the odd one that is, particularly the very large food chain store ones). If no actions, or only one or two small actions have taken place, it may be beneficial to go for a laboratory, the reasoning being that once things start happening in your area the labs, if any, will invest in more security measures. *There are still labs with only minimal security.* The animals are not necessarily in the labs at all times and there is usually an animal house in a separate building where animals are held until needed or in some cases are bred there. We can usually gain access to the grounds (we're not put off by the usual security fence with strands of barbed wire at the top, these can be climbed with practice--we use the concrete posts as a support and wear 2-3 pairs of gloves when learning), we usually find the building with animals have fans operating, pumping out the stale air in the unit and fresh air in. We can smell which one has animals within.

With factory farm units we can tell what kind of animals, if any, are in the units by simply placing our ear against an air duct on the side of the unit or at the door, listening and smelling. Or we try shining a pencil torch, with colored plastic held over the end by an elastic band, through any openings. In fact we double or triple the layers of plastic so that only the minimum of light gets through, not only reducing the chance of anyone else seeing but shine a bright light onto battery hens and they may well make a lot of noise. We always try the door handle etc. and have been pleasantly surprised a couple of times to find it is not locked. With experience one can often tell what animals are held in a particular unit by its shape, size and building materials used.
When looking at potential targets we don't take balaclavas etc. We also make a point of emptying our pockets of everything including door keys, discarding matching jewellery etc. before setting out, in case we drop anything. If we need to cover our faces a scarf is fine and we

a
b

wear gloves of course. We also carry bird watching books and binoculars.

The syringe-type applicator (a) handy, but expensive. Large tubes can have a small hole drilled in the cap (b) to direct a narrow stream of glue into the lock.

How do you carry out actions against shops involved in animal exploitation?
There are a number of ways in which we cause them financial loss. First is the length of time they are open, remembering the slogan "time is money" we place small pieces of wire, a half-inch long, or match sticks in Yale locks, screws/washers into mortice locks and then squirt in superglue, both to the locks in the front door and any side or back door. When completed any shutters on the windows have the locks similarly treated. A few days before the action we walk around the shops in the early evening to check what types of locks are installed so that we have an idea of how many pieces of wire/match, tubes of glue etc. we require. Returning on the night between 7-8 P.M. (we don't wander around the shops after the bars have closed when the police are expecting trouble, and shirt and tie doesn't go amiss), we walk up and down to check no police are standing in a doorway as they sometimes do in shopping centres. All clear and a bunch of us stand close to the door eating a bag of chips and talking, shielding the person gluing the lock, it only takes a few seconds. This is usually done by a female activist who has the materials in a small plastic bag under her clothing, if we were to be spotted acting suspiciously there is far less chance of a female being searched. We would of course be able to say which bar we have all just been to. Some stores have the type of handles on the doors that can be locked together with a bicycle lock. Any messages are written either with paint (not on widows which are easy to clean--we go for the brick/woodwork) or with a felt-tip pen. Where circus posters on walls are concerned we write the work "CANCELLED" twice on 8.5" by 14" paper in felt-tip pen, photocopy it, cut the copies in half so we have two "CANCELLED" strips and paste them over the posters. We also type up a "cancelled" note informing the shops that display posters in their windows of a mix-up of dates and asking them to take down the poster in their shop, also informing them that the complementary tickets they received for putting up the posters in their

A
B
C
D
E

shop will be honored when it takes place. To push up their insurance premiums we damage the windows. Up until recently this involved using a ball-bearing and Black Widow slingshot.

SLINGSHOTS

This versatile tool can be used to knock out any windows even put holes in so-called "shatter-proof" windows. In the illustration you see the compact and easily concealed type slingshot (a). Missiles must be small, dense, and relatively round (b). Avoid irregularly shaped objects (c) as they don't fly straight. Small rocks, steel ball bearings and large nuts (d) are suitable. In illustration (e) you can see how one or two catapulters can hit a target from a passing car. Be careful you slingshots do no extend out of the car window.

CRUSH THE HEADS OF

VIVISECTIONISTS

1. Wet a sponge.

2. Wrap the sponge tightly with a string and let it dry. When dry, it should be half it's normal size.

3. Remove the string.

4. Introduce the sponge into toilets or water drains to plug them up as the sponge swells.

Why and how do activists destroy vehicles and buildings?

We would first like to point out that damage to property does save animals. All the units at a factory farm can be destroyed in one night, a number of factory farmers have gone over to free-range egg production after a devastating action, some have been closed down. Laboratories have to spend more on security in order to retain their insurance, this money often comes out of their research budget, money that would have been spent on experimentation. Broiler sheds are a favorite target for destruction. Through modern growth promoting anti-biotics and various drugs the broiler hen reaches its maximum weight in an incredible seven weeks. The units are then cleared of the hens, many with broken limbs, which are slaughtered, processed for supermarkets and eventually the dinner table. The dirt and dead hens are cleared, the units disinfected and made ready for the new chicks. Shortly after the disinfecting is the time to burn them down as this disinfecting process scares away rodents. Some of the biggest destruction jobs have been successfully carried out by two people. A number of the buildings were worth half a million dollars plus also many vehicles have been trashed by just two people. The method used for factory farm units/laboratories etc. is for one person to carry two carrier bags full of torn-up clothes, the other person carrying a gallon container of gasoline in one carrier bag and boxes of firelighters in the other. Alternatively, rucksacks can be used (and disposed of afterwards). A newspaper and a box of matches are the only additions required. The container of gas and the boxes of firelighters are wrapped in cling wrap to eliminate any smell from them if we are using public transport, in which case newspapers cover everything in the bags. Everything, absolutely everything, has been carefully wiped(of fingerprints) including any crowbars used to gain access.

At the target area one acts as a look-out while the other gets into the building. If it's a wooden broiler unit (the doors are often left open when being cleaned) both carrier bags containing the old clothes are placed in a corner, the inflammable liquid is poured onto the old clothes drenching them, some can be poured on the wall for good measure. The boxes of firelighters are half opened and placed on top against the wooden walls. Using a piece of rolled up newspaper that is lit with a match, the firelighters are then lit while standing a few feet away. This is in case we have any inflammable materials on our gloves. The box of matches is tossed on top. If it's in a lab, slaughterhouse, etc. furniture is placed around one bag, the second one is placed in another room, again surrounded by furniture, and lit in the same way as above. Where there are a number of units/buildings either the largest building is destroyed or we go for the lot, transporting the materials by car. We will have already confirmed that there are no people or animals in a target building, our first job on the raid is to check the building(s) thoroughly.

Black plastic bin bags or sacks full of old clothes (one for each unit/building, more if possible depending on circumstances), half to one gallon of inflammable liquid to each bag/sack is required (the liquid being bought a gallon at a time from different sources). On top of each is placed a box of firelighters half opened (2 or 3 packets, even better, though not necessary). The sack is tilted so it leans against the corner of a wooden unit so that it can't fall away from the side panels while burning. The materials are driven to the units separately. If only one car is used, the sacks full of jumble can be stashed with a person left to keep an eye on them, then the gas, and finally the boxes of firelighters, newspaper and box of matches.

Trashing vehicles, all that is required is gasoline or paraffin. If the doors will open (as they often will with trucks) the gas is poured over the dash-board and seats, if need be a window is forced. If it's a car that is alarmed an old sheet is laid on top, inflammable liquid poured over and firelighters placed under each tire (a refinement that can be carried out against anything with tires, eg. tractor of a factory farmer). The firelighters are lit and the lighted paper tossed on top of the gas drenched sheet. If the fuel tank eventually goes up on a truck it may travel 20-30 yards. If the truck is not this distance away from a house or unit with animals in it we release the handbrake and push it beyond this distance.

If for some reason a truck cannot be destroyed outright and excellent tactic is to buy a tin of grinding paste, per truck, and mix the contents with oil. The resulting paste is poured down the oil pipe into the engine, this process ruins the engine. Once, sometime after one of these actions had been successfully carried out a particularly well made enclosure was built by the firm around the trucks with several dogs on the loose. Consequently a further raid would have proved difficult so a successful hoax was executed. Empty grinding paste tins were thrown over the fences, the firm informed of another raid. Finding the empty tins they had the engines stripped before finding it was a hoax. Also sugar, sand or water is added to fuel tanks.

ETCHING FLUID

ALF activists have discovered a new "weapon" which has successfully been used in some areas and will soon doubtless catch on in others. Sheffield ALF initiated the idea when they squirted "etching fluid" over more than fifty windows in the city in a continuation of their campaign against House of Fraser stores which have Edelson Fur departments. The stores attacked were Rackhams and Cole Bros. The fluid eats into the glass. Following the stir that this caused, the ALF in Merseyside used etching fluid on travel agencies where tickets were on sale for circuses using animals and the windows had to be replaced. There was also success with is in Stirling, Scotland, when the windows of two bloodsports shops and a fur shop had to be renewed after slogans were written on them with etching fluid. Then a dairy van had its windscreen doused with the fluid in London. The windscreens are particularly good targets, since they have to be replaced before the vehicles can be driven.

Glass etching fluid is available from craft and fine art shops. A small bottle costs about $20 but the expense is well worth it when one considers the reduction of risk to an activist using it—there is none of the noise.

[redacted]

How do you force locks open, to gain access to laboratories, etc.?

There are a few different methods the first is to try prying it off with a crowbar. Second method is to cut it off with a pair of bolt-cutters (keep them very sharp). The third is to use a battery-powered electric drill with a new 1/8 inch high speed drill bit. Depending on the hardness of the lock you may need more than one drill bit. Make sure you don't buy cheap bits–they will only let you down. Most keyed locks are pin-tumbler types whose basic operating principle can be seen in (A). When a key is inserted, it pushes up on spring-loaded pins of various lengths. when the tops of these pins are in perfect alignment with the "shear-line" the entire "plug" in which the key is inserted can be turned and the lock opened. In most locks, all of these parts are made of brass to prevent corrosion and it's relative softness makes drilling easy. As you can see in (B), the drill is used to destroy the pins along the shear line. You should be careful not to drill too deeply into the lock since this can damage the locking bar deep inside making it impossible to open. Drill in only to the depth of the keyway (3/4-inch in most padlocks and 1-inch in most doorlocks). A "drill stop" found with the power tools in a hardware store can be used to pre-set this depth and prevent drilling too deep. Now inserting a pin like a nail, will keep the damaged remains of the top pins above the shear line (C). Otherwise they will drop down and prevent the lock from opening. You may need to put the drill bit in a couple of times to chew up any pin fragments that might interfere with opening. You may need to put the drill bit in a couple of times to chew up any pin fragments that may interfere with opening. Finally, insert a narrow-bladed screwdriver (D) into the keyway and turn it to open the lock. Remember practice makes perfect, buy a cheap lock or two and practice at home.

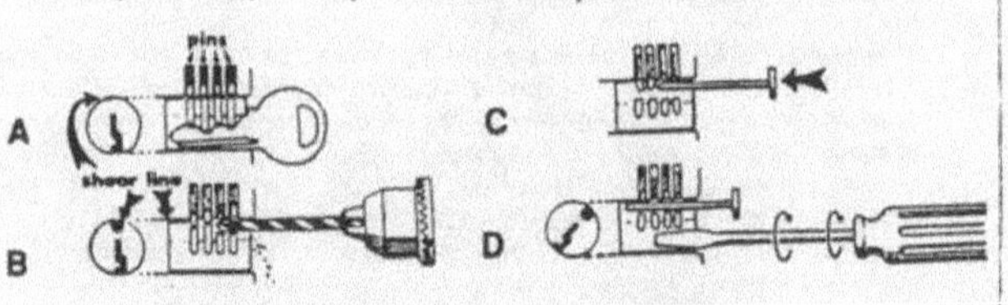
pins
shear line
A
B
C
D

CAUTION:
EXPLOSIVES
MAY BE HARM
UL TO YOUR
ALTH!!!

KEEP YOUR MOUTH SHUT

If you are arrested or taken in for questioning by the police–DO NOT SAY ANYTHING. Keep your mouth shut. The only information they are entitled to is your name, address and date of birth. If they ask any other questions reply "NO COMMENT" or "I DO NOT WISH TO SAY ANYTHING" and STICK TO THAT ANSWER.

The police may appear concerned,
"That was a silly thing to do wasn't it?"
"NO COMMENT"
They may be angry,
"Tell us what we want to know or we'll break every bone in your body."
"NO COMMENT"
They may appear friendly,
"Now if you just tell us what you did and why you did it, we'll forget about the charges."
"NO COMMENT"
They may try to glean other information from you,
"Do you know anything about so and so?"
"NO COMMENT"
They'll often tell lies,
"All your friends have confessed and have now been released. You're on your own now, and they've told us all about your involvement in it, so you might as well tell us yourself."
"NO COMMENT"

Remember–These bastards have been training for years in the art of extracting information from people. Any mood or feeling they put over is totally contrived, and aimed towards getting you to make a statement.

If they threaten to keep you in for longer if you refuse to make a statement, don't listen to them–they are lying. You will undoubtedly be kept in longer if you do make a statement, as once they have found they can crack you, they will push for more and more information.

Helping the animals extends far beyond damaging and liberating--it includes keeping your mouth shut in the police station. An imprisoned activist is a useless activist. Every time you open your mouth another animal dies because there is one less activist to save it. You are therefore doing the movement more harm than good. Remember this when you are taken in.

It is policy that any activist when arrested and questioned, gives names to the police of other animal rights activists will be given no aid from any of the Support Groups.

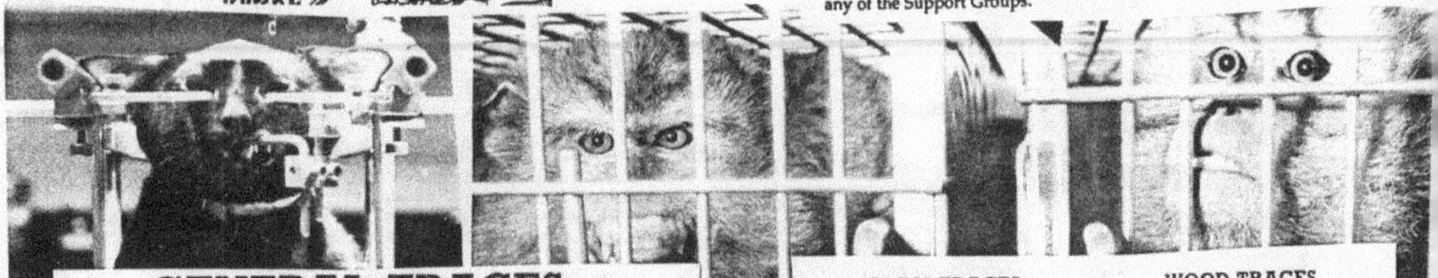

GENERAL TRACES

FINGERPRINTS

The science of fingerprint examination is called *dactyloscopy*. We are born with our fingerprints, and we'll never be able to change them or get rid of them. Whenever you touch something with your fingertips you leave behind your calling card. The police will have a varying degree of difficulty in reproducing your prints depending on the surface upon which it lies. Obviously surfaces such as glass, marble, chrome etc, will be the easiest, whilst it is almost impossible to lift prints from brickwork or untreated wood. A fingerprint is basically the fatty, acidic residue left on a surface in the exact shape of the *ridge lines* of your fingertips. Because a fingerprint is composed of sweat, which is an acid, in some instances it qwill etch itself onto metal. This is most likely to occur with crowbars, hammers, chisels, etc, and can be erased by rubbing down said tools with coarse wire wool after use. The police are continually perfecting their methods of print detection, because they are such a foolproof piece of personal identity. They can take prints from skin (if they really try), from tightly woven fabrics, especially synthetic ones, and paper.

To convict, the police need to show 12 matching features of a fingerprint. In practice, these can be found on just one square centimeter of skin area. Fingerprints are fairly hard to destroy, and even immersion in water will not do the job completely, so if you are going to throw something over the bridge, don't forget to wipe it down first. Unless an object is totally consumed, fire is also not a sure method of erasing prints, as a layer of carbon can cover them, and keep them recognisable. The older a print becomes, the harder it is to reproduce, although, in theory, it will last forever, as long as it has not been disfigured. Fingerprints are kept on the PNC in the form of encoded data, and as such, do not need to be visually checked to be found to match. A 'specialist' will analyse the fingerprint and turn it into a series of four digit numbers. These numbers are then entered into the PNC, which will return the location of any matching fingerprints held by the Fingerprint Bureau at New Scotland Yard. These matches will be examined further in detail to see if any of the candidates presented by the PNC *exactly* matches those found at the scene of crime. The PNC fingerprint index is

used roughly 300,000 times a year. A new system of fingerprint recognition has been developed which involves *hyper-computers*, and which can visually translate a single print into unique and complex computer data, thus making positive I.D. from a partial found print possible. This system is not yet in use, but should be in a few years.

The police show a great deal of interest in everyones prints, to the extent that babies are now being fingerprinted at birth in some countries, in case they should get'lost'. How touching! In the station, the police will always try and take your prints. Since the introduction of the Criminal Evidence Act, they have more or less complete freedom to do so, without having to go to a magistrate anymore. In theory, it is possible to smudge or blur our fingerprints. One way is to leave plenty of soap on your hands, after you've been made to wash them, and another is to try and 'help' the police. The idea is that you relax your fingers while they roll them over the sheet. If you apply too much pressure, or slide about a bit, you might smudge a couple. On the other hand, they might just tear them up and start again, or even tear you up and start again!

GLASS TRACES

Definitely one of the most important areas of forensics for people like us to know about. Every time that glass is smashed tiny shards of the stuff fly everywhere. For practical purposes it is wisest to assume that anyone even remotely near to breaking glass is covered in the stuff. It sticks to things like shit to a blanket, especially loose fibred cloth, such as woolen hats. The only way to get rid of it is to throw away anything that you may have been wearing. Glass also likes to get embedded in the soles of *shoes*. The police can identify different makes and types of glass, and therefore can put you at a certain place at a certain time. Fine, broken glass powder will stick to the smooth surfaces of tools, and fibres from your clothing will stick to the sharp edges of broken glass. The best way to break glass without covering yourself in traces is from a *very* long distance, using a powerful slingshot and marbles, or for toughened bank windows, steel ball bearings. Both ball bearings and marbles retain your prints well! Or why not try glass etching fluid? You can get it in craft shops, and with it you can write a message on a window that can never be removed, bar replacing the whole thing. N.B. *In certain hard hit towns you have to sign for etching fluid, and in some instances shopkeepers report sales to the police.*

DUST TRACES

For the police to convict you on the basis of dust traces takes a great deal of work on their part, involving painstaking work with powerful microscopes. The composition of dust in your clothes can tell them where you may have been (e.g. a metal foundry) and at what time of the year (by identifying the spores of seasonal plants). By just washing your clothes thoroughly you can get rid of most of these traces, but as always, the safest thing is to ditch them. It is unusual, though not unknown for the police to use dust traces to convict. These traces are more useful as a last resort for clues, when other avenues have failed. They are chiefly used to find out where and for how long something has been; e.g.guns, bodies, stolen goods.

In brief, the investigation of these traces is only likely to come up in a serious case, and should you start to worry about traces this tiny, then paranoia is taking over from sensible precaution. If the police threaten to use them against you, then it indicates that they most likely have nothing better to go on.

WOOD TRACES

Wood will yield some information to the forensic investigator. It is possible for him/her/it to match species of wood to each other, even from samples as small as sawdust or splinters. If someone has been introducing your local fascists head to a piece of 2 be 4, then a match can be made to the piece from which it was cut/sawed. When they remove said lump from your fascists head, it will be checked for foreign bodies, such as textile fibres, paint flakes, hairs, and other incriminating evidence. If a baseball bat were to be used instead, and it is not disposed of, then it can be linked to the 'crime' by comparison with the splinters it has left in the skull as well as traces of varnish or resin, and the bat itself will carry traces of skin, hair, blood, not to mention matching dental There is no point in keeping such weapons once they have been used.

SOIL AND PLANT TRACES

A forensic scientist can tell roughly where you have been from the composition of the dirt and soil that you will have picked up on your travels. If, let's say, you've been keeping warm by standing next to a burning portacabin on a Laings building site, then traces of sand, cement, gypsum, gravel, lime, etc, will have collected on your shoes and clothes. By the same token, if you have been watching Lord Anthony Wedgewood Benn's stately ancestral home burn to the ground, then traces of earth from his garden will be upon you, as will traces of plant life, such as pollen from the rare gladiolae that you may have brushed against. Once again, it is best to dispose of any clothing.

These traces are used to put you at a certain place, and in some instances, at a certain time. As with dust traces, don't let the police bluff a confession out of you by saying that these traces are cast iron evidence; they are certainly not and can be disputed in court.

HAIR TRACES

We all shed hair, and we shed it all the time. If we stay in one place for any length of time, than it is certain that we will leave samples of our hair in the vicinity. It is most likely to be lodged in the clothing of someone with whom we have had close contact (i.e. the bishop you just throttled). Hair will tell the forensic expert many things; where it came from on the body (scalp, beard, crotch, eyebrows, nose, armpit), how long your hair is, whether it has been cut recently, whether you have shaved recently, if you have been using any specific chemicals on it, such as dyes, oil, lotions, sprays, pommades, DDT, etc. They can also tell if you fall into the racial categories of Negroid, Caucasion or Mongoloid, or even mixtures of the three. They can tell your sex and blood type.

It is harder to tell the colour of your hair, as individual strands differ in hue from each other. It becomes easier if they possess more hairs. The good news is that conclusive proof of identity is *NOT* possible, *BUT* they can prove your innocence, in much the same way that parentage can only be disproved through blood tests. On the other hand, if they have a sample of your hair and it is 2 foot long, dyed green, and you've used superglue on it to keep your mohawk upright, than I'd imagine that they'd have a fair case for positive ID—Wear a tight fitting hat.

SHOE TRACES

There are thousands of styles and sizes of footwear and each one is distinctive, even more so when it has been worn for a while and picked up individual marks of wear and tear. Basically, a clear footprint is as useful to a forensic expert as a fingerprint. However, you can always throw away your shoes!

On hard surfaces, such as lino or marble, shoe *prints* will be left behind. On soft surfaces, such as mud, earth, dog shit, etc, shoe *impressions* will be left behind. From these marks identification can be made, and are watertight evidence if a comparison is made. The only sensible thing to do is to wear old shoes and to throw them a long way away immediately afterwards. Shoes will also carry traces away with them, such as oil, petrol, glass splinters and other such giveaways. Don't wear them in your home.

Tracker dogs will be able to follow the smell from your shoes, but not for more than 10 to 12 hours afterwards, and then only in favourable conditions. Roads that smell of exhaust fumes, petrol and rubber will mask your smell. The best conditions for tracker dogs are unspoilt meadows during moist and cool weather.

BLOOD TRACES

I can think of several instances where blood may be spilt, and for this reason it makes sense to know as much about it as possible. Blood is very hard to get rid of once it has got on you or on your clothing. Even dry cleaning will not remove it thoroughly. Should you be near to someone who has been punched in the nose or stabbed, you will be covered in a fine spray of blood droplets.

A forensic scientist can detect, retrieve and examine the minutest traces of blood, and the amount of information to be gathered depends on the circumstances. In the laboratory a fresh, warm pint of blood can show the type, the sex of the donor, any illnesses peculiar to the donor, any drugs or medication taken recently. In practice, however, the smaller the quantity and the older the sample, the harder the task. Importantly, a blood sample *cannot* be proved to be positively yours, although it can be proven that it isn't.

A new developement in the examinations has just been made in britain and it is rather worrying. It is called 'genetic fingerprinting' and has been perfected by a private company but has already been used once by the police. The use of this method in blood sample examination is supposed to be able to positively identify a person from a matching blood sample. It seems as if it will be several years before this is in general use, but it is the shape of things to come.

TEXTILE TRACES

There is not a lot to say about these traces that is not common sense.....just think of your clothing as blotting paper that will soak up incriminating evidence like crazy! Dust, soil, chemicals, blood, petrol, paint, the list is endless. Clothing will also leave behind particles of their fabric, and as with gloves, will leave *impressions* should you sit or lean on anything soft. Traces of fibre and debris from your own environment will be carried by your clothes aand left at scene. For instance, the fibres from your sofa, carpet, car furnishing, etc, will be carried by your trousers (say), and may be left wherever you go. To circumvent this, wear old clothes, and discard them afterwards. Remember, if you wear them back home, you will also be carrying back traces from wherever you may have been.

TOOL TRACES

In much the same way that a bullet will retain scratches from the barrel of the gun from which it was fired, then tools such as chisels, pliers, bolt cutters, knives, screwdrivers, etc, will leave identifying marks at the scene of an investigation. These marks can be matched to the tool at a later date using comparison or stereo microscopes. Most obviously, the shear marks on a cut padlock can be linked to the cutters that were used on the job. If the same pair of boltcutters has been going the rounds, and you find yourself nicked with it, then you might find yourself being held responsible for any number of previously unsolved 'crimes'. If such tools have been used to break into the Ministry of Defence, then it is courting disaster to hold on to them. For less dodgy instances, the working edges of tools can be given a new 'face' by filing or re-sharpening, but only if the tool is in good condition, and not badly pitted or scarred. Tools are not only made of metal; objects such as robe, string, tape, etc,are just as incriminatory, and lend themselves to comparitive analysis.

GLOVE TRACES

Although it is always wiser to wear gloves to avoid the risk of leaving any fingerprints behind, we should be aware that gloves can sometimes leave just as much information. Basically, gloves will almost certainly leave traces of the fabric from which they are made on anything they touch, especially broken glass, fencing, masonry, and rough wood. If gloves are not thrown away after use, then positive links can be made in the form of textile analysis. Plastic gloves, rubber gloves will keep your prints on the *inside* and some very thin surgical gloves will still allow your print*impressions* to show up on hard or shiny surfaces. If your discarded gloves are found, than traces of your sweat will be present (see Body Secretion Traces), as well as comparitive traces such as wood splinters, paint flakes, glass splinters, etc from the scene of crime. Remember also that you are going to look dead suspicious if you are found wearing gloves in mild weather, or even if you have them in your possession, especially if there is more thasn one of you, and you are all wearing them.

BODY SECRETION TRACES

The human body produces various fluids and secretions apart from blood. These are namely; spit, sweat, tears, earwax, urine, faeces and snot. Samples of these may or will be left at a scene of investigation. They don't tell the police a hell of a lot, but, as with blood traces, they help build up an overall picture. For the most part, body secretion traces will show blood type. In some instances the information can be more exact. From your snot and spit they will know if you smoke, or if you have a specific occupation (e.g. miner:black lung, docker: asbestosis, etc). From your urine, sweat and faeces, any illnesses that you have may be apparent. (Hepatitis, anaemia, NSU, etc) and any medication or drugs that you may have taken. From your shit they will be able to tell what you've had to eat.

For example, the analysis of urine at a scene of crime might show blood type A, presence of Hepatitis, and presence of Methadone. They already have a list of registered methadone users, therefore they already have a list of suspects.

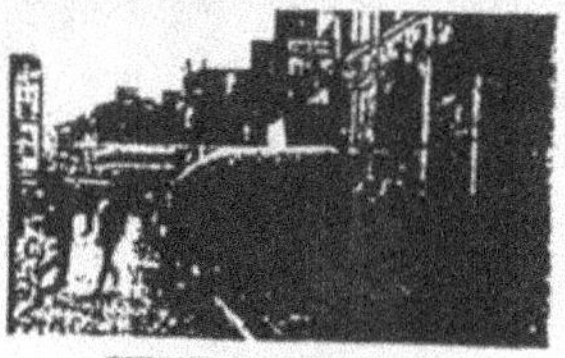

VEHICLE TRACES

Vehicle traces refer to any parts of forensic evidence that may be left by motor transport.

Firstly, the tyre tracks; these are usually left in soft ground, and not on hard top roads, although they may be found in soft tar, dog shit, etc, and in the case of a collision, sometimes on the *flesh of the victim(s)*. These traces will identify the make of tyre, and in most instances will prove unique to one tyre, due to the characteristic wear. The distance between tyre tracks will indicate axle width and chassis length, thus indicating the type of car. Some cars carry unique tyres, for instance imported, or small production runs.

Transfer traces are those which are left on the scene due to collision or contact. Most commonly this involves paint flakes. These are *always* left in the case of any contact. As well as indicating the exact colour of the vehicle, when studied microscopically they

Cruelty to lab animals exposed

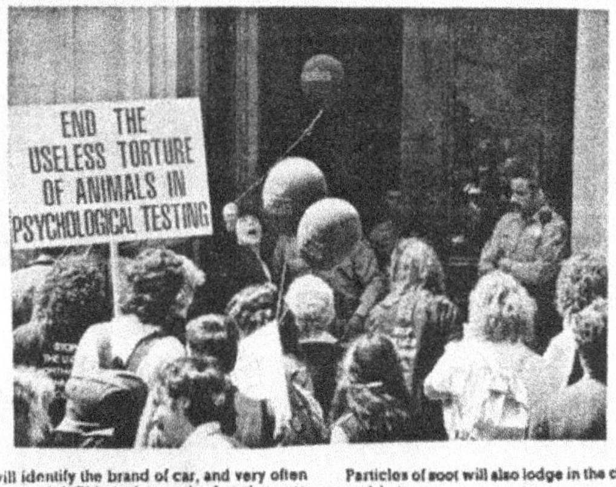
END THE
USELESS TORTURE
OF ANIMALS IN
PSYCHOLOGICAL TESTING

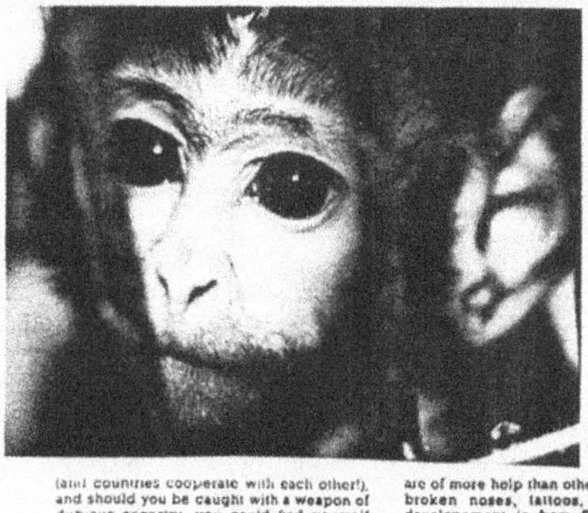

will identify the brand of car, and very often the model. This is due to the fact that auto paint can consist of over 14 layers of primer, paint, laquer, etc, which are unique to different manufacturers. Forensic experts carry detailed catalogues of paint samples. From one paint flake it is theoretically possible to know the make, the model, colour, previous colour(s), and the year of manufacture of a given car. Due to the extensive registration of vehicles this means that the police have a large amount of information to work on.

Other types of transfer traces chiefly consist of trim that may have been dislodged, such as hubcaps, bits of windscreen, light covers, door handles, those stupid rubber earth strips that hang off the rear bumper, aerials, coon tails, furry dice, etc. All these things lend themselves to comparitive analysis.

The direction and speed of a vehicle can be estimated from the direction of brake tracks, dripping oil, debris, etc.

In conclusion, as vehicles are so closely monitored in this country (M.O.T., license, insurance, tax, etc), the police have a good deal of evidence to work on *already*, before any crime has been commited, and this gives them the edge when it comes to tracking down cars. In practice, it is not a good idea to use your own car for anything dodgy. It may be spotted by the video cameras on potrol station forecourts, traffic control videos on motorways, or be checked on the PNC by the police without your knowledge. The stop proportionately more red cars than any other colour. Dull, fairly new fleet cars get stopped less, neutrally coloured and respectable looking are safest. A man and a woman get stopped less than single drivers, and flash sports cars succumb to the 'envy factor' in coppers, especially if driven by someone who is not an aryan true blue male brit.

ARSON AND FIRE TRACES

The assumption that evidence is destroyed by fire is incorrect. The Fire Investigation Unit will turn up if the origins of a fire are suspicious. They possess a large degree of skill and are able to determine the flashpoint of a fire and what caused it, (electrical fault, cigarette, candle, spontaneous combustion, deliberate arson etc). They also can tell the flammable substance which was used to start the fire (gasoline, paraffin, tallow, paper, etc.).

Chemicals used to start a fire will almost automatically end up on the person and clothing of the person(s) who started it. Particles of soot will also lodge in the clothing and hair.

Many arsonists have been caught because they wanted to come back and watch.

P.C. BLAKELOCK WALKS
ON WATER....

BALLISTIC AND FIREARM TRACES

In Britain, which has such a small number of private firearms, the forensic investigation of ballistics is considered of paramount importance. For this reason, extreme care must be taken when getting involved with them.

Firstly, the potential of the projectile (bullet). If it is recovered in good condition, then it will reveal the calibre of the weapon, the type, and often the manufacturer. A bullet will remain in good condition if it enters flesh or any other soft material. If it hits thick metal or concrete, etc, it will be disfigured, but will still retain many of its identifying characteristics. Certain types of bullets are designed to fragment on contact. These are bullets such as Dum Dum, Mercury Tip, Hollow Point or Explosive. Whilst this makes the job of the forensic investigator harder, it doesn't stop it. No matter what sort of bullet has been used, it is always safer to assume that it has left enough characteristic marks to make it identifyable. As we all know from watching Kojak, the barrel of a gun imparts unique markings to the surface of the bullet, which can be matched to specimens when viewed through a stereo microscope. What perhaps we don't know is that the shell casing or cartridge also carries unique markings, from the impact of the hammer or bolt,and from the ejection and breech mechanisms. Automatic hand guns, machine pistols, many rifles and some shotguns automatically eject their shells. A cage or trap fitted around the eject port enables these to be caught.

The police of every country keep a pictorial file of all bullets and weapons used previously

(and countries cooperate with each other!), and should you be caught with a weapon of dubious ancestry, you could find yourself having to explain a lot.

When a gun is fired, particles of gas and powder will DEFINITELY lodge themselves in any exposed skin and clothing. These particles can be found by a forensic examiner by the taking of ether swabs. In amerika an aerosol has been developed which can be sprayed on the hands and will show up as a coloured dye immediately should it come into contact with these particles. It is used to quickly eliminate suspects after (say) an assassination attempt. Gloves!

Once a gun has been used it is courting disaster to keep it. It should be thoroughly cleaned and dismantled and distributed into a deep lake, not forgetting that fingerprints can be preserved under water, especially if covered with a layer of gun oil.

In conclusion, firearms are an area in which forensics are advanced and extensive, thus giving the police the edge. Definitely not an area to get involved in without knowing what you're doing.

VOICE INDENTIFICATION

It is possible from a tape recording of a voice to compare it with another voice, and decide whether they are one and the same. This is because each persons voice is a combination of frequencies which can be analysed using a sound spectrograph. This is most likely to be called into use for anonymous phone callings, and to this end it should be assumed that *all* telephone lines are not secure. Most newspapers have facilities for immediately recording calls, and all emergency service calls are automatically taped. Changing your voice, dialect, or pitch won't make a hell of alot of difference to your 'voice print'. Speaking through a handkerchief has absolutely no effect! If you do have to use your voice over the phone, try everything from pinching your nose, stuffing your mouth with tissues and speaking with a Ukrainian accent. Perhaps the best way to phone in a message is to edit on tape together the words of famous personalities, in the same way as ransom notes are made from cut up mewspapers.......just imagine:-"This is Terry Wogan claiming responsibility on behalf of the ALF...."

FACE IDENTIFICATION

We have all seen Identikit pictures, and on the whole they just serve to give the roughest idea of someones face. Obviously, certain things are of more help than others....scars, moles, broken noses, tattoos, etc. The latest developement is from Sweden, where a computer takes a basic Indetikit picture and blurs the edge over, finally producing a computer generated image similar to a photograph. The police also use professional artists to make sketches from a witnesses description. It is hard to change the features on your face, but certain things help. Glasses, changes of hairstyle, haircolour, etc. Women can use a mountain of make up, heighten cheekbones, etc. Men can grow or shave facial hair. A man with very short hair and a moustache looks radically different from the same man cleanshaven with long hair.

RESPONSIBILITY NOTES

These are bit of an ego trip and just give the police more evidence to work on. In fact, it might be the *onlyevidence* the police will have, so why give it to them? However, if you do have to send them, there are some things you should be aware of.

Your blood type and other details can be taken from the spit used to moisten the stamp and the envelope flap.(See 'Body Secretion Traces').*Paper does carry fingerprints.* When handwriting use stylized block capitals:

JUST LIKE THIS

Only ever write on one sheet of paper at a time,preferably on a flat, hard surface such as glass or formica, which will not take the impression of what you are writing. Don't use sheets torn from a notebook, as comparisons can be made from the tear and from the type of notebook. Also, something innocuous already written in the notebook can be already transferred to the sheet you're using, providing more comparisons. Preferably use envelopes and writing paper of a very common brand, e.g. bought from Woolworths. Only write on one sheet at a time. Destroy any remaining sheets or envelopes. Don't keep any stamps from the same block. Don't post anything in your area. Be aware that minute traces of hair and fibre can easily be trapped in the glue of the flap and the stamp, especially if the letter has been in your pocket. This is even more likely if you have been cutting up newspaper words and sucking them down. When doing this, don't keep the glue, the scissors or the papers. When using a pen, use a 'Bic' ballpoint, as this is the most common, or use a felt pen, which is less like to leave an impression on sheets below. See also 'Typewriter Traces.'

TYPEWRITERS

Every typewriter carries its own unique identifying marks. Firstly these come from the keys themselves, which when enlarged, show individual peculiarities of style and wear. Secondly, the pressure that the keys have made upon the paper. Thirdly, the alignment (or lack of it) of the letters, both horizontallly and vertically upon the page. It is further possible to have an idea of the typist, from the pressure emphasis of certain letters. E.g 'hunt and peck' versus touch typing. This is most obvious on manual typewriters.

To avoid all this trouble, it easiest to use a machine with a seperate type element, such as a daisy wheel or golfball. These can be thrown away after use. Never type on to double sheets, as the entire text will appear as an impression on the bottom sheet. Carbon sheets also will retain the text, as will the ribbon, whether carbon or cotton. All things of this nature should be destroyed. (Don't forget erasion ribbons!)

The best way to avoid all this palaver is to buy a second-hand typewriter from a flea market. It should only cost a fiver. Use it once and then chuck it, not forgetting that your prints will be on every key!

With modern dot matrix computer print outs you can program your own typefaces. Perhaps this is worth trying out.

MAKING IMPRESSIONS VISIBLE AGAIN

It is sometimes believed that it is possible to remove identifying serial numbers by filing or drilling them off. The numbers stamped onto the frames of motor vehcles, guns and other metal objects can be made visible again by various forensic processes. This is because the initial stamping has changed the structure of the metal *beneath* the surface. The best way to obscure chassis numbers is to utilise this factor, by filing off the numbers and then banging hell out of the area with a hammer and cold chisel, before re-stamping.

Many government and business agencies, as well as private householders mark their property with an ultra-violet pen that is invisible to the naked eye. Ultra violet bulbs can be bought from specialist electrical shops, and these will help you read any numbers or marks.

TRACES IN PRINTING

When printing 'subversive' pamphlets, books, posters, etc, there are various proce... which lend themself to forensic compariso... Firstly, the typeface; this is as for typewriters, by studying the individual letters, their

allignment, etc, it can be told from what machine they came from. This is true for manual or cold type typesetters, but is much harder when a computer typesetter has been used, especially when using a very common typeface. Secondly, the artwork and negatives. They should be handled consistently with gloves, and destroyed immediately after use, as should be the printing plates. The paper should be of a very common type or brand and should be bought in small quantities from retail outlets, so as to avoid invoice traces from large paper suppliers. Thirdly, the printing machine(s); they impart individual marks on the paper from the gripper edge as they go through. These can be removed at the finishing stage with a guillotine. Fourthly, the guillotine; the cutting edge of the blade will uniquely mark the paper, but comparisons can be avoided by thoroughly re-sharpening the blade, unless it is badly worn, in which case it should be thrown away. Fifthly, the ink; it should be a very common brand (i.e. Pantone process black) so as to make comparisons useless. Sixthly, the distribution; should be done very quickly, leaving no stockpiles in embarassing places.

To avoid the labour of these above precautions, we typeset, laid out and printed this book abroad, and it was distributed over one long weekend.

EYE SPY

VIDEO SURVEILLANCE: HOW DOES IT AFFECT YOU?

We find video cameras these days in almost every public place: the Underground, shopping centres, car parks, banks, football stadia, rich houses, hospitals, as 'traffic control',etc,etc. These are all 'public' video cameras, which have some legitimate use, but must also be regarded as security measures. For the main part, these cameras serve to deter potential 'criminals', and instil a healthy sense of paranoia. 'If you have nothing to hide, you have nothing to fear'. 'This store is protected by video cameras', 'Big Brother is Watching You'. The purpose of cameras in such places as supermarkets and Tube stations is mainly preventative, although they occasionally are used evidentially. For example, in 1985 a penniless Nigerian student knifed to death an american banker in a

Mayfair street 'because he looked rich'. The murder was viewed and recorded by one of the many video cameras that festoon rich areas and *embassies*. He was convicted. We must be aware of the areas where video surveillance is used, for however innocous a purpose, and relate their importance to our actions.

VIDEO AND THE POLICE

These days the police are attaching a great deal of importance to video, and they have created special video teams, whose basic purpose is to monitor demos, pickets, riots, marches, raids, etc in order to to provide concrete evidence of crimes being committed and to be able to identify individuals and the groups to which they belong. You will no longer be able to go to a demo, march or mass picket without being recorded. In this way they build up a picture of affiliations, and they hope to spot 'trouble makers','ringleaders' etc. At a demo or picket it is common practice for the police to pose as newsteams and 'interview' those taking part. They can be spotted by the fact that their cameras do not carry the logos of any of the legitimate tv companies. If in doubt, you can always ask to see their press cards!

VIDEO AND THE PRIVATE SECTOR

Because of the apallingly low clear up rate that the police have for crimes against property (and from the upper classes point of view, these are the most serious crimes), rich individuals and companies are resorting heavily to private security firms. This applies particaulary to companies that suffer from expensive vandalism. For example Barclays, sequestrators, arms companies, the nuclear production and waste industry, fur farmers, butchers vivisectionists, etc.

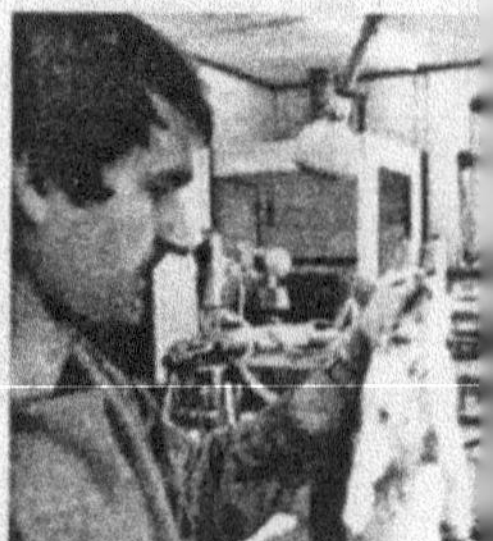

HOW TO DEAL WITH VIDEO SURVEILLANCE

Obviously the most important thing is to be unrecognisable. For the most part this involves keeping your masks and balaclavas handy, but in situations where this may look too suspicious, such as a march or a daylight picket, hats and glasses can be worn. Try to

avoid wearing *conspicous* clothing, as this makes you stick out.

It is is possible to burn out the *cone* of video cameras by simply pointing the flash gun of a camera directly into the lense, and giving them a burst, thus leaving them unusable. The best place to try this is with the cop cameras at demos, and the cameras of TV crews (for all practical purposes, the two are indistinguishable). Try the same thing on private security cameras, just for the harassment value, but this will not always work, as many have anti glare coatings on their lenses, or are keyed for night-time use, and in both cases will not register high levels of light. Many security cameras will work at night, either with the aid of floodlighting, or with infra-red. You can be seen in pitch darkness.

CONCLUSION

Camera surveillance is entering our lives increasingly, and because of their numbers, we often simply fail to notice them. They are used and monitored by two seperate groups. Firstly, the police and state security agencies, and secondly by the propertied classes, who are unhappy with the level of service that they are getting from their security guards (the police). Video cameras should be vandalised at every possible chance. Spraypaint onto the lense, stickers, glass etch fluid, a lump hammer, etc. Big Brother *is* watching you!

POLICE HELICOPTERS AND THEIR VIDEO CAPACITY

The Metropolitan police in London have at present two helicopters stationed at Lippins Hill, but they will be getting more in the future, and their technology will be improving. As it is, the helicopters carry radio receiving and transmission capabilities on microwave frequencies, video surveillance equipment, night searchlights, loud hailers and on board computer terminals.

The radio equipment allows tthem to be on constant contact with the ground, and their response time is very fast. they can fly across London in 15 minutes. The pilots are police officers, and not privately hired (flying pigs?). The video camera is mounted to the side of the fuselage in a globe cover. The cameras are remote, and can be pointed in any direction, and are of a quality that can can focus, pick out and *record* a face in a crowd. The picture is monitored on board, but using microwave transmision it can also be monitored on the ground, from vans or a command centre at New Scotland Yard. This system is called 'Hele-Tele', and in practice it means that an individual in a crowd can be isolated, followed, identified, and police on the ground can be directed to him/her by radio, even when he/she is only visible from the air. At night time, the camera is complemented by a very powerful directional searchlight, although it can use existing light, or work on infra-red frequencies, but with a distinct loss of quality. This technology has long since been used by the occupation army in Ulster for spotting night time movements, especially along the border. In places where there is a large amount of residual heat, such as in built up areas, image intensifiers lose much of their effectiveness.

The on board computer that these helicopters carry is a *terminal*, which means that they have all the information on the PNC to work with. This makes it autonomous. In practice they can spot a car from the air, zoom in on its plates, and find out the name, address of the owner/previous owners, criminal record of the owner, in fact all information available on the PNC.

Police helicopters carry a lot of heat sensitive equipment, and they really don't like things like rockets and distress flares being fired at them, so this is all I can suggest to annoy them, short of building a microwave radio jammer, or firing a SAM missile at them.

FIELD NOTES

* Medicine for monkeywrenchers: Ecoteurs have fallen into ditches, scraped knuckles on heavy equipment, cut themselves on glass, and otherwise suffered numerous minor injuries. Usually there is so much adrenaline pumping through your system that you are scarcely aware of the injury. You must make it a point to examine the wound at the first safe opportunity. A penlight flashlight can be carefully used for the examination. Each member of the team should carry a dark, clean bandanna to use as a bandage.

* Disposing of tools: *Never* bury tools used in ecotage on your own land or that owned by friends or associates. Police agencies are experienced in the use of metal detectors to uncover buried caches. Metal detectors can be thrown off, nevertheless, by burying metal tools in old landfills that have other metal present or by scattering nails and scrap metal through the soil where you do bury your "monkeywrenches."

* Water: Monkeywrenching can be hot, dry work. Keep a water jug in your vehicle. If you carry a canteen on your person, remember that a partially full canteen can make a loud sloshing noise. If you're traveling at night under strict security precautions, you should drink all of the water in your canteen or pour out the remainder when you first drink in order to keep it from sloshing and revealing your position.

*Psychology: Learn to play your hunches and be aware of subtle feelings. Life in the underground sharpens the senses to the point where you can develop a protective "sixth sense" that defies rational explanation. Dreams and "feelings" with no basis in fact or observation have saved many an outlaw or monkeywrencher from arrest. Nevertheless, under no circumstances should you allow this to become a substitute for proper planning and preparation. On the other extreme, make sure that neither you nor your associates slips into paranoia. If fears and pressures seem to be mounting, take a vacation.

Another type of behavior for which to be on alert, particularly among experienced operatives, is euphoria. This energetic, go-getting, "nothing-can-stop-me-now" attitude almost inevitably follows periods of depression. The pattern will be acted out by even the most highly motivated individuals after prolonged exposure to danger. First comes a slow, creeping depression when the individual loses enthusiasm and begins to question his or her basic motivation. It begins to seem as though nothing will ever change for the better, regardless of what one may do. After a few days or weeks, the mind snaps out of this way of thinking but then overcompensates by making the individual feel invincible. This is euphoria. Locked in its heady grip, experienced monkeywrenchers have been known to charge forward without taking even elementary security precautions. This is a dangerous state of mind, and team leaders, in their coordinating role, must remain on the alert for it (even in themselves!). The solitary Earth defender must carefully evaluate her or his own moods. A break or vacation will help to restore proper balance.

*Keep in mind that police, Forest Service and other government agencies, and ... specialists will study this book in the hope of developing countermeasures. Be thoughtful and inventive. Do not leave this book lying around your home or car in plain view.

* If you have suggestive bumperstickers on your car, you can cover them with masking tape and duct tape while "on the job" or visiting unfriendly towns like Escalante, Utah. Cover your sticker with masking tape first, then cover the masking tape with duct tape. The masking tape will protect your bumpersticker from being peeled off or torn when the duct tape is pulled off. When your need for maintaining a low profile is over, simply peel off the duct tape and there is your bumpersticker proclaiming its message to the world.

*Regardless of what you are doing, or where you are operating, remember that your abilities are cumulative and only acquired through experience. The prospective monkeywrencher should read and re-read pertinent sections of this volume before attempting an actual operation. It is then recommended that one start with simple tasks and easy targets, and only gradually work one's way up to major monkeywrenching.

*Power tools, chainsaws and oxy-acetylene or propane torches all bear serial numbers (sometimes not readily apparent). A tool such as these dropped at the scene of a hit can be traced from the manufacturer to the retailer who sold it. There must be no paper trail linking you to the tool purchase.

*In all of your monkeywrenching endeavors, do not be afraid to constantly experiment, improvise and practice your techniques. Monkeywrenching is a highly creative field in the fight to preserve wild country. Use your imagination!

*When driving in rough country or on jeep trails, try not to leave evidence in passing. If you scrape a rock, the paint chips you leave can be compared to the FBI's National Automotive Paint File to determine the year and make of your vehicle. Also, grease smears rubbed off on the high-centers of such roads can sometimes be linked to the remaining crud on the undercarriage of your vehicle. Whenever you leave such a sign, stop to brush it away.

*Get a black, dark green or camouflage fanny pack and fill it with basic survival gear (space blanket, matches, candle, candy, pocket knife, first aid kit, small flashlight, etc). Strap it around your waist as soon as you leave your vehicle for operations such as tree-spiking in the woods. Do not remove it. In case you are confronted by Forest Service law enforcement agents or deputies, you can k. h-tail it through the woods to escape and be sure that you have the minimum survival requirements on your person to get back to safety even if you have to spend several days in the backcountry.

SABOTAGING THE FUR INDUSTRY

-BY TELEPHONE AND THROUGH THE MAIL-

This information is being distributed with the hope that it will be used to further the liberation of non-humans from their imprisonment, torture and murder by the hands of selfish humans. What you are holding here is a call to action, steps all of us who care about animals can take to help free them while putting ourselves at little, if any, risk of punishment.

All forms of animal exploitation are morally indefensible. A small portion of the population (VEGAN POWER!) understands this, but the masses of human society are indifferent to the suffering of anyone but themselves and their own species. There are, however, a few types of animal abuse which larger numbers of humans oppose or at least understand the immorality of. Fur is one of these issues. It's not too hard find people who are digusted by fur yet they themselves eat meat, wear leather, drink milk, etc. Public opinion is very favorable on the anti-fur issue at least when compared to most other forms of animal abuse. Because of this it's reasonable to say that the fur industry can be abolished before the turn of the century. IF, we make a conscious effort to work towards that goal. The fur industry is not that powerful. It can and will be destroyed. But we need you to help us. Consistent calling of "800" numbers destroys mail order businesses. If the caller keeps them on the line with inquiries about their products, their phone bills go up and they don't get any business in return. If the caller tells them they're murderers, they eventually get fed up and take their phone off the hook. Either way you're tying up their phone lines, running up their bills, preventing legitimate business calls from being answered, and wasting their time. They get really frustrated, believe me. Certain companies get more calls from animal liberationists than they do from furriers and trappers. This has destroyed their businesses. This information is being distributed to animal rightists throughout the nation so that the successes of our small groups can be multiplied by the thousands so that every number, every business on this sheet can be shut down, or crippled. When phone bills are combined with the costs of returned packages the frustration and economic losses to the furriers/trappers are even more substantial. The first time you call, request a catalog be mailed to you. (To be on the safe side use a false name.) Then when you receive the catalog call again and again placing C.O.D. orders to whatever adress you can think of (other fur shops are a good choice-check the yellow pages). They have to pay the postage and the C.O.D. fee, so the larger the order the better! After they know your voice continue to call them and tell them how evil they are. This system has already proven it's effectiveness. If you're worried about security you can always call from a pay phone, but it's not always necessary. The worst that can really happen is for the business or their phone company to call your house and ask you about it. Just deny it and don't call that number from your house again. A final note can be added on the use of business reply cards. They can be taped to packages and they have to pay the bill. Mail them rocks, bricks, anything heavy you can find. THINK OF THE ANIMALS!! YELL AT FUR WEARERS!! AND CALL THESE NUMBERS!!:

(ALL NUMBERS BEGIN WITH "1-800")

FUR STORES

872-3699 - USA FOXX AND FURS
275-4387 - FUR VAULT
347-7040 - TENDLER FURS
521-2037 - HENIG FURS
423-6465 - FURS BY WEISS
331-5255 - LINGENFELTER BRILL FURS
221-8826 - ERWIN GOODMAN FURS
248-5332 - JENSEN FURS
437-6465 - MINK SPECIALTIES
445-6465 - AMERICAN LEGENDS

DEPT. STORES

272-2450 - DAYTON'S
374-3000 - CARSON PIRIE SCOTT
343-0121 - MACY'S
777-8910 - ROBINSON'S
284-3900 - HOME SHOPPING CLUB
626-4800 - BROADWAY
528-8000 - AMERICAN EXPRESS
634-6267 - NEIMAN MARCUS
345-3454 - SAKS FIFTH AVENUE

(Note: We probably won't shut down these large companies, but we can get them to stop selling fur!)

FUR PROCESSORS

772-3277 - NATIONAL SUPERIOR
282-6387 - D. COHN FUR PROCESSORS

TRAPPING SUPPLIERS

356-6730 - TOM MIRANDA'S
800-1819 - WOODSTREAM TRAPPING SPLY
523-4803 - NORTHERN FUR AND SPORT
245-6483 - DUNN "FUR TAMER" KNIVES
828-7077 - DOG PROOF TRAP CO.
373-8097 - SNARE SHOP
279-4252 - KOCH TRAPPING SUPPLY
742-8727 - STERLING FUR AND TOOL
626-2894 - FUNKE TRAPS
423-9526 - HOOSIER TRAPPING
545-8737 - RUSS CARMEN LURES
344-2923 - F.C. TAYLOR FUR CO.
247-7709 - SHEDAS TRAPPING SPLY
762-2706 - RP OUTDOORS
458-5647 - RIGGING AND WEAR
282-5663 - PETE RICKARD LURES
368-5924 - SE OUTDOORS

TRAPPING PUBLICATIONS

258-0929 - TRAPPER AND PREDATOR CALLER (Free sample issue, answ. mach. at night)

TAXIDERMY

488-3256 - NEW IA SHCOOL OF TAXIDERMY
228-2291 - J.W. ELWOOD TXDMY SUPPLY
736-2104 - HIGH COUNTRY ANTLERS
334-8012 - WASCO TXDMY SUPPLY
722 -2327 - COOMBS TXDMY SPLY

HUNTING SUPPLY

888-3006 - THE SPORTSMAN'S GUIDE
558-8815 - KESTER'S GAME FOOD
441-3036 - J. STUART WILDLIFE CALLERS
654-3825 - BOWHUNTER'S VIDEO
451-4572 - BURNHAM BROS.
767-9168 - BOAR HUNTING VIDEO

HUNTING & FISHING GUIDES

235-7764 - COLORADO TROPHY HUNT
289-0474 - WAYNE GATLING GUIDE SERVICE
437-2474 - G. LAMOUREUX ALASKAN GUIDE
665-0240 - PLUMMER'S LODGE HUNT/FISH
344-8173 - HAYWARD L. SIMMONS
666-2619 - DEER/TURKEY HUNTS
356-7453 - R. & FRED BETTSCHEN

Thanks for your help! If a large number of you receiving this mailing call consistently it's guaranteed that all these numbers will be gone within a year. To make that goal even more tangible we have one final suggestion on how to get the general public to call. Certain numbers match up to certain words. For example, Russ Carmen Lures number is 1-800-545-8737, which could also be said as 1-800-LIK-U-737. If this number is written on pay phones, in bathrooms, etc. with a message such as "FREE PHONE SEX!" attached to it, you can be sure lots of people will call! Another example we've found is that all numbers ending in "MINK" (6465) can be changed to "OINK", 1-800-HER-OINK (Mink Specialties) for example. You could also just use the regular number without words. People will still call. In any case, CALL THESE NUMBERS! and remember these numbers are run by murderers. They don't deserve to profit from the death of innocent lives. If they deserve anything at all it's a noose around their necks to prevent them from destroying more innocent lives. Running up their phone bills is the least we can do.

REPRODUCE AND DISTRIBUTE AT WILL!

FUR COATS ARE OFTEN WORN TO OPERA HOUSES AND CHURCHES!

VEGAN REVOLUTION IS COMING

Meat eatin' Bambi hunter speaks out

Many times during my stay in the People's Republic of Boulder, I've defended my red meat fixation to those whiny liberal vegetarians. I've been told that animals have as much right to live as I do, that wearing their skin as a belt is barbaric and that eating "animal flesh" is disgusting.

Really? You know what disgusts me? Bothering somebody about what they eat.

Yeah, they treat the calves cruelly to make veal, but so what? I'm about to graduate, I've got a ton of bills, I have no idea what I'm going to do with my life and I'm supposed to worry about a flippin' cow?

Rich Stark

Hey, maybe cows are secretly masochistic and enjoy it! Besides, veal is without a doubt one of the finer pleasures our planet offers.

And another thing— if I hear one more hippy tell me how cruel it is to hunt and slaughter our sweet, "innocent" little forest brethren, I'm officially opening up hunting season on liberals.

Some concepts for ya' here, people:

1) Hunting is not murder, and it won't be until they pass a law against it.

2) Hunting is a great way to enjoy the outdoors.

3) Hunting has been around even longer than prostitution.

4) Since we can't legally kill most of the things we hate, why not take it out on animals? They don't fight back, you can't get sued if you only wing 'em and you can eat 'em when you're done.

5) Killing your dinner puts you in touch with your ancestors.

6) You have no idea how fun it is to drive past a VW busload of hippies with a deer strapped to your hood.

In the comparatively short lifespan that we humans enjoy, taking away the right to hunt would just make life that much worse — because the feeling of killing your dinner and preparing it is simply without equal.

I'm a simple man, and I have simple needs: sleep, nicotine, Mountain Dew and red meat.

When you come down to it, the only thing that separates us from animals is that we shop, cook and screw indoors.

So until deer evolve enough to shoot back, I think I'll have another helping of venison.

Stark swerves for squirrels and bunnies.

.....AND THIS IS THE ENEMY

THE MILITANT VEGAN

ISSUE #2 AUGUST 1993

In This Issue:

AS LONG AS THERE ARE SLAUGHTERHOUSES, THERE WILL BE BATTLEFIELDS

THE MILITANT VEGAN-ISSUE #2 AUGUST 1993

Like the first issue, The Militant Vegan is being produced to provide coverage of issues and events that are ignored by both the media and the mainstream animal liberation movement. We try to bring together news from various publications and newspapers to show that militant action for animals is growing in North America.

Our second goal is to build support for imprisoned animal activists. While Johnathan Paul is free, Rik Scarce and several others are behind bars. Show them all your support by writing them letters!

If you are new to the ideas of animal liberation and veganism, write PETA at PO Box 42516/ Washington, DC 20015 for literature and recipes. The book Diet For a New America by John Robbins is an excellent vegan primer.

Two publications which report ALF-type actions are: Earth First! Journal/ PO Box 5176/ Missoula, MT 59806 and Profane Existence/ PO Box 8722/ Minneapolis, MN 59806. Mail them both news clippings of direct action.

The only ALF Legal Support Group in North America is at: ALFSG/ Box 75029, Ritchie Stn./ Edmonton, Alberta /T6E 6K1 CANADA.

In England, the ALFSG is at: BCM 1160/ London, WC1M 3XX/ ENGLAND, and the ALF Press Office is at: BM 4400 / London/ WC1N 3XX. The Swedish ALFSG is at: DBF/ Box 2051/ S-265 02/ Astorp 2/ SWEDEN.

An excellent animal liberation magazine is Arkangel/ BCM 9240/ London/ WC1N 3XX/ ENGLAND.

In this issue, we hope you will enjoy the "History of Direct Action in the U.S." We spent many long hours in various library microfilm rooms, looking through old newspapers from around the country!

Again, we are remaining anonymous, so there is no return address for more copies. We encourage and beg you to reproduce this magazine and distribute it around the U.S. and Canada. Let's get the news of militant veganism heard!

Neither this magazine or the publishers intend to encourage crime. The Militant Vegan is for informational purposes only!

'Eco-vigilantes' head for Norway

Whaling ban lifted; ...wn braces for ...ip of saboteurs

Leonard Doyle
...DON INDEPENDENT

...REINE, Norway — Deep inside ...Arctic Circle, in the far north of ...rway, the whaling community is ...iously awaiting the arrival of ...Edward Abbey, a fast ocean-...ng ship with a reinforced prow ...ramming whalers.

...The vessel, manned by eco-vigi-...tes from the Sea Shepherd Con-...vation Society, is expected to ...ck Norwegian whaling vessels ...top "environmental atrocities" ...inst the minke whales.

...The sabotage alert comes in the ...e of Norway's declaration on ...day that it is authorizing a lim-... resumption of commercial ...ling in defiance of the latest ...ernational Whaling Commis-...'s decisions.

...For five years, Norway has ob-...ed the international moratori-... on hunting minke whales. ...w, it contends, minke whale ...ks have recovered sufficiently ...sustain a limited hunt. The ...ntry's small fleet of whaling vessels from northern coastal communities is awaiting the green light to hunt and kill 800 minke whales.

The anti-whaling campaign already has brought changes to the Lofoten Islands. People known for their welcoming ways have become suspicious of strangers.

Leif Arne, a pony-tailed crewman on the Jwol whaling ship, said residents now make mental notes of the license plates of cars they do not recognize. "If I ever catch a saboteur, I'll belt him over the head and then hand him over to the police," said the Jwol's skipper, Geir Andersen.

The anti-whalers are a constant topic of conversation. A mere rumor that they had left their base in Marina Del Rey in Los Angeles County was a lead item on the television news, and Norwegian newspapers have sent correspondents to track down and interview Paul Watson, the Canadian who heads Sea Shepherd.

The first attacks on Norway's whaling community began last winter when Watson, the world's most notorious animal liberationist, slipped across the Swedish border to northern Norway with two confederates.

On Dec. 26, according to the Norwegian police, Watson and his companions boarded several whaling boats in the towns of Steine and Skrova, then opened the seacocks to scuttle a whaler named the Nybraena.

In his letter to Norwegians after the attack, Watson said he was speaking "on behalf of the cetacean nation" and was "representing whalekind in an effort to reach a state of coexistence with humankind."

He takes credit for sinking or permanently disabling nine whalers since 1975. He warned that "we will continue to scuttle Norwegian ships. ... We will also confront Norwegian whalers with our ships in the Norwegian Sea in the spring of 1993."

Mariette Korsrud, wife of a whaler-fisherman who spends up to six months a year between cod fishing and whaling, expresses the anger that residents of the region feel toward the anti-whaling movement.

"I used to get hurt when they called our husbands murderers and barbarians, but now I just get angry," she said. "Our men risk their lives going out in dark, rough weather to earn their livelihood, while we are being told what to do by people in polluted Los Angeles. And they are calling us barbarians?"

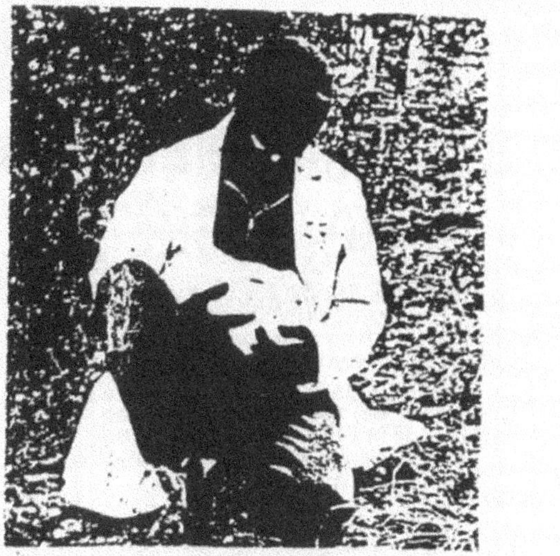

Grad student refuses to testify

Washington State University (WSU) graduate student Rik Scarce may spend the next nine months in jail for refusing to testify against radical environmentalists who were the subject of his dissertation.

The subjects, who call themselves the Animal Liberation Front (ALF), raided a WSU animal lab in August 1991.

While Scarce is not implicated in any of the ALF's actions, one of the men suspected of organizing the raid, Rodney Coronado, was living at Scarce's house at the time of the raid.

Authorities want him to testify about his knowledge of Coronado and the ALF but Scarce, despite the threat of being in jail until December, refuses to testify.

"Journalists have certain protections about testifying about their sources and social researchers and academicians deserve the same protection," he said.

But Scarce does not condone the ALF's actions.

"The researchers affected by the raid were denied their full right to research, which is exactly what I'm protesting about, but I do not think my research about what motivates people to commit such acts should also be damaged."

Although he will begin serving his time, Scarce and his lawyer are appealing the judge's decision.

— The Daily Evergreen

Animal rights activists suspected in firebombing

Minneapolis Star-Tribune 11/9/92

By Susan Feyder
Staff Writer

Five trucks belonging to a Minneapolis meat wholesaler were firebombed Sunday after being spray-painted with slogans including "Meat is murder" and the initials of an animal rights group.

The five trucks were destroyed, said LeRoy Mann, owner of Swanson Meats Inc., 2700 26th Av. S. Mann, who has operated the business for 12 years, estimated the damage at about $100,000, and said insurance will cover some of that.

The firebombing appears to be the worst local case of vandalism related to protests against the meat industry.

Mann said this is the second time in recent weeks his business has been targeted by vandals who left messages behind claiming they support animal rights. Four weeks ago, the windshields of all his delivery trucks

Vandals continued on page 4A

...On Nov. 8, ALF ...ebombed trucks ...ned by a Minne-...olis meat whole-...ler, causing ...00,000 in ...mage.

Vandals/ Police say they have no leads in fire

Continued from page 1A

were broken and some trucks were spray-painted with slogans and the initials ALF. Mann and others believe that stands for the Animal Liberation Front, a loose-knit group of animal protection supporters.

Minneapolis police said yesterday they have no leads in the case.

After the first incident, Mann said, he moved the trucks from an open parking area in back of his business to an area closer to 26th Av. That's where the trucks were about 3:30 yesterday morning when a cab driver passed by, noticed they were burning and called police, Mann said.

The only other damage at Swanson Meats was quick-hardening glue put into the locks of the building. That's similar to the damage suffered by other meat companies and other businesses in recent years from vandals who leave messages claiming to be part of animal rights groups.

Last year Ready Meats, 3550 NE. Johnson St., had its windows broken, siding smashed and locks glued shut. "Don't kill the animals" was spray-painted on the Johnson Meat Co. building at 1735 Nicollet Av. in Minneapolis. Also last year, workers at Simek's Meats and Seafood, 905 45th Av. NE. in Hilltop, found the words "Meat is dead and you are next" spray-painted on the store's back door.

Summit Meats and Deli, 14637 County Rd. 11 in Burnsville, has been vandalized several times in recent years. On one occasion, a pet store and restaurant in the same mall as the market were vandalized the same night.

The Animal Liberation Front is considered a loose federation of activists in the United States and Great Britain that has been classified by the FBI as a terrorist organization. ALF members have claimed responsibility for numerous acts of vandalism at animal laboratories costing millions of dollars, thefts of lab animals and the bombing of at least a half-dozen stores in England.

No spokesperson for the group could be reached last night. An official of the Animal Rights Coalition (ARC), a separate Twin Cities-based animal-protection group, condemned the firebombings.

"ARC does not condone violence, even to property," said Dan Oldre, a board member of the group. "We're against animal suffering, and we speak out against industries like the meat industry, but we're definitely against that kind of action." The group has demonstrated against the meat and fur industries as well as practices in animal research that it believes are inhumane.

Last year the meat industry in the St. Paul-Minneapolis, MN area alone was the recipient of at least six attacks, not all identified with ALF or Earth First.

Hunt demo boy killed

A 15-YEAR-OLD hunt saboteur was crushed under the wheels of a lorry yesterday.

Thomas Worby was among a 40-strong group trying to disrupt the Cambridgeshire Hunt, at Waresley, Cambs.

The tragedy happened as the hunt truck passed protestors. The boy, from Milton Keynes, Bucks., was on his first demo.

On Saturday, April 3, 1993, a fifteen-year-old hunt saboteur was murdered by a hunter named Tony Ball in Waresley, England. After a successful sab in which a fox was saved from death, the hunt boxed up its hounds in a van and began driving down a narrow lane. Saboteurs, numbering around 30, blocked the path of the van until Ball revved his engine and pulled forward slowly. Thomas Worby's jacket caught on the side mirror, and he was dragged along the lane until he grabbed the sideboard of the vehicle. Worby beat on the window of the van to try to get Ball to slow down, but Ball refused and Worby fell under the van. His head was crushed as the van sped away and other hunters taunted the sabs who rushed to the boy's body.

Like the murder of Mike Hill under similar circumstances in February of 1991, the hunter faces no charges. Alan Summersgill, the man who killed Mike Hill, went unpunished as six men were jailed for threatening the sick degenerate. Fortunately, Summersgill's house and hunt club were set on fire. Hopefully, justice will also be dealt to Tony Ball, and any other animal abuser who dares assault an activist. Closer to home, a recent article in the Earth First! Journal detailed the more than 200 attacks against environmental and animal activists in the past few years. This will only escalate as we become more and more successful in our fight for the lives of innocent animals. Let's face it, the battle for animals and the environment will be a war, with casualties on both sides. While we would all like to see animals freed without violence, the truth is that most animal abusers will attack us when we try to put a stop to their greed. Every vegan in this country should get off drugs and alcohol, get in shape, and learn self-defense. If you want to stop animal abuse, be prepared to fight. Don't ever let Mike Hill and Thomas Worby be forgotten.

Adopt-a-McDonald's ALF-Style

Jeremy Rifkin's group, Beyond Beef has urged activists to "Adopt-A-McDonald's" by handing out flyers, buttons and balloons in front of McRestaurants to persuade burger-eaters to cease their misguided ways. The Animal Liberation Front has taken the campaign a step further.

In the early morning hours of December 25, 1992, Animal Liberation Front activists in Victoria, British Columbia, paid a Yuletide visit to McDonald's on Pandora Avenue, delivering gifts of painted walls and broken windows. One week later, early on New Year's Day, we descended upon Williams Quality Meats on Blanshard Street, supergluing bits of toothpick into their locks. As far as we, know, these are the first ALF actions to occur in Victoria. But ALF attacks do not just "occur." They are the work of womyn and men who are no longer able to sit back and allow terrible, cruel things to happen. Now, more than ever before, we must remember the four-leggeds and the scaley ones. We will continue our war; but alone, we cannot possibly do enough, fast enough. Animal oppression is everywhere. Involvement in the Animal Liberation Front begins with your first liberation or act of economic sabotage. Do not try to find us, get together with a groups of friends whom you know you can trust. Animal liberation is virtually a stone's throw away. Careful...No evidence.

—SOURCE: ANIMAL LIBERATION FRONT

Activists Desperately Seek Headlines With Paint Panther Vandalism

Apparently desperate because heir movement is losing steam and fur sales have increased this eason, animal-rights activists ppear to have launched a new rganization, which two weeks ago aunched a series of vandalism ttacks on fur retailers across the Jnited States in order to grab headlines.

The Fur Information Council of America (FICA) recently warned furriers to increase their security precautions in response o an activist group calling itself he Paint Panthers, which claimed responsibility for spraying stores the weekend before Christmas in Washington, DC, Denver, Miami and Aspen.

"We anticipate that more furriers will be target in the coming weeks as this group desperately tries to use the media," said Bill Outlaw, FICA's executive director of media relations. "I think it's a reaction to the fact that fur sales are increasing so far this year.

"The important thing for furriers to remember is to contact police immediately, clean the affected area (if painted) and to contact FICA and let us handle the media calls," Outlaw said.

"Everyone in the industry should bear in mind that these type of actions actually work against the activists because it turns the public off to their approach," he added.

There are strong indications that People for the Ethical Treatment of Animals (PeTA) is promoting the activities of the Paint Panthers by making contact with the media to try to generate publicity for the incidents.

"One reporter told us that she was sent a fax about the incident by PeTA," Outlaw said.

Dan Mathews, spokesperson for PeTA, told the *Denver Post* that, while the Paint Panthers are not connected with PeTA, PeTA does not "condone or condemn them" as long as their methods remain non-violent.

"We understand the frustration that drives activists to do stuff like that," Mathews was quoted in the paper. "It sends a stronger message."

In the Denver area, Lloyd's Furs, Irv Ringler Furs and Mark's Furs were hit early Sunday, Dec. 17, by vandals who smashed paint-filled ornaments against the buildings and spray-painted graffiti on them.

All three cases are being investigated by the police.

Five Washington, DC-area fur salons — Saks Jandel, Skandia Furs, Furs of Kiszely, Miller Furs and Rosendorf Evans — were spray-painted with anti-fur slogans on the morning of Dec. 20.

Activists claim they also sprayed paint in Aspen and Miami.

FICA did interviews with the media in Washington and Denver after being contacted by furriers in each place.

"We want to help furriers handle the media on this because we want to be consistent in what is being said to the media in response to this action," Outlaw said.

"They claim to have sprayed people as well, but we do not have confirmation of that," Outlaw said. "It's really just part of their intimidation campaign."

"Our best approach when this happens is to remind the public that these actions are not what freedom of speech is all about," he continued. "I'm convinced that the public is on our side on this.

"I'm also convinced that these tactics are another indication that the activists are losing steam and they know it."

Fur Age Weekly 1/4/93
(Fur Age Weekly is a shitty trade journal for the fur industry and is always a laugh!)

Outdoor Life November 1992

Rodeo Roped In By Bomb Threat

Rodeos became an animal rights target on July 5 when the Park Rapids Rodeo was the recipient of a bomb threat. According to Putting People First, the American Horse Council reported that a threat was called in to the Park Rapids, Minnesota, police department from an individual who identified himself as a member of the Animal Rights Coalition Force. Three thousand spectators had to be evacuated; a search of the grounds did not turn up any explosives.

Activists Go On Desperate Vandalism Spree

Animal-rights activists lashed ack recently at pro-fur media posure by urging vandalism on tional television and then carrying it out against several New rk City fur retailers.

On NBC's *Saturday Night Live* b. 6, series regular/activist evin Nealon used his "Weekend pdate" news parody segment to display a photograph of Aretha Franklin performing during one of the Presidential Inauguration concerts, showing her wearing her golden sable coat.

Nealon said that the coat was reportedly worth $60,000. Then he quipped, "Did I say $60,000? I meant $2!" as he took out a can of spray paint and defaced the photo.

This was all accompanied by Nealon's trademark smarmy grin, but most people in the audience didn't get the joke. They remained largely silent.

The following night, under cover of darkness, the PeTA offshoot group Paint Panthers spray-painted epithets on the storefronts of seven Manhattan fur salons.

There were no serious damages, only messages like "Murderers," "Fur Scum," and "Blood Money."

The majority of retailers immediately cleaned up the mess so a not to attract publicity or frighten customers, but *Newsday* captured The Fur Vault's disgrace in a photo the following day.

Apparently the entire act was a publicity stunt, since a story was on the newswires by 3 a.m. Monday morning. Besides *Newsday*, only the *New York Post* and two local television news broadcasts (CBS and NBC) carried brief stories.

Besides the Fur Vault, only

Continued on page 5

Activists Go On Desperate Vandalism Spree

ontinued from page 3

hers identified by police and ewspaper reports were: the Ritz rift Shop, Elizabeth Arden, loomingdale's, Fendi Bergdorf oodman and Harold J. Rubin.

There was obvious frustration oth in Nealon's and the Paint anther's actions, as if now, since ey obviously cannot make peo e believe in animal rights, they ill try to intimidate them into t wearing fur.

Nealon, whom furriers will member as the celebrity leader last year's New York City day ter Thanksgiving parade, peared as some kind of petty, venile delinquent.

The Paint Panthers told New ork's CBS affiliate, Channel 2, at they felt their actions were e only way to get their point ross to fur wearers.

Sandy Blye, executive vice esident of the New York City-based American Fur Industry (AFI), said, "It's too bad they have to resort to these tactics in light of the fact that people are wearing fur. I think they're desperate because people are obviously not paying attention to them."

Asked if it was possible there was a connection between Nealon's stunt and the vandalism the next night, Blye said "There could be."

Bill Outlaw, media relations director for the Fur Information Council of America (FICA), said he didn't think there was a connection.

"The Paint Panthers started their activities several months ago here in Washington, DC," he said.

Despite the fact that Nealon's ploy could promote violence to fur wearers and to women, Outlaw said that if any legal action were to be taken, it would be up to Aretha Franklin.

As it did following Paint Panther attacks in Washington, DC recently, FICA is actively pursuing the media to give them "equal time" when covering the vandalism. The FICA staff is writing letters to members of the press who covered the story and demanding that the fur industry side of the story be heard.

"We have a positive story to tell now," said Outlaw. "Of course we'd rather they not cover the vandalism at all, because it might intimidate consumers, but now we can show that fur sales are up, people are choosing to wear fur, and these kinds of desperate acts actually work against the animal-rights movement. Also, we can make the media understand that they are being used by thee people to promote vandalism."

Outlaw cited a recent column by "Miss Manners" in the *Washington Post*, in which she chides various activist groups for their methods, saying violence never wins converts.

Activists in the San Francisco Bay Area have been busy, as several people have mentioned to us that during the months of April and May, egg, cheese, milk, MacDonald's, and other animal abuse advertisements on billboards have been defaced all over the city of Berkeley and in north Oakland. In some cases, the billboards have been splashed with red paint, and slogans such as "Go Vegan!" "Vegan Power!" "Animal Torture," and so on have been painted. Many of the billboards were in highly visible areas and some remained for weeks.

HISTORY OF DIRECT ACTION FOR ANIMALS IN THE U.S.

This list was mostly taken from "The Liberator" and old Canadian ALFSG newspapers. The rest is taken from news articles, and movement and opposition magazines.

All of the actions before 1991 were listed in movement publications or mainstream media. But with magazines such as the Animals' Agenda becoming more moderate and no longer covering direct action, many of the recent actions (such as the Park Rapids, Indiana, Utah/Montana, and Paint Panther actions) were only to be found in opposition publications. It's a shame that anti-animal groups do a better job of covering direct action than activists do-- so we're publishing this magazine to gather news of direct action for the movement.

It is also worth mentioning that while this list probably covers all the major raids, it's a safe bet that hundreds of minor actions have gone unreported around the country.

1977

May 29 Honolulu, HI- 2 dolphins liberated from a U. of Hawaii marine lab.

1979

March 14 New York, NY- 1 cat, 2 dogs, and 2 guinea pigs liberated from NY U. Medical Center.

1980

December 4 Tampa, FL- 55 gerbils and 35 rats liberated from the U. of Southern Florida.
December 9 Venice, FL- circus traliers spray painted.

1981

October Amherst, MA- 2 rabbits liberated from U. of Mass. Hatch Lab.

1982

April 2 College Park, MD- 42 rabbits liberated from U. of Maryland.
June 26 New Rochelle, NY- 1 calf liberated from New Rochelle Fatt Calf.
December 25 Wash. DC- 30+ cats liberated from Howard U. $2640 damage.
December 27 Bethesda, MD- 1 dog liberated from US Navy Medical Research Institute.
December 27 Berkeley, CA- 3 cats liberated from UCB psych lab by the Urban Gorillas.

1983

January 14 Bethesda, MD- 3 dogs liberated from same Navy lab.
December 22 Dade County, FL- 6 furriers attacked with spray paint and jammed locks.
December 24 Baltimore, MD- 6 rats liberated from Johns Hopkins U. Psych. Dept.
December 25 Los Angeles, CA- 12 dogs liberated from UC Harbor Medical Center.

1984

? Gainesville, FL- Rats liberated from U. of Florida.
May 16 Sacramento, CA- 23 rats liberated from Cal State U. Psych. Dept.
May 28 Philadelphia, PA- 60 hours of videotapes taken and $60,000 damage done to U. of PA Head Injury Clinic.
June 30 Sacramento, CA- Folsom Rodeo spray painted.
July 22 Philadelphia, PA- 1 dog liberated from U. of PA School of Veterinary Medicine.
July 26 Philadelphia, PA- 4 cats, 1 dog, and 8 pigeons liberated from U. of PA School of Vet. Med.
August 12 Springfield, CA- 1 rabbit and 3 racoons liberated from George's Livery.
September 5 Davis, CA- fake bombs delivered to UC Davis vivisectors.
September Tucson, AZ- Fur store attacked.
October Vernon, CA- Murals on a slaughterhouse defaced.
November 12 Stockton, CA- Knudson Facility, a "B" dealer, had broken windows and paint splattered, ALF message left in box.
December 9 Duarte, CA- 115 animals (cats, rabbits, dogs, mice) liberated from City of Hope Medical Center. $500,000 in research damage and $7000 sabotage.
December 12 Tampa, FL- store spray painted.

1985

January San Diego, CA- bomb left in fur store restro
January 14 San Diego, C death threat to UC San Dieg vivisector forces cancellati seminar.
January Minneapolis, MN dog liberated from U. of MN
February 13 Davis, CA- beagles liberated from UC Energy-Related Health Lab
February 16 Napa, CA- City of Hope rabbits re-liber from Napa County Animal Shelter.
March 10 Los Angeles, C Animal Control Director's ho and Porche splattered with
March 13 Sacramento, C $5000 damage done to a fu store.
March Honolulu, HI- 2 mongoose liberated from Honolulu Zoo.
April 11 Davis, CA- UC D vehicles spray painted at la
April 20 Riverside, CA- 1000 animals (a monkey, c oppossums, rabbits, pigeo gerbils, mice, rats) liberate documents taken, and sev hundred thousand dollars o economic sabotage done a Riverside.
August 10 Bethesda, M leather shop spray painted
September Cleveland, C number of horses and racc were liberated from a riding stable.

1986

January Berkeley, CA- number of rabbits liberated captivity at the Tilden Regi Park.
June 4 Hartley, DE- 25 h liberated from Sydel's egg
July Oregon- 66 silver fo were freed from a fur farm.
July In seven states and around California, ALF cel attacked fur stores.
October 26 Eugene, OR animals (hanpsters, cats, rabbits, rats, and pigeons liberated and $50,000 dam done to U. of Oregon bree facility.

November 24 Sacramento, CA- 127 turkeys liberated and $12,000 damage done to 2 turkey farms.
November 26 Arizona- 10 fur stores attacked.
December 6- Rockville, MD- 4 chimpanzees liberated and documents taken from SEMA Corp.

1987
January San Jose, CA- fur store attacked.
January 19 Williamsburg, VA- 6 mice liberated from William and Mary College.
February Palm Springs, CA- An I. Magnin's billboard was cut down because they sell fur.
February Beaumont, CA- A Kentucky Fried Chicken was spray painted and its billboard was cut down.
March 19 San Jose , CA- fur store attacked.
April Colinga, CA- Harris Ranch had slogans painted and spikes left under truck tires.
April 16 Davis, CA- Animal Diagnostic Lab under construction was burned down and 18 UC vehicles were damaged. $4.5 million damage.
April 17 Delaware- 40 hens liberated from a battery unit by Farm Freedom Fighters.
April 17 Bloomington, CA- 115 rabbits liberated from Universal Animal Care.
April 18 Riverside, CA- 50 rabbits liberated from a breeding farm.
April Lake Havasau City, CA- 4 animal abuse businesses attacked.
April Fresno, CA- fur store attacked.
April Milan, PA- 40 hens liberated from Wolfe Poultry Farm.
May 20 Sacramento, CA- Grau Hall Scientific Corp. was spray painted.
May 24 Litchfield, CA- 300 wild horses freed from Bureau of Land Management.
June 13 Davis, CA- 7 turkey vultures liberated form UC Davis lab.
August 12 Las Vegas, NV- 3 goats liberated from U. of Nevada.
August 23 Beltsville, MD- 36 cats and 7 pigs liberated from USDA lab by the Band of Mercy.
September 1 San Jose, CA- San Jose Valley Veal, Inc. had a warehouse burned by the Animal Rights Militia. $10,000 damage.
October Fairfield, CA- hunting club billboard paint bombed.
October Fresno, CA- fur store and taxidermist attacked.
October CA Olivera Egg Farm spray painted.
November 9 Marysville, CA- rodeo billboard cut down.
November 14 Ceres, CA- 38 hens liberated and equipment sabotaged with slogans left at Faith Home Poultry.
November 17 Fairfield, CA- Hunting club spray painted and billboard cut down.
November 19 Gilroy, CA- Truck spray painted at Davis Egg Ranch.
November 26 San Jose, CA- A grain building at the Ferrara Meat Co. was burned down by the Animal Rights Militia. $230,000 damage.
November 27 Wash. DC- 2 fur stores had windows smashed.
November 27 Bethesda, MD- 4 fur stores had windows smashed.
November 28 Santa Clara, CA- A poultry warehouse was set on fire.
November Tucson, AZ- Fur store receives a bomb threat, which prompts the owner to give up after 3 years of vandalism.
December 5- Bethesda, MD- Fur Vault has windows smashed and reports to the Justice Dept. that its chains have had $50,000 damage in the past year and a half.

1988
January 29 Irvine, CA- 13 beagles liberated from UC Irvine, 13 year project ruined.
March 6 San Jose, CA- A meat company had its trucks paint-strippered.
March 21 San Jose, CA- The same meat co. had its windows etched with acid and trucks spray painted.
March 27 Hayward, CA- 64 rabbits were liberated from the Nitabell Rabbitry.
April 2 Gilroy, CA- 63 chickens liberated from the Davis Egg Ranch.
April 5 San Jose, CA- Meat shop spray painted.
April 27 Colinga, CA- Harris Ranch spray painted.
May 10 Colinga, CA- Harris Ranch spray painted.
June San Jose, CA- several animal abuse businesses were attacked.
June 4- San Jose, CA- The Sun Valley Meat Co. was burned to the ground.
June 23 Santa Rosa, CA- 2 veal calves liberated from Santa Rosa veal farm.
August 15 Loma Linda, CA- 7 dogs and 2 goats liberated, $10,000 sabotage, and hundreds of documents taken from "Baby Fae" lab at Loma Linda U.
August 21 Atlanta, GA- Two fur stores attacked with etching fluid.
October San Jose, CA- several animal abuse businesses were attacked.
October 1 San Francisco and San Bruno, CA- 7 animal abuse businesses were attacked.
October 15 Escondido, CA- 3 trainers who beat an elephant had their homes splattered with paint and their cars paint-strippered.
November 12 Manteca, CA- 33 turkeys liberated and slogans painted at a ranch.
December Palo Alto, CA- A fake bomb was left in a lab under construction.
December 17 Philadelphia, PA- 4 fur stores were splattered with red paint.

1989
January 6 Tucson, AZ- 3 dogs liberated from Veteran's Admin. Medical Center.
March 10 Soquel, CA- 40 rabbits liberated from EL Laboratories.
April 3 Tucson, AZ- 1,131 animals were liberated and 2 labs and a vivisector's office were burned down at the U. of Arizona.
May Dixon, CA- The Dixon Livestock Auction Warehouse was burned bown jointly by the ALF and Earth First!

July 4 Lubbock, TX- 5 cats were liberated and $70,000 damage done at Texas Tech U.
? Santa Rosa, CA- The front of a fur store was set on fire.
? California- Butcher shops and a KFC had smashed windows and slogans painted.
December Miami, FL- Fur stores splattered with paint.
December Long Island, NY- Police arrested a woman after she smashed the windows of a fur store.
December 25 Memphis, TN- The Southern Meat Market was attacked.

1990

In 1990, the ALF carried out 2 unpublicized raids in Pennsylvania and upstate New York.
Memphis, TN- large numbers of animal abuse businesses were attacked during 1990.
January 14 Philadelphia, PA- Documents, tapes, and discs were taken from the office of vivisector Adrian Morrison at the U. of PA.
Early 1990- An FBI agent told the Nat'l Cattlemen's Assn. that animal activists were doing widespread damage to ranches.
April New York area- A vivisector at Columbia University had his house set on fire.
Summer Florida-6 rabbits were liberated from the Dawson Research Corp.
Summer San Francisco, CA- 7 incendiary devices left in 5 fur selling Department stores over a 3 month period were all found.
June 9 New York, NY- 15 fur stores had their locks glued.
Fall Morgan Hill, CA- 100 guinea pigs were liberated from Simonsen Laboratories.
Fall Kensington, MD- 3 meat sellers were attacked.
October 29 Buffalo, NY- Hundreds of rats, mice, and hamsters were liberated from SUNY-Buffalo by Animals Now.
November Tucson, AZ- Supermarkets pulled turkeys after a man said they had been contaminated. None were.

1991

Minneapolis, MN- During 1991, at least 6 meat dealers were attacked with painted slogans, smashed windows, and/or locks glued.
Memphis, TN- During 1991, large numbers of animal abusing businesses were attacked.
January 1 Chicago, IL- 11 rabbits and 10 guinea pigs were liberated from Cook County Hospital's Hektoen Laboratory, and dried fruit and bananas were given to imprisoned baboons.
June 10 Corvallis, OR- Oregon State University's Experimental Fur Farm was broken into, and activists destroyed equipment and a data base and set fire to a storage shed. $62,000 damage.
June 15 Edmonds, WA- Incendiary devices were planted at the Northwest Fur Foods Cooperative, a major supplier of fur farms and the OSU program. $800,000 damage.
July Memphis, TN- McDonald's Regional Office had a dozen windows and two doors smashed.
August 13 Pullman, WA- At Washington State U., 7 coyotes, 6 mink, and 10 mice were liberated and $50,000 damage was done to 2 labs.
December 21 Yamhill, OR- An incendiary device destroyed the processing plant at the Malecky Mink Ranch.

1991-2 ? Attempted break-ins at fur farms in Utah and Montana.

1992

Memphis, TN- Several attacks on animal abusing businesses.
January 13 Walnut Creek, CA- "Corrosive chemical" thrown on the windows of a fur store.
February 28 Lansing, MI- $125,000 damage done to Michigan State's mink research program as documents are taken and offices burned.
June Memphis, TN- Fur stores attacked.
? Indiana- Hoosier Trappers was spray painted, and a fur delivery van in Indianapolis was damaged.
? South Carolina- The Vegan Front attacked a fur store.
July 5 Park Rapids, MN- 3000 people were evacuated from the Park Rapids Rodeo after a bomb threat by the Animal Rights Coalition Force.
July 7 Chicago, IL- An attampt was made to burn a fur billboard.
August San Francisco, CA- Anti-fur protestors noticed that fur and leather shops in the Union Square area had their windows chemically damaged.
August Memphis, TN- Fur stores attacked.
August 9, Memphis, TN- Police arrested 3 Hardliners after 3 people were caught spray painting a fur store.
October Minneapolis, MN- Swanson's Meats had windows of its delivery trucks smashed and slogans painted.
October 24 Milville and Logan, UT- Two Animal Damage Control labs at Utah State were burned and 29 coyotes were liberated. $150,000 damage.
November 8 Minneapolis, MN- 5 trucks at Swanson's Meats were firebombed and the locks to the building were glued. $100,000 damage.
December Miami, FL- Fur stores attacked by Paint Panthers
December Aspen, CO- Fur stores attacked by Paint Panthers.
December 17 Denver, CO- 3 fur stores attacked by Paint Panthers.
December 20 Wash. DC- 5 fur stores attacked by Paint Panthers.

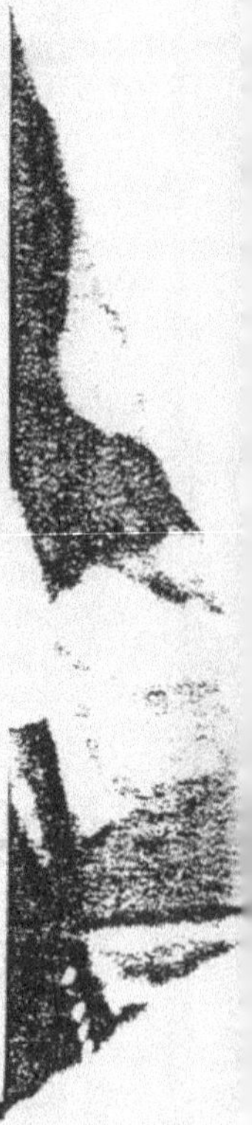

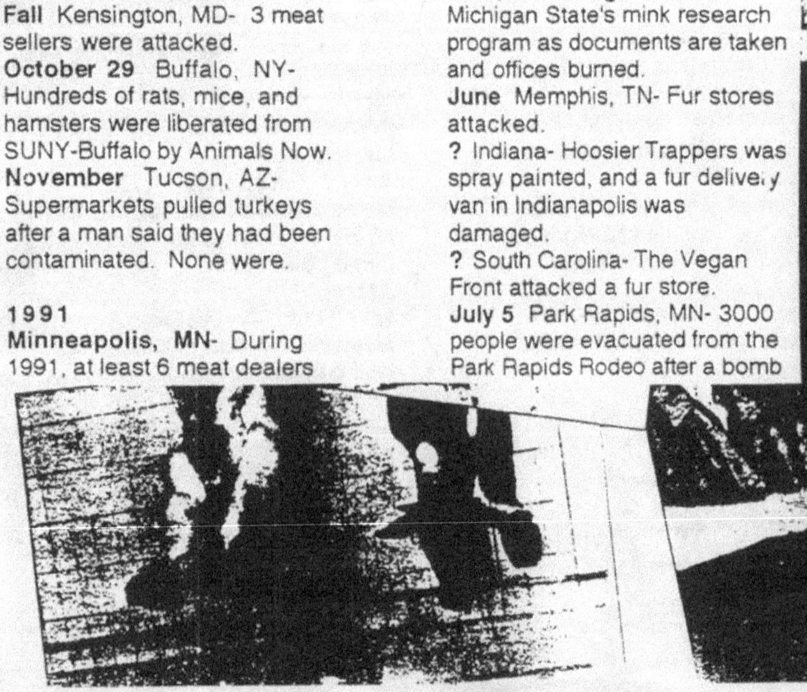

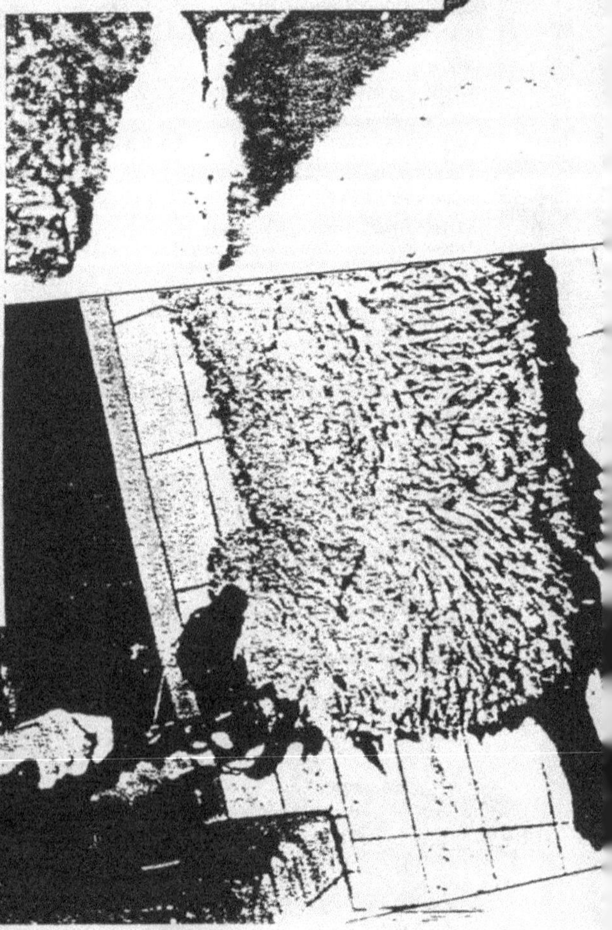

VEGAN PHONEBOOK

Amnesty Zine, P.O. Box 25144, Washington, D.C. 20007-8144

The following are the toll free 1-800 phone numbers of various animal exploiters. Every time you keep them on the phone for thirty seconds, it costs them a dollar. The longer you talk, the more they pay. Be creative: order their catalogs, make C.O.D. orders to fake addresses, etc. Carry this list around with you and make a few calls every time you pass a pay phone. Copy it and pass it around. Call for animal liberation!!! (All numbers begin with 1-800.)

American Feeds & Livestock, 323-7553
American Legend Fur Auction House, 445-MINK
Atlantic Seafood Direct, 227-1116
Atlantic Veal Corporation, 221-6988
Auth Brothers Meats, 424-2610
Beck Sausage, 543-6328
Big Game Fishing, 458-2879
Bio-Serv Lab Animal Supplies, 521-3368
Birchwood Livestock Genetics, 892-6342
Blossomland Bee Supply, 637-5262
Bowhunting Safari Consultants, 833-9777
Brisken Berk Furs, 241-7243
Bristol-Myers Squibb, 468-7746
Brushy Mountain Bee Farm, 233-7929
Buffalo Meat, BUY-BUFF
Burger King, YES-1-800
Burnham Brothers Predator Callers, 451-4572
Burkshire Corporation Lab Animal Supplies, 443-6379
Butterball Turkey, 323-4848
Carolina Biological Supply Company, 334-5551
Cattlemen Meat Company, 832-6595
Certified Prime Meats, 257-2977
Charles Rivers Lab Animal Supplies, LAB-RATS
Church's Fried Chicken Catering, 635-5394
Clifty Farm Country Meats, 238-8239
Colgate-Palmolive, 338-8388
Country Fed Meat Company, 637-7559
D. Cohn Fur Processors, 2-TAN-FUR
Diamond's Leather, 426-6105
Diamond V. Fur Mills, 373-7234
Dipcraft Housing Manufacturers, 245-6145
Double J. Limousine Beef, 544-5893
Dog Proof Trap Company, 828-7077
Dunn's Knive Company, 24-KNIVE
Eel Skin Elegance, 922-2188
Eel Skin Unlimited, 243-8335
F.C. Taylor Fur Company, 334-2923
Frantz Sawdust Company (for pelt drying), 262-8700
Fresh Seafood Express, 654-1366
Funke Mink Farm and Trap Supplies, 626-2894
Furs by Weiss, 423-MINK
Fur Wardrobe, 424-3877
Glazed Honey Hams, 458-7682
Harvard Apparatus Lab Animal Supplies, 272-2775
Hazleton Research Products, 345-4114
Heavenly Ham, 262-8545
Heger Feed Supply Company, 688-1990
Henig Furs, 521-2037
Henry J.'s Meat, 242-1314
Hilltop Lab Animals, 245-6921
Holt Products Veal Hormones, 369-4658
Honeybaked Ham, FOR-A-HAM
Honeycrust Hams, 423-4267
Hoosier Trapper Supplies, 423-9526
J.W. Elwood Taxidermy Supply Company, 228-2291
Jerky Hut, 223-5759
Johnny Stewart Wildlife Callers, 441-3036
La Budde Feed and Grain, 776-3610
Lakeland Vet Veal Antibiotics, 328-0652

Lamb Pasta Sauce, 237-LAMB
Lapps Bee Supply Center, 321-1960
Leather Center, 525-0952
Leather Factory Corporation, 233-7155
Lingenfelter Brill Furs, 331-5255
Lobster Express, 624-6301
Look's Live Lobsters, 446-4009
M&F Meat, 334-5396
Malcomb Meats, 822-6328
Merit Nomac Furs, 323-0449
Midwest Turkey Call Supply, 541-1638
Mills Fur Farm Supplies, 722-6455
Minden Meat Market, 272-3529
Myer's Meats, 635-3759
Nashville Poultry and Egg, 662-3447
National Beef Company, 835-9180
National Fur Feed, 558-5803 (in WI, 242-5902)
National Superior Fur Processors, 77-BEARS
Nebraska's Choice Steaks, 255-5944
Northern Fur and Sport, 523-4803
Oklahoma Cattlemen's Association, 622-2776
Omaha Steaks International, 228-9055
Padows Hams, 344-4267
Pharmaceutical Manufacturers Association, 538-26
Proctor & Gamble, 543-0485
R.P. Outdoors Trapping Supplies, 762-2706
Research America, FON-CURE
Rigging and Wear Trapping Supplies, 458-5647
Riverdale Mills Cages, 762-6374
Robbins Livestock Auction, 336-7753
Robertson's Hams, 458-4267
Russ Carman Lures, 545-8737
Sabal Meats, 527-2825
Safari Land Hunting, 624-5988
Sav-A-Caf Veal Hormones, 468-2472
S.C. Johnson, 848-2588
Shatz Brothers Meats, 541-3898
Shultz Meats, 842-0297
Sir Loin Meat Shoppe, 541-5933
Sportsman's Guide, 888-3006
Strauser Bee Supply, 541-8908
Susquehanna Industries Veal Feed, 232-8325
Talicor Furs, 433-4263
Taxidermy How To Videos, 334-8012
Tom Miranda Great Outdoors, 356-6730
Trapper and Predator Caller Magazine, 258-0929
Tri-County Taxidermy, 521-2825
United Vaccines, 283-MINK
U.S.A. Foxx and Furs, USA-FOXX
U.S.D.A. Meat and Poultry Hotline, 535-4555
Veal Hotline, 323-0955
Venison Etc., 338-4868
Ward's Biological Supply Company, 962-2660
Weaver Chicken, 233-6332
Wisco Fur Foods, 235-9656
Woodstream Corporation Trapping Supplies, 800-1
Woodward & Lothrop Fur Department, 955-0020
World Hunts, 448-6846
...mmo Meat Company, 672-1688

VEGAN REVOLUTION IS COMING

Soul food

A fast-food tycoon pushes chicken and praises the Lord

Chick-fil-A

FILE PHOTOGR

Truett Cathy runs a major business based on the principles of faith, charity and love.

An engraved plaque containing that goal greets all visitors to Chick-fil-A's Atlanta headquarters: "To glorify God by being a faithful steward of all that is entrusted to us; and, to have a positive influence on all who come in contact with Chick-fil-A."

In 1964, Cathy hired Chick-fil-A's first employee. Today, its 365 restaurants rank No. 3 nationally in chicken fast-food sales. Its California restaurants include one in Sunnyvale and one in Santa Rosa.

Ideas come from God, Cathy says, but "they won't keep. They have to be acted upon." And act is what Cathy did when he experimented with pressure-cooking a boneless chicken breast and serving it as a sandwich.

Cathy's round face, gentle smile and relaxed Southern accent depart from the stereotype of the harried executive. But his determination is certainly intact. Behind it lies a vigorous faith rooted in the belief that succeeding in the fast-food chicken business is God's mission for his life.

For more than 30 years, Cathy has taught a Sunday school class of 13-year-old boys at First Baptist Church in Jonesboro, Ga.

But on Sunday, don't look for Cathy or his employees in a Chick-fil-A restaurant. They're closed. He says he attracts the kind of employees who want to attend church on Sunday and spend time with their families.

.....AND THIS IS THE ENEMY

THE MILITANT VEGAN

ISSUE #3

OCTOBER 19

In This Issue:

A.L.F. HITS HARD IN WISCONSIN AND TENNESSEE

USED TO BE WE ONLY HAD TO WORRY 'BOUT NIGGERS MOVIN' INTO TOWN.
YEAH, WHEN I FIRST HEARD OF ANIMAL RIGHTS PEOPLE, THEY WERE JUST A BUNCH OF DAMN HIPPIES.
YOU REMEMBER WHEN THOSE QUEERS STOOD OUTSIDE MY BUTCHER SHOP HOLDING SIGNS? IT WAS FUCKIN' HILARIOUS!
HEH, HEH, HEH!
BUT NOW, THEY'VE CHANGED. THEY CAME BACK TO PROTEST LAST WEEK.
SO I CALLED SHERIFF TOOMBY AND HE SAID TO LET MY SON MAVIS KICK SOME ASS!
HEH, HEH, HEH!
BUT THIS TIME THEY FOUGHT BACK!
EARL'S MEAT
STOP THE KILLING
VEGAN POWER
I PICKED UP MAVIS FROM THE HOSPITAL TWO DAYS LATER...
DAMN...
THEN, SOMEBODY BLEW UP THAT POULTRY PACKING PLANT!
AW, HELL!
I ADMIT IT, COOTER...
I'M SCARED!

THE MILITANT VEGAN-ISSUE 3-OCTOBER 199

Welcome to the third issue of The Militant Vegan. Once again, we have clippings of direct action animals from around North America, support for vegan prisoners, and news of the radical anir liberation movement. Starting with this issue, we'll be adding our own articles and opinions on the st of the movement and how people can get involved.

The Militant Vegan has three goals: To provide news of direct action, to build awareness and support for those who imprisoned in the cause of animal liberation, and to unify and inspire a small but rapidly growing wing of the environmental animal liberation movement.

Over the past few years, small groups of young radicals have sprung up across the country. These new vegan activists enthusiastic and ready to act for animals, and it's about time we do for the mainstream animal liberation groups what Earth F did to the mainstream environmental groups at the beginning of the 1980's. Let's be the radical energy that pushes ani issues into the minds and values of the public and saves millions of lives-there's no question of what the situation is for anim and there's no time to lose. Get organized, get active, avoid infighting, and act!

If you are new to the ideas of veganism, we recommend reading Diet For a New America by John Robbins and get information and recipes from PETA at PO Box 42516/ Washington, DC 20015. Remember that health food stores are a rip and better prices and food can be found at Asian and Indian groceries. Copy recipes out of cookbooks at the bookstore.

Yes, this is a single issue magazine. We all have been and will continue to be involved in various human rights environmental issues. But we refuse to discount animal issues and we will stand up against any sort of animal abuse wherev appears. We represent no political ideology, just a common sense value system where the rights of the innocent are alw defended against exploitation and abuse.

A lot of people around the country have been getting free "subscriptions," as we try to reach people we've seen listed in o publications. Also, distributors have gotten packages with multiple copies for their store or mail order service. Still, we can afford to make a few hundred copies of each issue, which is a shame because there are thousands of people interested in kind of information. So we beg you to **make copies of this magazine** and sell it, give it to your friends, etc. We've alre heard of people in three cities selling the copies they made. Also, if you read about direct action in your area, save the clip and mail it to those who will publish it: Earth First! Journal/PO Box 1415/ Eugene, OR 97440, Profane Existence/ PO Box 8 Minneapolis, MN/ 59806, and Out of the Cages/ PO Box 2960/ Santa Cruz, CA 95063.

One important thing to realize is that we are not an ALF Support Group. We simply print what we read elsewhere. The ALF Support Group in North America is at ALFSG/ Box 75029, Ritchie P.O./ Edmonton, AB/ T6E 6K1/ CANADA. They rec action claims by ALF groups and take donations for accused ALF members in prison. They also sell various publications.

In England, the ALFSG is at: BCM 1160/ London, WC1N 3XX/ England, and they do the same as well as selling t-sh buttons, and publishing a quarterly prisoner support magazine. The English ALF also have a separate Press Office w receives action claims and acts as a media spokesperson. They can be reached at: ALF Press Office/ BM 4400/ London, WC 3XX/ ENGLAND. The Swedish ALF (DBF) can be reached at: DBF/ Box 2051/ S-265 02/ Astorp 2/ SWEDEN.

The Animal Liberation Front seeks to end all human-caused animal suffering by nonviolently liberating animals from abu conditions and by destroying the property of animal abusers. Any group of vegans and/or vegetarians who carry out acti according to these guidelines have the right to consider themselves an ALF group. The ALF is non-hierarchical and operate cells with little or no intergroup communication.

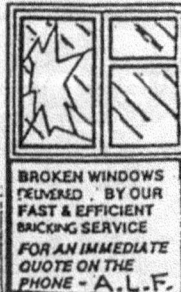

BROKEN WINDOWS DELIVERED . BY OUR FAST & EFFICIENT BRICKING SERVICE
FOR AN IMMEDIATE QUOTE ON THE PHONE - A.L.F.

THE MILITANT VEGAN #2
8 1/2 x 11 - copied - 12 pgs
While magazines that consist mainly of clippings normally do not get the standard review, this information is important so therefore... This consists of clippings of A.L.F. atttacks from around the worlds. news, a history of direct actions for animals in the U.S., contacts, 1-800 numbers, and adresses of jailed activists. Vital. (MA)

Glance at the library racks and you'll find such edifying publications as *The Militant Vegan, Better Homos and Gardens,* and *Anarchy: A Journal of Desire Armed.*

read thousands of undergroun zines such as "The Militant Vegan"

We're pretty excited about this issue as we've packed a lot more information into it than we with previous issues. We hope you all enjoy it! We remain committed for a lifetime of work to f innocent animals and restore natural biodiversity and ecological balance.

The Militant Vegan and the publishers do not intend to encourage crime. This magazine is informational purposes only.

AS LONG AS THERE ARE SLAUGHTERHOUSES THERE WILL BE BATTLEFIELDS.

DIARY OF ACTIONS

Every single night, the women and men of the Animal Liberation Front carry out direct action to stop animal cruelty at its sources somewhere in the world. England sees thousands of attacks a year, and ALF units are active across the industrialized world. Whether it's the Black Ravens in Russia, the DBF in Sweden, Animal Rescue in Japan, or the ALF in New Zealand, Canada, Israel, Poland, Italy, Spain, France, etc., the goal is the same: to liberate the suffering and destroy the property of those who kill for profit.

DIARY OF ACTIONS FOR THE U.S. AND CANADA, 1992-1993

The following reports are taken from news media, movement, and opposition publications, except for one reported on a computer bulletin board, one eyewitness report (the Berkeley/Oakland billboards,) and two from Tennessee TV reports. It is very likely that most actions are never reported, or that we have missed many which only appear in small, local newspapers. We keep coming across additions to the 1992 report, so chances are that we won't find out all that has happened in 1993 for a while!

So this list is probably not a complete account-help us out by mailing news clippings of action in your town or state to the addresses on the inside cover.

CANADA

(We have very little Canadian news-all but one of these reports come from ALFSG-Edmonton. It looks like the action subsides in February 1992 but that's just because the last issue of Combat stopped there!)

1992

January 1-Edmonton, Alberta- Ouellette Packing Plant was spray painted and had paint bombs thrown at it. Their van was spray painted, had its tires slashed,and was set ablaze. *ALF*

January 3-Calgary and Edmonton, AB- The *Animal Rights Militia* claims to have poisoned 87 Canadian Cold Buster chocolate bars because of University of Alberta vivisector Larry Wang's 16 years of animal experiments that led to the invention of the bar.

January 4-7-Calgary, AB- 4 fur stores and 4 meat sellers were attacked with spray paint, window smashings, and/or etching fluid. *ALF*

January 8-Edmonton, AB- A delivery truck of Ouellette Packers had its tires slashed. *ALF*

January 9-Edmonton, AB- Billingsgate Fish had all three replacement delivery trucks spray painted and 18 tires were slashed. *ALF*

February 7-Calgary, AB- Fur stores were damaged. *ALF*

June 1- Edmonton, AB- 29 cats were liberated from the University of Alberta. Research documents were taken and equipment was destroyed. *ALF*

December 25- Victoria, BC- A McDonalds was spray painted and had its windows smashed. *ALF*

1993

January 1-Victoria, BC- Locks were jammed at Williams Quality Meats. *ALF*

?- Ottawa, Ontario- Fur stores have had their windows smashed. This was listed on an animal rights computer bulletin board, so we have no dates or details.

May 4- Montreal, Quebec- Paradise Furs and another fur store were spray painted with slogans. *Paint Panthers*

UNITED STATES

1992

Memphis, TN- Numerous attacks on animal abusing businesses.

January 13-Walnut Creek, California- "Corrosive chemical" thrown on the windows of a fur store.

February 28-Lansing, Michigan- $125,000 damage done to Michigan State's mink research program as documents are taken and offices burned. *ALF Great Lakes Unit*

June-Memphis, Tennessee- Fur stores attacked.

?-Indiana- Hoosier Trappers was spray painted and a fur delivery van in Indianapolis was damaged.

?-South Carolina- The Vegan Front trashed a fur store.

July 5-Park Rapids, Minnesota- 3000 people were evacuated from the Park Rapids Rodeo after a bomb threat was phoned in. *Animal Rights Coalition Force* ?

July 7-Chicago, Illinois-An attempt was made to burn fur billboards-one was slightly damaged.

July 28-Memphis, TN- A TMX store had its locks glued, and a truck had its tires slashed and was spray painted. $934.58 in damages.

August-San Francisco, CA- Anti-fur protesters noticed that fur and leather shops in the Union Square area had their windows chemically damaged.

August 4-Memphis, TN- The same TMX store had its windows smashed locks glued, and slogans spray painted. $2,994.74 in damages.

August 5-Memphis, TN- Motes Furs was spray painted and splattered with paint bombs. $3,086.65 in damages.

August 9-Memphis, TN- J.P. Holloway Furriers was being spray painted when police, who had been staking out the store, arrested 3 Hardliners at the scene.

October- Minneapolis, MN- Swanson's Meats had the windows of its delivery trucks smashed and slogans spray painted on them. *ALF*

October 24-Milville and Logan, Utah- Two Animal Damage Control labs at Utah State were burned down and 29 coyotes were liberated. $150,000 in damages. *ALF*

November 8-Minneapolis, MN- 5 delivery trucks at Swanson's Meats were firebombed and the locks to the building were glued. $100,000 in damages. *ALF*

December-Miami, Florida- Several fur stores were spray painted. *Paint Panthers*

December 17-Denver, Colorado- Lloyd's Furs, Irv Ringler Furs, and Marks Furs were spray painted and paint bombed. *Paint Panthers*

December 18-Aspen, Vail, Breckenridge, Keystone, Denver, CO- 30 fur coats were damaged by having red paint spayed on them. *Paint Panthers*

December 20-Washington, D.C.- 5 fur stores were spray painted and splattered with paint-filled Christmas ornaments. *Paint Panthers*

1993

San Francisco, CA-ALFSG has word of action but no details.

Chicago, IL- ALFSG has word of action but no details.

Seattle, WA- ALFSG has word of action but no details.

Los Angeles, CA- ALFSG has word of action but no details.

January 13-Cleveland, Ohio- Ciska Furs spray painted and splattered with paint. *Paint Panthers*

February 8-New York, New York- The Fur Vault, Ritz Thrift Shop, Elizabeth Arden, Bloomingdale's, Fendi Bergdorf Goodman, and Harold J. Rubin Furs damaged with paint bombs and spray painted slogans like "Fur Shame," "Blood $," "Scum," "P.P.," and "Murderers." *Paint Panthers*

April-Berkeley and Oakland, CA- A large number of animal abuse billboards were spray painted with slogans such as "Go Vegan!" "Vegan Power!" and "Animal Torture."

April 14- Bethesda, Maryland- Three McDonald's, two Kentucky Fried Chickens, and Honey Baked Ham were spray painted with slogans. *Meat Free Mission*

April 27-MD- Five vivisectors had their homes spray painted with slogans like "Animal Torturer," etc. *Animal Avengers*

May-Berkeley and Oakland, CA- More animal abuse billboards spray painted.

June 10-Memphis, TN- The owner of Gilbert Kay Furs had his home spray painted and its locks glued. A taxidermy was spray painted and its windows were broken and door locks glued. A meat shop was spray painted. *ALF*

July-Manchester, TN (1 hour east of Nashville)- A meat market was spray painted with slogans and "ALF." The same night, an empty stockyard was set on fire and burned to the ground. The fire was so big that it took firefighters 4 hours to put it out. Bulldozers have cleared the ruins. The Tennessee Bureau of Investigation is looking into the case, but the fire destroyed all traces of whatever was used to start it. *ALF*

July-Memphis, TN- An unsuccessful arson attack was made on Jack Lewis Furs, and the store was spray painted. The store had a new $3,000 security camera, but it proved worthless as the attackers were well disguised. It did record the time the attack was made.

July 23-Berkeley, CA- An article on the harassment of a University of California vivisector mentioned that the campus had spray paintings appear calling him a "killer."

July 30-Bloomington, IN- After 4 delivery trucks at a poultry store had their refrigeration units unplugged and were spray painted, police arrived and saw two men. When they went after one, the other shook a fence to create a diversion and he was arrested instead. His trial is set for sometime in October.

The Diary of Actions is continued on page 3.

Anti-meat vandalism hits Sims

H-T Report

A Bloomington man was arrested Friday morning when vandalism to a dock was discovered behind Sims Poultry Co. on North Madison Avenue.

David [redacted] 19, [redacted] Bryan St., was booked into Monroe County Jail at 4:10 a.m. on preliminary charges of criminal mischief and resisting law enforcement. He was released on $1,000 bond.

The arrest came after someone reported noises coming from the dock, police said.

Officers saw "Meat is murder" spray-painted on the dock door as well as "Meat is death" on the side of a delivery truck. "ALF" was painted on another truck and "We will stop you" on the back of a third, police said.

In addition, the refrigeration units on four delivery trucks had been unplugged, police said.

Police then spotted two males in the area wearing dark clothing; they chased and caught one of the men. The man, later identified as [redacted] said he had met two other men at the Waffle House the night before and they all were vegetarians. police said.

No other arrests have been made.

DIARY OF ACTIONS CONTINUED

August-Madison, Wisconsin- At the University of Wisconsin, th ALF broke through a door at the building housing all the camp vivisection offices and set files on fire. We have no further details y but the University does farm animal research and does research f the fur farm industry, among other things. *ALF*

August-Milwaukee, WI- A meat delivery van was set on fire. *ALF*

August-Milwaukee, WI- On the outskirts of town, a chicke restaraunt was set on fire. Both of these actions were reported o local television. *ALF*

August-Memphis, TN- A Kentucky Fried Chicken and anoth animal abusing business were attacked.

We hope to have more details on these recent actions in th next issue.

The A.L.F. strikes again

DARREN THURSTON

The trial for accused ALF activist DarrenThurston was set to start on September 22, but we have no news on his case so far.

He was arrested and imprisoned over a year ago after being under police surveillance for at least a few weeks. He is charged with the liberation of 29 cats from the University of Alberta in Edmonton in June 1992, the arson attack on the Billingsgate Fish Company in December 1991 and several other actions. Donations for his court costs are needed and can be sent to the Edmonton ALFSG (make checks payable to ALFSG.)

ADDITIONS TO THE U.S. ALF HISTORY FROM LAST ISSUE

In November 1988, the ALF set a fur store on fire in Santa Rosa, CA. Damages topped $100,000 and the store had to close.

As of December 1988, the Yerkes Primate Research Center at Emory University in Atlanta, GA had undergone 2 bomb threats and 5 attempted break-ins.

In January 1990, there was an attempted break-in at John Orem's Texas Tech lab, the site of a successful ALF raid in 1989.

The fire at the Columbia vivisector's house was in January 1990, not April.

STOP THE PRESSES! LATE BREAKING NEWS!

1) Slingshot, an underground newspaper, received the action claim quote below:

"GREETINGS FELLOW ACTIVISTS,

The Animal Liberation Front, Golden Gate Unit, claims:

March 26: Oakland. Butcher shop spraypainted.

May 26: San Francisco. 3 chicken restaurants, 2 butchers, and 2 leathe shops had slogans painted and locks glued shut.

mid-June: San Francisco. 3 fur shops had locks glued.

July 9: Albany. A KFC had all its locks glued, slogans painted on 3 walls an all windows etched with acid.

July 16: San Francisco. City Meats (sells veal) had its front lock glued an slogans painted. A Burger King had its front lock glued.

July 31: San Francisco. 2 trucks at Robert's corned beef had all locks glue and slogans painted all over them. At United Meats, a back fence was cu through, and 3 trucks had all locks glued and slogans painted such as 'Mea is Murder.'

WE FIGHT FOR THE ANIMALS!" *(Source: Slingshot magazine)*

2) On the morning of July 6 in Montgomery County, Maryland, fake bomb were left on the front steps of 4 vivisectors. The bomb squad found that th packages contained a brick, a plastic mouse with fake blood, and threatening note. *(Source: Putting People First)*

3) On July 16, the grand jury in Michigan indicted Rod Coronado on severa counts for the 2/28/92 ALF raid on Michigan State's mink lab. They say h could face 50 years in jail, but the problem is, they can't find him! Stay fre Rod! Notice how the murderers, child molesters and drug dealers who rul our streets get out of jail in months or 2 years, while the FBI hunts dow those who stand up to barbarism and the real criminals running our societ go untouched. *(Source: Putting People First)*

We apologize to our friend whose article on vegan philosophy was supposed to go in th space. It'll be in the next issue.

Further proof that our enemies are every bit as depraved as we say they are:

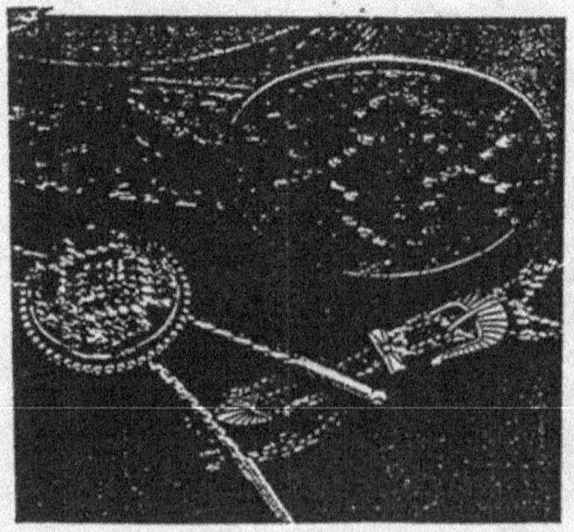

SNAKESKIN SET FOR THE MACHO MAN
One rattlesnake gave up a lot so you could dress up in his skin. Choose a watchband, a bola tie with silvered string tips and a belt with even the belt buckle covered with rattlesnake skin. Belt available in sizes 34, 36 & 38.

#924302 RATTLESNAKE WATCHBAND, $29.95
#924304 RATTLESNAKE BOLA, $9.95
#924305 RATTLESNAKE BELT, $45.00

ORDER TOLL FREE
24 HOURS A DAY 7 DAYS A WEEK
1-800-237-2559

THE GOOD LIFE CATALOG 1915 THOMPSON MFG. INC. TAMPA, FLORIDA

5401 Hangar Court, P.O. Box 30303
Tampa, FL 33630-3303

MALE CHAUVINIST T-SHIRTS
Black and blue shirt says, "Wanted! Good woman able to clean, cook, sew, skin deer, cut meat. Must have shotgun, duck blind and 4-wheel drive. Please send picture of 4-wheel drive." Black and yellow shirt wants a good woman to cook, sew, dig worms, clean fish and must have boat and motor. Says, "Please send picture of boat and motor." 100% cotton, machine-washable. Made in USA. M, L, XL.

#920755 HUNTERS, GOOD WOMAN T-SHIRT, $13.95
#915220 FISHERMAN, GOOD WOMAN T-SHIRT, $13.95

WANTED!
GOOD WOMAN
WANTED
GOOD WOMAN
PLEASE SEND PICTURE
OF BOAT AND MOTOR.

LLOYD'S FURS&GEMS

The Denver Post / Glen Martin

ACTIVISTS ACT UP: The exterior of Lloyd's Furs, 2780 E. Second Ave., was sprayed by activists.

Cherry Creek furriers vandalized

'Paint Panthers' smash ornaments, spray graffiti

By Sarah Ellis
Special to The Denver Post

Three Cherry Creek-area fur stores were hit early yesterday by vandals who smashed paint-filled ornaments against the buildings and spray-painted graffiti on them.

An anti-fur protest group calling itself the "Paint Panthers" took credit for the acts, according to Dan Mathews, spokesman for the People for the Ethical Treatment of Animals.

The group is not connected with PETA, Mathews said, but as long as their methods remain non-violent PETA does not "condone or condemn them."

"We understand the frustration that drives activists to do stuff like that," Mathews said. "It sends a stronger message."

In a telephone message to the Washington offices of PETA, the Paint Panthers threatened to spray-paint fur wearers on both the streets of Denver and Colorado ski slopes this weekend. They also claimed responsibility for similar actions earlier this week in several south Florida cities, Mathews said.

The three furriers who were targeted by the new underground group were reluctant to discuss the incidents.

"I do not care to give these people any publicity," said Fred Schelm, manager of Lloyd's Furs, 2780 E. Second Ave.

Police verified that, in addition to Lloyd's, reports were received from Irv Ringler Furs, 310 St. Paul St., and Mark's Furs, 263 Josephine St.

All three cases are under investigation, officer Harlan Walker said.

The Fur Information Council of America advises members to avoid media attention to protest actions such as yesterday's vandalism.

"We believe activist groups are entitled to their opinions," council spokesman Bill Outlaw said. "But they cross the line with acts of vandalism. The public becomes turned off, and they damage their own cause the most."

From The Denver Post, December 19, 1992.

Animal-Rights Activists Vandalize 5 Area Fur Salons

Five Washington area fur salons were vandalized early yesterday by a group that spray-painted storefronts with anti-fur slogans.

The group, which called itself the "Paint Panthers," said it was responsible for spray-painting the words "shame," "blood money" and "fur scum" on the windows and awnings of Saks Jandel in Chevy Chase, Skandia Furs of Vienna, Furs of Kiszely in McLean, and Miller's Furs and Rosendorf Evans, both in the District.

Area police said they are investigating the incidents.

Animal-rights activists said it is the fourth such attack in the last week by the group on fur stores across the country, with similar incidents occurring in Miami, Denver and Aspen, Colo. Some of the earlier attacks involved squirting blood-red paint on people wearing furs.

"We don't begrudge them the right to their opinion, but they don't have the right to vandalize property to make their point," said Bill Outlaw, a spokesman for the Fur Information Council in Herndon. "People have the right to wear fur without [having to fear] undue intimidation."

From The Washington Post, December 21, 1992.

NEWS

Anyone heard anything about the federal grand jur in Louisiana? Supposedly they are investigating ar ALF plan to liberate the Silver Springs Monkeys fror Tulane University in New Orleans, and a PET undercover investigator at Wright State in Ohio had he equipment seized by the FBI. That's all we know.....

There is also a federal grand jury called in Utah a the end of last October, after the Utah State raid. Nc news on that either.

The Oregon State Experimental Fur Farm was closec in June. When a member of the Mink Farmer Research Foundation was asked if the closure ha anything to do with the June 1991 ALF raid there, he said, "Probably, but we can't say that publicly or they' get ideas."

CVS
Bag
OF death

Billboard in Berkeley, CA, May 1993. Thanks to a friend for the photo.

DeValois reported some of the harassment to UC Berkeley police.

"There has been graffiti calling him a killer that's appeared on campus. He has also received hate mail regarding his research," said UC Berkeley police Lt. Bill Foley.

Foley added that the cases are under investigation in order to find the perpetrators.

DeValois said the Federal Bureau of Investigation has investigated some of the letters and threats that he has received.

Law targets animal rights activists

WASHINGTON — A new law aimed at the militant, underground animal liberation movement makes violence against farms and research labs a federal crime. Farmers and researchers say they hope the law has a chilling effect on the radical elements of the animal rights movement. But activists who sympathize with the Animal Liberation Front say the attackers will not be deterred. The law targets raids on labs, livestock facilities, aquariums, zoos, circuses and rodeos in which damages total at least $10,000.

THE COMMERCIAL APPEAL
MEMPHIS, SUNDAY, JUNE 13, 1993

Furrier, taxidermy are hit by vandalism

Vandals spray painted the Ea Memphis home of Gilbe Kirschner, owner of Gilbert K Furs at 4540 Poplar, and al painted the wall of Hataway Taxidermy Inc. at 880 S. Coop some time Thursday night, a cording to police reports.

Kirschner said three peopl were arrested recently for sim lar vandalism and he believe the painting was retaliation.

He said the vandals painte "Fur Is Dead" on his garage an "ALF" on both his house and g rage. And, he said, they splashe paint on the front of his hous Glue was also squirted in hi house and garage door locks.

Kirschner said the vandalisr will not put him out of business "I'll just paint over it."

Members of the so-called Animal Liberation Front have caused similar damage throughout the country.

Johnny Hataway, owner of the taxidermy, told police "A L F" was sprayed on his store wall and two windows were broken. And, he said, glue was also put in his door locks.

"Meat Is Murder" was sprayed on Ashford's Mid-Town Meats at 643 N. McLean Thursday night, according to police.

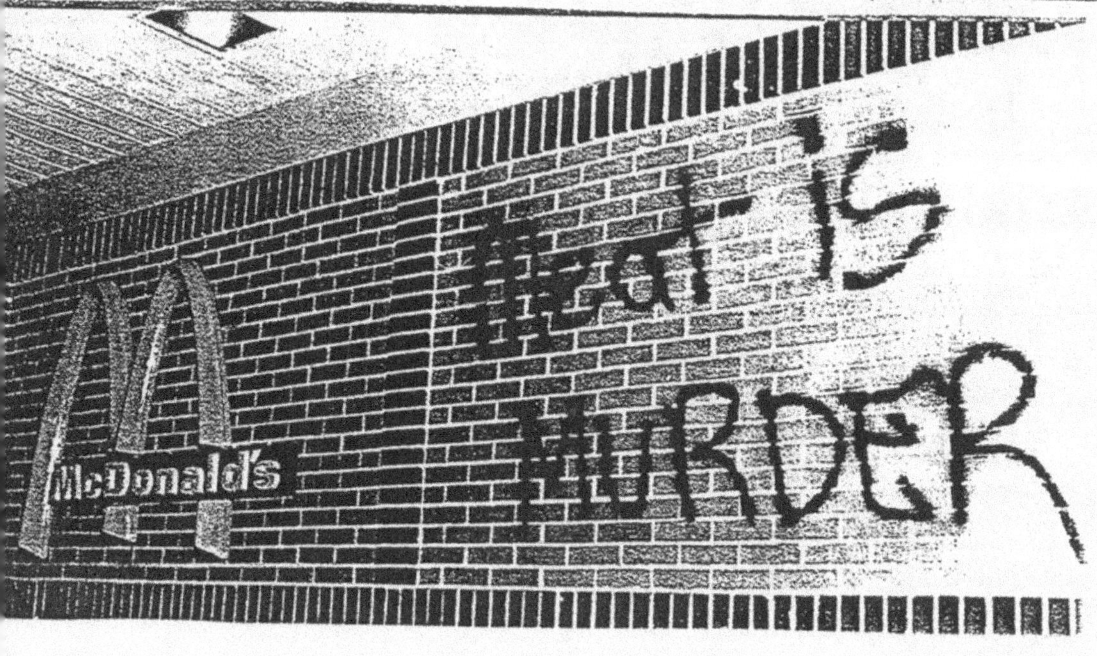
McDonald's
Meat IS MURDER

From PETA News, Summer 1993.

THE MEMPHIS THREE

Memphis is in western Tennessee next to Arkansas. For the past several years, animal abusing businesses have been under continuous attack, with over 100 reported instances of direct action. On August 9, 1992, two young women and a young man were arrested while spray painting a fur store. The two women implicated two other men in four attacks on fur stores during July and August, and they were arrested the next day. After waiting months for a trial, the three were sentenced to 11 months and 29 days in jail for the 4 actions. They were released on June 5 after 3 weeks in jail on appeal. The appeal will be heard in November, and for now the three have to wear electronic monitoring devices and obey a curfew.

The three defendants are members of Hardline, and as stated in the last 2 issues, we oppose parts of their ideology, especially their anti-gay views. Due to their positions, many publications haven't reported their case.

Why then, do we? One, because action speaks louder than words.

Second, because we are a news magazine reporting on the vegan movement.

So, you decide whether to support them.... We will continue to report on their case while hoping that with the departure of Sean VR and the growing political sophistication of Hardline, they will take a closer look at some of the reasons why so many decent activists disagree with them. We encourage members of Hardline to contact gay animal liberation groups and read the several recent studies (not funded by gays) which show that homosexuality is biologically natural in a portion of any given population.

If you decide to support them, they need donations badly to cover court fees. You can also write and talk to them if you disagree with them. Write J.P., Jesse, and Mike at PO Box 241532/ Memphis, TN/38124.

'Payday' arrives for 3 sent to prison

By Lawrence Buser
The Commercial Appeal

Three animal-rights activists who broke windows, glued locks and spray-painted fur stores last year were sent to prison Monday by a judge who said their "payday" had arrived.

The three were ordered to begin serving a sentence of 11 months and 29 days for their guilty pleas last month to four counts of vandalism under $500. They were sent to the Shelby County Penal Farm where they must serve about six months before release.

Several of the city's furriers urged the judge to show no mercy, saying they have been terrorized by such acts since 1987.

"This will have ramifications nationwide," said state Prosecutor James Lammey Jr., who said the three espoused the beliefs of terrorist groups. "I'm sure they didn't appreciate the enormity of what they did, but I'm sure they do now."

Defendant John P. Goodwin, 20, was described as the ringleader. Co-defendants Michael S. Karbon, 20, and Jessie Keenan, 19, are Minnesota residents who said they moved to Memphis last summer, in part, to join animal rights causes.

Friends, employers and relatives testified for the defendants, who said they regretted their actions, which caused at least $7,000 in damages.

"I was trying to help animals, but it was totally shortsighted," Karbon said. "I never fully thought it through."

The three said they are Vegans, a vegetarian group that shuns the use of animal products. The 3½ hour sentencing hearing in Criminal Court also included discussions of People for the Ethical Treatment of Animals (PETA), the Coalition Against Fur Farms and the Animal Liberation Front (ALF).

The latter group has been investigated by FBI offices across the country for violent crimes, including firebombing and arson, Lammey said.

The defendants denied any affiliation with ALF, although they admitted spray-painting those letters on the fur compan-

Please see VEGANS, Page B2

From Page B1

Vegans

ies they vandalized last July and August. They also admitted other acts of vandalism for which they were not charged.

Police said there have been about 100 similar incidents of vandalism at furriers and meat markets in the past three years. Graffiti often included slogans such as "Fur is Dead," "Meat is Murder," "Ban Fur" and "ALF."

The vandalism stopped after their arrest by police.

"You may not be the Klan, but you wanted to intimidate someone," Judge W. Fred Axley told them. "The First Amendment does not extend itself to violence and when you cross that line you belong to me. I believe in payday. Step out."

The three pleaded guilty to vandalizing TMX Stores at 6122 Macon Road on July 28 and Aug. 4; Motes Furs, at 4273 American Way, on Aug. 5, and J. P. Holloway Furriers at 673 Avon on Aug. 9.

"I received a phone call and was asked if I liked being treated the way animals are being treated," said Janice Dowell. "We lived in fear every time we walked into the store."

One furrier, Steven Ballin, said a threatening message was stapled to his downtown furrier, King Furs, last year.

The message, "Communique #1 From The Vegan Front" said in part: "No longer shall your crimes against the people, animals and the environment of this planet go unpunished. Judgement day is at hand."

Attorney Mac Dickinson, who represented all three defendants, said there was no evidence they wrote the message.

Suspects in fur vandalism free on bond

Three animal-rights activists imprisoned May 17 for vandalizing fur stores were granted release on appeal bonds Friday.

John P. Goodwin, 20, Michael S. Karbon, 20, and Jessie Keenan, 19, were serving a sentence of 11 months and 29 days at the Shelby County Penal Farm.

Criminal Court Judge W. Fred Axley set the bonds and ordered a 10 p.m. nightly curfew while their attorneys appeal the sentence.

The three are Vegans, a group that shuns the use of animal products. They pleaded guilty in April to breaking windows, gluing locks and spray-painting four fur stores.

Bond for Karbon was set at $5,000 because his permanent residence is Minnesota. Keenan's was set at $2,500 and Goodwin's at $1,000.

—*Lawrence Buser*

Continue Protest, Albeit Legally

Among those attending the Good Earth Fe[stival] June 5th was animal-righ[ts] activist J.P. Goodwin — whi[ch] surprised many of his acquai[n]tances. They thought he was [in] jail.

In fact, Goodwin had bee[n] released that very morning fro[m] the penal farm, after three week[s] of incarceration. He and his tw[o] cohorts, Michael Karban an[d] Jesse Keenan, had originally re[]ceived a one-year prison term fo[r] vandalism, but they'd gotten ou[t] on bond and were awaiting a[n] appeals hearing.

"Right now we have a 1[0] p.m. curfew and we're on elec[]tronic monitoring," says Goodwin. "We hav[e] no idea when we'll go to appeals court, but w[e] expect that our sentence will be overturned an[d] we'll get probation."

Goodwin's legal troubles began last yea[r] when he was charged with vandalizing fou[r] Memphis fur stores. He and his friends broke windows, threw paint, and put Super Glue i[n] the locks. All were teenagers at the time. They pleaded guilty, paid a $2,000 fine, apologized and offered to pay restitution. Nevertheless Goodwin says, local fur merchants pushed fo[r] a felony charge.

"They had furriers that we hadn't vandalized get up on the witness stand and say we deserved the maximum sentence, though they admitted we had never been near their stores. Their lawyers also presented evidence that did not pertain to us — FBI files about laboratory break-ins in Oregon. They were trying to set a national precedent."

Goodwin feels that Criminal Court Judge W. Fred Axley was trying to make an example of the young men. Axley permitted all of the evidence to stand, even though some of it implied the defendants were part of a terrorist-style group such as the Animal Liberation Front.

"We are not involved in any kind of organized conspiracy," insists Goodwin, "though we use the same tactics that are used by animal-rights people around the country. Just because somebody spray-paints something on a wall doesn't mean they're involved in any serious crimes. We were trying to show the judge that we have high moral character—we don't smoke or use drugs or drink." He claims that Axley belittled their vegan beliefs, asking whether they wore leather shoes.

Calling himself "a thorn in the side of the furriers," Goodwin says, "It's a hollow victory for them, because this has gotten the animal-rights people up in arms. I think the public agrees the sentencing was unnecessarily harsh."

Goodwin adds that local animal-rights groups plan to launch a major educational campaign and hold many fur protests this winter. "Through *legal* means," he emphasizes. "You *can* have radical action — such as sit-ins — that doesn't destroy property or hurt anybody. Civil disobedience generates a lot of attention, and I think that's beneficial."

But is it worth going to jail for? "If it creates publicity," Goodwin replies, "it's okay with me." ■

Three face jail, fines in anti-fur vandalism

By Lawrence Buser
The Commercial Appeal

Three animal-rights activists Monday pleaded guilty to vandalizing three stores last year because the stores handle furs.

They slashed truck tires, spray-painted "Fur is Dead" and tossed red bell peppers filled with paint on store walls.

John Paul Goodwin, 20, who was described as "the ringleader," Michael Karbon, 20, and Jessie Keenan, 19, pleaded guilty to vandalism under $500.

They were sentenced to 11 months and 29 days in jail, fines of up to $2,000 and full restitution under a plea agreement.

They remain free until May 17, when Criminal Court Judge W. Fred Axley will decide whether to grant their request for probation. "The First Amendment protects free speech, but not vandalism," said state prosecutor James Lammey Jr. "They can write their congressman or go on TV or carry signs to make their point."

The defendants said they did not want to comment while their sentence is pending, but at least one of them did just what the prosecutor suggested.

Goodwin was one of about 20 people who protested in front of local McDonald's restaurants over the weekend as part of a nationwide anti-beef campaign urging the fast-food chain to offer a vegetarian burger as an alternative.

The three were arrested last summer after a special police task force staked out one of several fur stores that had been vandalized. One juvenile who was arrested implicated the others and said she followed the beliefs of the "Vegans," a vegetarian group that shuns the use of animal products.

In one incident, the defendants spray-painted a truck with the letters "ALF," apparently for a national group called the Animal Liberation Front.

Court records show the incidents and damages included:

■ TMX Stores at 6122 Macon Road on July 28, where slogans were spray-painted on a truck, tires were slashed and door locks were filled with glue. Damages totaled $934.58.

■ TMX Stores at 6122 Macon Road on Aug. 4, where plate-glass windows were broken, glue was sprayed in the locks and walls were spray painted. Damages totaled $2,994.74.

■ Motes Furs at 4273 American Way on Aug. 5, where walls were spray painted and splattered with paint-filled red bell peppers. Damages totaled $3,086.65.

■ J.P. Holloway Furriers at 673 Avon on Aug. 9, where a roll-down metal curtain was spray painted. Damages totaled $800.

"If they have a difference of opinion, they shouldn't use vandalism to express themselves," said trapper Kenneth R. Jones, who attended the proceeding.

The Militant Movement for Animal Liberation in England

Wednesday December 21 1988

Firefighters battle to control the blaze which wrecked Dingles, the House of Fraser store in Plymouth, on Monday night. Police suspect arson PHOTOGRAPH: MARC HILL

On all levels, from the number of local animal liberation groups to the amount of attention the government pays to animal issues, there is no comparison to the amount of activism in the United Kingdom. This has been true for more than a century, as the Western concepts of the rights of animals were developed by English philosophers (After influences from Eastern philosophies.) While we have little space to cover the militant wing of the English movement in detail, the following is intended as a brief and inspiring sketch.

The first group who carried out direct action for the animals were the Band of Mercy, who damaged hunters' rifles in the 1870's. The Hunt Saboteurs' Association was founded in 1962 with the purpose of disrupting bloodsports on the field. A member of the Hunt Saboteurs decided to go a little farther, and in 1972 Ronnie Lee founded the Band of Mercy, which would carry out illegal direct action for animals like its namesake. Members of the Band of Mercy burned hunting vehicles and a seal hunting boat, and burned down a laboratory under construction in Milton Keynes. Lee was caught in late 1974 and was sent to prison for a year. During his sentence, other activists liberated dogs who were being forced to smoke cigarettes in a laboratory. In 1976, Lee reorganized the group and gave it a new name-the Animal Liberation Front. The first ALF attack was on Charles River Laboratories. Lee was again jailed for a year, this time for liberating hundreds of rats from a lab, in February 1977. Over the next few years, the ALF continued to carry out several laboratory raids and many other attacks a year.

In the meantime, the Hunt Saboteurs continued to grow as well. The anarchist punk movement began supporting direct action for animals, and brought thousands of people into the movement. Bands such as Conflict and the Apostles detailed ALF tactics in their songs.

While the ALF and Hunt Saboteurs remained committed to nonviolence, the Animal Rights Militia sent letter bombs to the leaders of political parties and several vivisectors in 1982. One vivisector was injured. The same group carried out the "Mars Bar Hoax" in 1984 where ARM claimed it had poisoned the candy bars on shelves because its parent company carried out vivisection. All the candy was pulled off store shelves across England and the company stopped testing on animals soon afterwards.

With a vast increase in actions during the mid-80's, the meat industry began to bear the brunt of ALF attacks. Butchers' shops and delivery vans began to be firebombed across the country. Smaller actions such as the usual window smashings, glueing of locks, and so on were reported regularly in large cities, small towns, and rural areas. Now that the ALF was a serious threat to animal abusers, the British government began to take

ARSON ATTACK ON BASC's HQ

Left: Firemen fight the blaze at the British Association for Shooting and Conservation headquarters. Thousands of pounds worth of damage was caused Photo: Shooting Times and Country magazine 7/2/91

ALF
G503ADC

Slogans daubed on one of the Simpson vehicles, among them 'Meat is Murder.'

On 16th September the Northern A4 ALF cell raided Adlington Poultry Farm, a battery unit near Stockport. After drilling through walls and cutting locks to gain access, and then dealing with seven security cameras, the activists rescued eighty-two hens, smashed hundreds of eggs and painted slogans.

notice. The Scotland Yard set up the Animal Rights National Index in 1984 to monitor the movement and identify ALF activists.

As a result, Ronnie Lee, Vivien Smith, and several others were arrested on conspiracy charges after what was described as a major ALF firebomb factory was discovered in Sheffield. The prisoners were accused of being the leadership of the ALF, and they were sentenced to long prison terms by a judge who had been a Fascist organizer in the 1930's. Lee received 10 years, the longest sentence. During the trial, he said, "Going to prison in order to stop the imprisonment of animals may seem a peculiar concept, but then their prisons are so much worse than ours...." The ALF showed that it was a non-centralized group under no leadership by carrying out a number of attacks and liberations in the weeks after the trial.

The Hunt Saboteurs also continued to grow, with fox hunts being harassed in most areas. As a result, hunters began to regularly use violence to defend their sadistic bloodsports. One scumbag hunter told an Essex court in 1986 that beating a hunt sab "is rather like wife beating, they are both private matters."

1987 marked the beginning of the English ALF's most famous campaign. To smash the fur trade, the ALF began setting off incendiary devices in fur stores and department stores that sold fur to turn on fire sprinklers and destroy the coats. On July 12, one of the devices left in Debenham's department stores in three cities caused three million pounds damage to the store in Luton. Smaller attacks targeted fur stores again and again until they went out of business. Then, on December 20, 1988, the ALF set off firebombs in 5 cities, sent letter bombs to fur stores, and had incendiary devices discovered in several more. The biggest fire completely destroyed a gigantic department store in Plymouth which sold fur. In the wake of these attacks, most department stores in the U.K. stopped selling fur. The ALF is credited with decimating 70 to 90 percent of Britain's fur industry in these years.

February 1989 saw a further increase in militancy as the ALF used plastic explosives for the first time to blow up a university building in Bristol. While this action was exceptional, firebombings and arson bec[a] much more common ALF tac[tics]. Delivery vans were the most com[mon] targets, as the meat and d[airy] industries found to their dismay. liberations continued, with thous[ands] of animals liberated every year.

In the most direct attack [on] vivisectors so far, an unknown gr[oup] placed bombs under the cars of prominent torturers in June 1[990]. Both received minor injuries, b[ut a] small boy was injured by flying m[etal] after vivisector Patrick Head['s] Volkswagon exploded. This hor[rible] result showed the danger in us[ing] such tactics.

The Hunt Sabs began to actu[ally] force hunt clubs to give up, as m[any] major hunts faced constant sab[otage] whenever they went out. Viole[nce] against sabs increased, and

At Howells, in Cardiff, which has been attacked by animal rights extremists three times before, the incendiary was concealed in the menswear department. Stock valued at £170,000 was destroyed.

February 1991, 18 year old Mike Hill was murdered when hunter Alan Summersgill knowingly accelerated his truck when Hill was on the back of it. This April, 15 year old Thomas Worby was murdered by hunter Tony Ball, who crushed his head with the hunt van. Scores of sabs have been seriously injured by hunters and hired "escort" thugs. As a result, direct action against hunters has increased and many sabs have begun to fight back despite the HSA's official pacifist stance. Summersgill's house and hunt club were burned down, and numbers of hunters have had their cars destroyed by incendiary devices. Smaller attacks have increased as well, and hunts and hunting balls are often the scene of vicious confrontations.

A big upsurge in activity made 1991 and 1992 the most active years ever for the ALF, and 1993 is shaping up the same way. Literally thousands of animal abusers have been targeted, from a series of firebombings in Scotland, to arson attacks in Northern Ireland, to laboratory and factory farm liberations around the U.K., to hundreds of delivery trucks burned, to arson attacks against the fishing industry. Of course, government repression continues, as the Operation Fox arrests show. Scotland Yard carried out extensive surveillance for months before arresting Vivien Smith, Keith Mann, and several others in October of 1991. But Ronnie Lee was released in November 1992, and very few arrests are made considering that several attacks take place every single day.

From the looks of it, direct action in the U.K. will probably make that country the leader in animal liberation in the industrialized world. While moderates claim that ALF actions detract from the movement, the solid gains made by the ALF in England show what direct action can do. For the billions of animals still to be liberated from their cages of hell, we thank all the activists in the U.K. for their tireless work. Keep it up!

e foie

term m
of force
to six po
oat every
natural siz
e-fed for
The tr
straddlin
t, and p
packing
On mech
d stretch
can be inserted into the goose's throat. On farms, an elastic band is placed around the neck to prevent it from retching up the food.

Animal Liberation Front Supporters' Group

Diary of Actions

Nov. 1987 No. 2

August — November 1987

ALF bite back

BUTCHER SHOPS HIT BY ANIMAL RIGHTS GROUP

ANIMAL LIB GUN ATTACK

Furriers threatened as gang hurls smoke bombs

Rape and the New Woman...

ARKANGEL

FOR ANIMAL LIBERATION

Number 8 Summer 92 £1.80

NORTHAMPTONSHIRE

Half an million pounds of damage was caused at Europe's biggest slaughterhouse - Midland Meat Packer, at Crick - when 10 incendiary devices, placed in the cabs of 10 lorries ignited. 20 police officers are apparently working around the clock to catch the 'mindless thugs' responsible for the MMP attack and 'for spate of attacks' on shops in and around the Northampton and Kettering areas, including 23 the night after the fire at Crick.
One butcher, Derek Hands said 'we had a brick hurled through the window by some idiots...they have no brains, animals are put on the Earth for one purpose - to eat'...yes Derek...and the ALF were put here for one purpose. Stan Weston, another butcher said 'we care for animals'.

Bombers won't stop me, hunt woman vows as sister escapes car blast

Defiant: Sarah Godley

A HUNTSWOMAN vowed yesterday to defy animal rights extremists after a bomb exploded under her car.

The incendiary device which damaged Sarah Godley's Ford Sierra went off seconds after her 24-year-old sister had walked by with her boyfriend.

By DOMINIC KENNEDY

Miss Godley, a member of the Surrey Union Hunt, blamed animal extremists for the blast outside her home in the village of Westcott, near Dorking.

'They have said they want to kill me,' she said. 'And this nearly killed my sister, Joanna. It proves to me that the anti-hunters are hypocritical, violent, vicious and intolerant.

'It makes me more determined than ever to go hunting. Even if I feel like lying in bed on a Saturday morning, I shall join the hunt to defy them.'

The 31-year-old secretary, who has been hunting for seven years, clashed with campaigners after recording their demonstrations for a film, The Unacceptable Face of Protest.

She received 3am telephone calls labelling her a 'hideous, perverted trollop'. They stopped when she rang anti-hunt activists in the early hours to complain.

Earlier this year, her car and the large country house she shares with her parents and sister were daubed with red paint and paint-stripper.

Building the Vegan Movement

We're at an exciting juncture in the history of the animal liberation movement. Large numbers of young vegans are getting involved the fight for saving animals, which means that we will start to see changes in a movement that has been made up of older activists for the past decade. So at this time, it's important that we organize this new energy in the most effective manner to save as many animals as possible. **Here are our ideas.**

First, we need people who are compassionate, hard-working, intelligent, and physically fit. We need activists from all races and all economic and social backgrounds, vegans who stand against all forms of oppression and injustice. Fortunately, we have many such vegans working for animals now, and with enough communication, we will attract many more enthusiastic activists.

Unlike other radical movements, the vegan movement will avoid attracting the type of violence-loving thugs who are often drawn to political movements of many types. I think we've probably all seen people who join movements because they are looking for conflict and a place to blow off steam. The animal liberation movement will never appeal to most such people simply because a vegan diet takes a personal commitment. Most likely, it will be our opponents who will be psychotic and prone to sadism. After all, animal abusers like trappers, hunters, and so on are some of the most violent, ignorant, bigoted scum in the entire country.

The most important thing we can do now to build our movement is to communicate. Get a PO Box, and let us all know you're out there. We need vegan contacts in every large city and in every state and province. This will allow for the trading of ideas and information, and for vegan activists to travel from state to state, educating and inspiring others.

Use the PO Box to spread information through flyers and 'zines. **We need positive, exciting calls to action that look good and are well written.** Use computer bulletin boards to spread ideas, and make sure the message is constantly heard and repeated at your school, on your campus, at music shows, and in neighborhoods where students and young adults live or hang out. This can be done with flyers, posters, stickers, etc., all of which can be designed and made cheaply. (For stickers, simply xerox a sheet of your designs onto sticker paper, available at copy and office supply shops.)

Keep up with the movement, and encourage potential vegan activists to read books like Eco Warriors and Free the Animals!. Pass around copies of *Arkangel*, *Howl*, the *Earth First! Journal*, and others to inspire vegan activists and show them that they are not alone. Serious activists can study the abolition movement of the mid 1800's for ideas and tactics. Also, keep up with what the filth are doing by reading hunting magazines at the public library and sending off for newsletters by animal abusers.

At the same time that radical vegans are organizing around the country, we need to stay in contact with and get along with the mainstream movement. There's too much infighting as it is, and we need to remember that different types of people will play differing roles in the fight for animals' lives.

So let's get going! Each animal saved is a success, and every small victory adds up. We've got a long and hard struggle ahead of us, but the day will come when no redneck degenerate will stand in the way of an animal's freedom. **We will win- kindness, strength, and perseverance.**

How We Can Deal With Government and Private Surveillance

The extent of government spying and collusion with industries it approves of in harassing political groups may come as a surprise to many activists. But since at least the 1910's, various federal agencies have spied on and disrupted, often violently, political groups ranging from pacifists to urban guerillas. While we cannot go into n detail here, all radical vegans sh read "War at Home" by Brian Glick, COINTELPRO Papers" by Churchil Vander Wall, and "Break-ins, D Threats, and the FBI" by F Gelbspan. All can be ordered South End Press/ 116 St. Botolph Boston, MA 02115. These bo describe in detail tactics used to dis activists' efforts.

So what can we expect to face in near future? On the low level, we expect mail to be read or "misdeliver phone tapping, threats, and camera video surveillance at demos meetings. All of these tactics regularly used by state, local, federal agencies all over the coun and the FBI and many others, incluc private spies, keep files on activists

On a more serious level, we expect infiltration attempts, burglar police searches and hassles, activ being followed, and in the rare ca violence or an assassination attemp

While we know of other moveme facing disruption, how do we know the government and others spy on movement? We only have to remem the infiltration of Mike Fain into D Foreman's Earth First! group a Sapone and Mead's setup of Fran T to realize how serious things can g Judi Bari and Darryl Cherney we almost killed by a bomb with alm certain FBI involvement. The office Friends of Animals in Connecticut w robbed of Rod Coronado's videotap of fur farms. The old US ALFSG c because their houses were broken i so often and their phones were tapp Six agencies, including the FBI a Michigan police, copied every single in Darren Thurston's apartment after was arrested, and his phones had be tapped for months.

It seems that we must be prepar for harassment, so what can we d First, assume that all phone calls a mail to your home or PO Box a monitored. To communicate witho hassle, use PO Boxes under fa names on both ends. Next, never tru anyone with confidential informati unless you've known them outside the movement or for years. Keep yo files safe from burglary and learn s defense. Don't draw attention yourself as a radical at mainstrea meetings. Take pictures of spies demos when you're sure they are, a never talk to any police agency. It important to disregard all threat rumors, gossip and insults from insic the movement because that has ofte been the government's most effecti way of splitting movements.

Even with these precautions, do get paranoid! Remember, the FBI ha totally failed to catch the ALF or Ro Coronado-they simply don't have th resources to watch us all!

WARNING: ...G EIGI... EXTREMELY GRAPHIC NATURE. OUR COVER STORY ENDS ON PAGE 65.

This is from the booklet "Without A Trace" available for 3$ from DSFA/ c/o Box 8, 82 Colston St./ Bristol/ U.K.

AN INTERVIEW WITH AN ALF ACTIVIST

How do you go about carrying out actions?
There are a number of aspects that one has to take into consideration. First and foremost it's important to look round the region at all the targets, laboratories, and as many of the factory farms as one can find, hunt kennels, fur shops, abbatoirs, etc. If actions have taken place already in your home area it's a good idea to go for the most straightforward, squirting paintstripper from a lemon juice squeezy, or a washing up liquid squeezy bottle over the van(s) of an animal exploiter, gluing up fur shop locks to start with, then progress to factory farms which generally are not alarmed (there is the odd one that is, particularly those that belong to the large chain stores). If no actions, or only one or two small actions have taken place, it may be beneficial to go for a laboratory, the reasoning being that once things start in your area the labs wil start investing in more security measures. There are still labs with only minimal security. The animals are not necessarily in the labs at all times and there is usually an animal house in seperate building where animals are held until needed, or in some cases are bred there. We can usually gain access to the grounds, (we're not put off by the usual security fence with with strands of barbed wire, as these can be climbed with practice - we use the concrete posts as a support and wear 2-3 pairs of gloves when learning. N.B. Razor wire is much more tricky/dangerous - be careful!), we usually find the buildings with animals have fans operating, pumping out the stale air and the fresh in. We can smell which one has them within.

With factory farm units we can tell what kind of animals, if any, are in the units, simply by placing our ears against an air duct on the side of the unit or at the door, listening and smelling. Or we try shining a pencil torch, with coloured plastic held over the end by an elastic band, through any openings. In fact, we double or treble the layers of plastic so that only the minimum of light get through, not only reducing the chance of anyone else seeing, but shine a bright light onto battery hens and they may well make a lot of noise. We always try the door handle, etc, and have been pleasantly surprised a couple of times to find it is unlocked. With experience one can often tell what animals are held in a particular unit by its shape, size, and building materials used.

When looking at potential targets, we don't take balaclavas, etc We also make a point of emptying our pockets of everything, including door keys, discarding matching jewellery etc. before setting out, in case we drop anything. If we need to cover our faces a scarf is fine and we wear gloves of course. We also carry bird watching books and binoculars. Usually a lad and a girl will go by public transport or be dropped off at a prearranged time. We avoid parking a car in an area where a future target is being looked over, unless it's hidden. We try to limit our visits to any target to one or two and we do not leave any trace of our visit. We find we can make a totally silent look round by removing our shoes, though this is usually unnecessary. During the day we explore the approaches to the target with the help of an Ordnance Survey (O.S.) map, looking for a suitable dropping off point/place to stash the vehicle(s), emergency meeting point if necessary, noting any guard dogs at the target or in the gardens of houses along the route in. After dark we walk the route to ensure there are no guard dogs, go in and examine the units, check if there are any animals in them, can we climb in through an air duct, if not, what types of locks will we have to deal with.

If it's a lab, and not straightforward, we need to know the times of security patrols, then we'll do a spot of camping nearby.

In our group there are four people and over a period of time we have equipped ourselves with ordinary scarves for covering our heads and faces, gloves, two crowbars (one small, roughly a foot long, the other roughly a yard), a large screwdriver, a well oiled brace and 1" auger bit (it's a wood boring drill, the type used to make the hole in your door for the Yale lock), two mortar drills (one being extra long), two sledgehammers (a 14lb one with full handle and a 10lb one with the handle cut to 20" for working in a confined space), a pair of boltcutters, two 35mm SLR cameras with flashguns (with diffuser and tilt - occasionally we can bounce off the ceiling to get natural shadow). Duracell batteries are used in the flashguns—recharge is then much quicker. We use 400 ASA B+W film in one, and 100ASA colour slides in the other. When we carried out our first raid there were three people with scarves, gloves and a large screwdriver. We rescued 36 hens. Four sacks each, one carried on each shoulder by their draw strings and one in each hand, 3 hens in each sack.

We have since found that cardboard boxes are fine for chicks, etc., if the 'items' involved are rodents we sometimes find the cages in which they are housed are portable and we place the lot in our boxes or rucksacks. For hens and rabbits we use fairly large sacks (approx. 24" wide x 36" long) with rope nylon drawstrings in the middle. The rope is threaded in and out of the sack at 6" to 8" intervals and the length, when knotted together is the same as the circumference of the sack. We seal the double knot of the rope by using a match and literally lighting the two ends. As the nylon melts we blow out the flames and the resulting black blobs keep the strands together.

Another useful item that we make from a sack is a guard sack. Two brush poles are sprayed a dark colour, then placed inside the sack, one either side, and stitched securely into place. Roughly 6 - 8" of the handles protrude. One or two of these act as good barriers when you have to deal with a guard dog. The protruding poles are placed under the armpits and are held as high as possible. If anyone asks what they are they would be told that they are hides for photographing wildlife.

The actual day chosen for the raid is considered well in advance. A full moon and no cloud means a well-lit night which is undesirable, as are hot muggy nights when people find it hard to get to sleep. Overcast nights are good, and any rain is very welcome. With a particularly difficult target, everyone is made aware that we are expecting 'bad' weather and to expect very short notice. It is also important not to work to a pattern (e.g. actions every Friday/Saturday night). Weekend *evenings* are good because of the amount of people travelling to and from pubs/clubs, but for *night* raids weekdays are more approriate because of the amount of early morning traffic. Saturday nights are the worst possible, the roads early Sunday are dead. On the day of the raid a planning meeting takes place and a thorough briefing/discussion takes place. Details dealt with include the transport of equipment of activists, time of raid and departure, while studying a plan of the target - who will be responsible for being a lookout, breaking in, taking the animals, holding the sacks/boxes, where to meet up if things go wrong, who will be acting as back up by sitting at a phone, ensuring everyone has a few ten pences and some emergency money - while the raid may go OK, a car could break down. Everyone empties their pockets. We do take a container of water if the raid is likely to take a long time - wearing a mask for lengthy periods results in dry throats and coughing .

Before the tools are transported everything is wiped first with a rag soaked in warm soapy water and then again with a dry drag. This also goes for the cameras (and battery), flashgun (and batteries), everything, even glasses if worn. A further refinement is to cover our clothes with something like a boiler suit or old baggy clothes over our normal clothes and have a spare set of footwear. These items virtually eliminate the risk of us carrying traces home. These items can be discarded when we return to the vehicles(s), placed in a black bin bag it all looks like jumble. Someone has the responsibility of thoroughly washing the scarves, gloves, boiler suits/old clothes and shoes immediately upon returning after a raid. This person is not directly involved in the actions and stores the clothes and equipment. In other words we use a 'safe house'. Generally speaking, the arrangements for events after the action are just as important as the precautions beforehand.

Before setting off we make sure that everyone has a plausible reason for travelling in that direction or homewards, we consult the music press to see if there are any concerts applicable. If a male activist is driving, a female member will sit behind him. The police have a habit of glancing into cars and mixed company is far less likely to be stopped.

Choosing the time for the raid can be crucial. If possible we carry out the raid mid-evening so that we are home before 10:30-11:30 pm. Once the pubs close, and particularly after midnight there is always the chance of a spot check by the police looking for burglars. If travelling by car (we avoid hired vans, hired cars are OK, the police take less notice of new cars) we try to arrange for the tools, and hoods if used, to be well hidden in the target area mid-evening by just two people, a girl and a lad using public transport if possible. We take only the minimum amount of equipment.

The raid may need to be at night. Battery hens often make quite a din, though we are not put off by this. Unless we carry out the action while the house is unoccupied or is some distance away we raid the unit at 3-4am while everyone is fast asleep. We never travel between 12 midnight and 6-7am there or back. We arrive in the evening and hide out in a wood (we avoid the local pubs for the obvious reasons) and time the raid so that we arrive back at the transport after the raid shortly before dawn. Generally speaking, by planning well ahead we tend to concentrate on late evening raids during the summer and nighttime raids during the long nights of autumn and winter. the transport will often be a minimum of one mile away from the target and probably two or three miles away hidden in a field or wood (we carry a good quality compass in case we have to leave in a hurry, though it's generally not required). Vehicles are never parked in country lanes as the police will generally treat them as stolen vehicles that have been dumped, or certainly suspicious. Anyone sitting in such a vehicle will certainly be questioned. We push the car(s) down a track into a wood or similar. Pushing does away with driving with lights on and resultant noise and thus alerting any locals out walking the dog. We have parked in a nearby housing estate, leaving the vehicle(s) locked and empty, the drivers returning in couples to pick up the vehicles, and later the raiders. If the target is in an awkward area the raiders can be picked up by vehicles returning at a prearranged time or called in by portable C.B.s (again Duracell baterries are used).

If there are a number of cars hidden in a field/wood for an evening raid, depending on circumstances, it may be prudent for drivers to remain hidden nearby and watch that no dog walkers/courting couples stumble across them. If this were to happen and the dog wlaker/couple take a lot of notice , the vehicles(s) are moved to the emergency meeting place. When the raid is over one person travels ahead and checks that the transport is o.k.

The first thing we do during an actual raid is for the look out(s) to get into position. Binoculars are a very useful addition that can be used at night. They may take a little getting used to, focussing and time for ones eyes to adjust but it's well worth persevering. We find the usual long, thin straps on binoculars are unsuitable. They not only leave them dangling, and thus banging on fences being climbed, etc, but they are also uncomfortable to wear after a time. We substitute wide camera straps, suitably shortened. If portable C.B.s are being used they are tested beforehand to make sure they are in working order and tuned in. Because of the noisy static when both units are switched on, the raiders will have their C.B.s switched on all the time while the look-out(s) will have theirs switched off. This gives total silence; if the look-out needs to reach the raiders, a flick of the switch and it's on and ready to use. However, we do not rely on the C.B.s alone as sometimes they we may be working in a spot that gives poor reception. The look-outs should be positioned so that they can also warn the raiders directly and quickly. Usually bleeps are used rather than voices on the C.B.s, two bleeps to keep still and quiet, four for 'all clear' and continous bleeping if it's time to run for it, though we've not had to use this last sequence so far.

We have once or twice locked a gate using a plastic covered bike lock. This method is both quick and silent and ensures security vehicles cannot pursue us.

Usually we do not cut the telephone wires but occasionally this is necessary. Either they are cut near the house or office, if this is not possible a piece of brick is tied to a nylon rope and is thrown over the wire between two poles and two people will pull the wire down. It's usually a struggle and requires two people to use all their weight to yank it down. Wires are not cut at the big commercial labs as they are likely to have alarms connected via the phone lines to the nearest police station.

When entering the target area we usually have to deal with a fence of some sort, two people go forward and deal with it. The ordinary 3 strand barbed wire farm fences have the bottom 2 strands cut only. The top one prevents cows or horses following us or straying in the road. On the other hand, anyone pursuing us will be in for a shock. If it's a chain link fence we cut a strand at the very top, following that strand down through the others to about thigh height from the ground and cut it again. Then, holding the strand where it is cut at the bottom we force it to twist and 'corkscrew' it out. We can then part the fence and climb throught he gap. We leave the bottom part uncut if there are guard dogs, if disturbed it would be harder for them to get out after us, particularly if the top half is also blocked by one of the guard sacks with the poles jammed in the netting. The same two people then check out the unit and immediate area.

When actually breaking in to (say) a factory farm unit, usually is required is a large screwdriver and a couple of crowbars to deal with a Yale lock on the front door (straightforward) or to deal with the inside bolt(s) on the back door. In the case of the back door, if it's a tight fitting one we first pull it from the bottom, we can then judge where the inside bolt or first bolt is. We force the first screwdriver roughly 12" from the bolt and force the opening until the small crowbar can be inserted. Further force is exerted until the large crowbar can be put in by a second person, who puts their full weight behind it and rocks it to and fro, forcefully yet gently. the idea is to make the screws which hold the lock/bolt eventually pop out, not to take the door off its hinges.

For padlocks we may need to use boltcutters, we ignore the lock and go for the hasp which is often mild steel. With the cutters in place, a wet towel is wrapped round the cutters and hasp. This helps to deaden the sharp crack noise. If we are unsure about a door being alarmed the two people who dealt with the fence will also break in and then rejoin the rest of the group for 30-40 minutes to watch for any reaction, from a couple of fields away.

If the animals being liberated are battery hens all the group enters very quietly, then closes the door. A torch covered with coloured plastic is switched on. The cages are opened. A variety of different types of cages are used, common sense tells us if they unclip, slide up or across. A last resort is simply to tear them apart with our hands. We are not put off by the noise the hens will be making by now. Due to the barbaric conditions it's not unusual for fighting to break out so factory farmers are used to outbreaks of noise. Having closed the door most of the noise is absorbed by the usual wooden building.

Working in twos, one person clasps a hen (remembering their wings are quite strong) so that the head is facing away from us, while the other holds the sack which is rolled down to the drawstring beforehand which helps to keep the neck open. The hen goes in head first, we don't let go until the bird is sitting comfortably at the bottom of the sacktwo more follow. To try and simply drop them into the sack just does not work, they will get their feet caught up in the sacking and flap their wings about. If this happens, it's taken out and the precedure repeated properly. We are very careful not to injure the hen. The three hens safely in, the draw string in the middle of the sack is drawn closed and the resulting loop goes over the shoulder. We take as many hens etc as we have good homes for.

With experience it's possible to work in total darkness which usually reduces the amount of noise the hens make. When working in a broiler unit with full grown birds with move more slowly, otherwise 10-15,000 hens may start off. We don't panic if they do though, it may sound loud in the unit but outside it's surprising how much the wooden units deaden the noise.

With rabbits we select single mothers with well-developed young. Large rabbits on their own often indicates a pregnant female, and for obvious reasons rabbits with small young are not disturbed. Rabbits go into the sack back end first because of their large rear feet. Sacks are ideal carriers because the material is comfortable and keeps the animals warm, and with plenty of fresh air. Following the raid we ensure the door is closed so that the cold night air doesn't result in a sharp drop in temperature and discomfort for the animals left behind. For buildings that are alarmed we try to gain direct access into the room holding the animals by going through a wall. Using a well oiled brace and mortar drill long enough to drill out the mortar from around one or two bricks, we then lever them out with a large screwdriver or small crowbar. We then simply cut bricks along the mortar with a padsaw and literally cut bricks out. Squirting water from a squeezy bottle onto the padsaw reduces the noise of cutting the mortar (3-4 squeezy bottles are usually required).

To go through a door that may be alarmed we use our brace to drill a series of overlapping holes using a 1" auger bit until a square can be removed big enough for us to get in and out of with our boxes etc. We have also been able to remove a window from an animal house by taking out the putty using one of those screwdriver sets that has a pointed implement. On another occasion we gained access to an animal house during the day when the alarms were switched off. During the lunch break we gained access using a skeleton key. We had already established on a previous visit at night that it worked, by unlocking the door, but not opening it, then relocking it.

Old type alarms can be dealt with by removing the bell with a screwdriver or forcing it to one side with a crowbar so that that the hammer can be cut off or bent so that it cannot possibly strike the bell. Another method with the klaxanhorn type is to spray cavity wall insulation fluid (the type that sets in 15 minutes) into the horn and through the vents into the alarm box. Once enough time has elapsed for the animals to be got away it's time to deal with the labs and offices. As these premises may also have alarms we crawl along the floor. The aim is to quickly smash up enough equipment to put it out of action or plant incendiary materials to burn it down once satisfied there are no people or animals in there and, if possible, to obtain any documents relating to the experiments, who supplied the animals, names and home adresses of the vivisectors/animal technicians etc.

With the big commercial labs there is always the chance of a silent alarm connected to the local police station. By going through a wall into a room with animals we usually find this is no problem, but later when entering the actual labs, to destroy it or rescue animals undergoing experiments we prefer to go for a smash and grab effort. Sledgehammers then come into their own. A 14lb hammer is aimed at the mortice lock repeatedly. We save vital time by going through the outside wall first or smashing in through a window and then dealing wih the internal doors with the sledgehammer. In a confined space a 10lb hammer with the handle cut down to about 20" is the answer. Crowbars are also of use. In planning this type of action we have to be totally practical. Those fit enough to run some distance after the raid carrying dogs, etc and rucksacks full of documents will be responsible for taking the animals, papers, for destroying equipment and if possible, the lab itself. For the most part, raiding labs is straightforward, only a handful of the very big labs have more elaborate security equipment.

We never paint the letters ALF on a unit or lab, at most we will spray 'Animal Liberation' or 'Animal Belsen'. We paint slogans in dark colours and where they are visible to any reporters following up the story—this helps confirm the action has taken place when the owner or manager denies it. Where the noise of a spray can may alert a guard dog a large felt tip pen is sufficient.

If everything goes well we do of course mention it was an ALF group to the media so that everyone concerned is aware who was rsponsible.

If we have to carry potentially noisy animals, e.g. dogs, a long distance over fields, etc, particularly after a smash and grab, we carry some anti-mate (as used by hunt-sabs to put hounds off the scent of foxes). We give a good squirt after crossing a stream, road, etc, for obvious reasons.

When returning to the vehicles on no account do we walk along roads at night. If something went wrong we would at most walk in the fields parallel with roads to help direct us to the meeting up place.

Much of what I've said may appear to be processes that would take some getting used to but we found after a while that they became second nature. We've never been discovered carrying out a raid and the four of us had no previous experience. It is simply down to common sense.

YES SIR!!

THE MILITANT VEGAN-ISSUE 3-OCTOBER 19
NEXT ISSUE OUT IN FEBRUARY OR MARC

FIGHT THE FURRIERS BY PHON

Fall is the time when fur season begins. Fur scum have started a r media push to try to stem their losses of the past few years. Many fu and trappers have toll-free mailorder phone lines. So call them for and politely tell them what you think of them. Of course, many of t numbers are shut off in various cities and most of northern California many get disconnected nationwide becasue hooligans call from phones (still toll free) and hang up on them over and over again, co them money and driving them crazy. In those cases, you can' through to them.

All numbers start with 1-800.

Fur Vault-ASK4FUR or 548 2908 or 451 3733	LaBudde Feed/Grain-776 361
	Tom Miranda Outdoors-356 6
Custom Furs-257 FURS or 735 FURS	Woodstream Co.(Traps)-800
Lingenfelter Brill-331-5255	RP Outdoors-762 2706
USA FOXX-USA FOXX	Koch Supplies-279 4252
Henig Furs-521 2037	Diamond V Mills-373 7234
Erwin Goodman Furs-221 8826	National Fur Foods-558 5803
Merit Nomac Furs-323 0449	Wisco Fur Foods-235 9656
Revilion Furs-248 2664	United Vaccines-283 MINK
Brisken Berk Furs-241 7243	Mills Fur Farm Supply-722 64
Hoosier Trapping Co.-423 9526	Dipcraft Manufacturing-245 6
Russ Carmen Lures-545 8737	Heger Co.-688 1990
Funke Mink Farm/Trapping-626 2894	......*More scum next issue...*

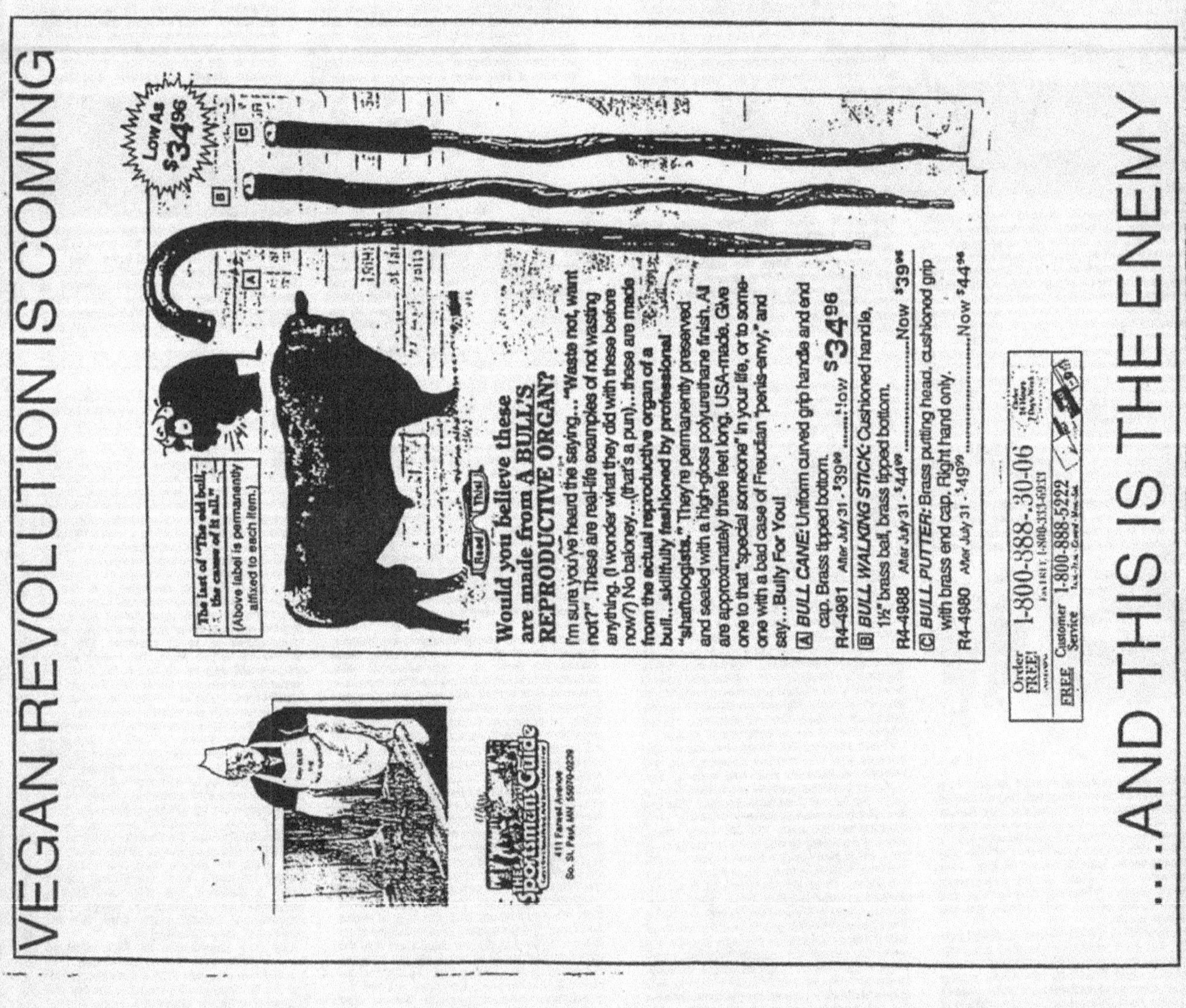

VEGAN REVOLUTION IS COMING
Low As $34.96
Would you believe these are made from A BULL'S REPRODUCTIVE ORGAN?
I'm sure you've heard the saying... "Waste not, want not?" These are real-life examples of not wasting anything. (I wonder what they did with these before now?) No baloney... (that's a pun)...these are made from the actual reproductive organ of a bull...skillfully fashioned by professional "shaftologists." They're permanently preserved and sealed with a high-gloss polyurethane finish. All are approximately three feet long. USA-made. Give one to that "special someone" in your life, or to someone with a bad case of Freudian "penis-envy," and say...Bully For You!
A BULL CANE: Uniform curved grip handle and end cap. Brass tipped bottom.
B BULL WALKING STICK: Cushioned handle, 1½" brass ball, brass tipped bottom.
C BULL PUTTER: Brass putting head, cushioned grip with brass end cap. Right hand only.
The last of "The odd ball, the cream of it all."
(Above label is permanantly affixed to each item.)
Order FREE! 1-800-888-30-06
FREE Customer Service 1-800-888-5222
Sportsman's Guide
411 Farwell Avenue So. St. Paul, MN 55075-0239
...AND THIS IS THE ENEMY

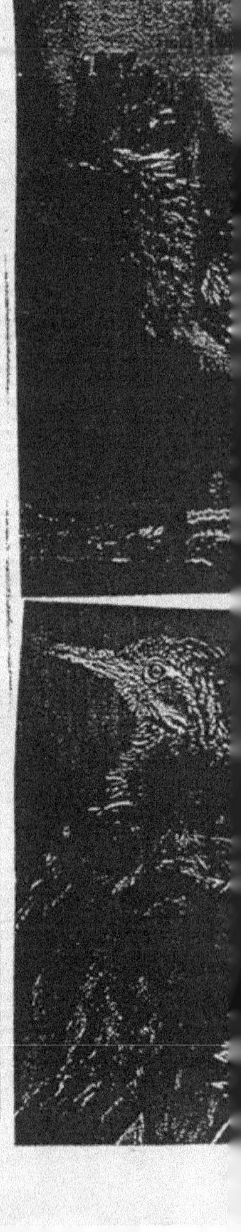

THE MILITANT VEGAN

SSUE #4 JANUARY 1994

FURRIERS ATTACKED IN CHICAGO

lso In This Issue:

)rganizing for Hunt Sabotage

ighting the Fur rade

Actions in alifornia

More Strategies for the Grassroots nimal Liberation lovement

lews, Opinions, nd More!

WE FIGHT
FOR THE ANIMALS
VEGETARIAN RESTAURANT
CLOSED
MEAT IS MURDER
KILLER

THE MILITANT VEGAN-ISSUE #4-JANUARY 1994

first anniversary issue!

Welcome to our fourth issue-we published the first one last January, thinking it would just be a one-off project to inform people about issues and actions that neither the mainstream press or the moderate animal liberation magazines were covering. We printed about 25, which we sold in less than a week. It was then that we realized how strong the interest is in these issues.

All around the country, grassroots vegan activists are getting organized with a new sense of urgency and determination. We all support the big groups, because we won't be sidetracked by infighting and every tactic has a place in the struggle. But we know that a more radical, more active, and completely non-compromising movement is necessary to defeat the animal abusers. Just since our last issue, we have seen more and more people communicating around the country, spreading ideas for new tactics and inspiring one another. 1994 will be our strongest year yet-the year that animal killers everywhere will fear the animal liberation movement.

If you are new to vegan ideas and want to save animals, we recommend reading Diet For a New America by John Robbins for starters, and contacting PETA at PO Box 42516/ Washington, D.C. 20015 for recipes and information about animal abuse. Avoid all the overpriced health food stores, as Asian and Indian groceries have better food at cheaper prices. Copy recipes out of cookbooks at the bookstore.

For the most part, we've gotten nothing but praise for our efforts. But to answer a couple of small criticisms, the magazine is only 12 pages per issue because we have very little money and we try to keep it where postage rates are lower for the hundreds of free copies we mail out. And as to why we mostly focus on the ALF when not everyone can partake in direct action, we understand. We will try to cover other tactics as well from now on.

Again, this is a single issue magazine. That doesn't mean that we see animal liberation as any more important than many othe issues, and we are in full support of the battles against fascism, patriarchy, and all other forms of social injustice. At the same time, we do not represent any ideology, just a basic value system of compassion, equality, and justice.

We have been sending out lots of free issues, and distributors have been getting packages to sell. But due to our lack of money, we only print a few hundred copies of each issue. In several states now, people are xeroxing the magazine and selling the copies. So in your area, PLEASE help get this information out by <u>making copies of this issue</u>. There are thousands of people who care about animals and might be inspired to do more if they realized all that is happening out there.

The Militant Vegan is not an ALF Support Group, and we have no contact with illegal units. So if you see articles about direct action in your area or if you are a member of an ALF cell, send the clipping or a report of your actions to the North American ALF Support Group/ Box 75029, Ritchie P.O./ Edmonton, AB/ T6E 6K1/ CANADA.

In England, the ALFSG is at BCM 1160/ London, WC1N 3XX/ ENGLAND, and they print a quarterly magazine for prisoner support (20$ a year for a subscription,) sell t-shirts and other items and take donations for ALF prisoners. A separate ALF Press Office takes action claims and provides a spokesperson to the media after ALF raids. They can be reached at ALF Press Office/ BM 4400/ London, WC1N 3XX/ ENGLAND. The Swedish ALF is at DBF/ Box 2051/ S-265 02/ Astorp 2/ SWEDEN.

To keep up with the movement, read the Earth First! Journal/ PO Box 1415/ Eugene, OR 97440 and Out of the Cages/ PO Box 2960/ Santa Cruz, CA 95063. All activists should also read <u>Free the Animals!</u> by Ingrid Newkirk, <u>Eco Warriors</u> by Rik Scarce, and the new third edition of <u>Ecodefence</u> by Dave Foreman.

We hope you enjoy this issue, but remember, without action, all our hopes for animal liberation will never be realized. Let's get moving and make this the year the movement hits hard across the country!

The Militant Vegan and the publishers do not intend to encourage crime. This magazine is for informational purposes only.

Clinton Trying Tofu Diet

Washington

President Clinton is shifting from burgers to bean curd in a bid to better his health, his wife, Hillary Rodham Clinton, told reporters

Sorry, Bill, that's not good enough. Ban the fur trade and maybe we can talk.

IF NOT YOU, THEN WHO? IF NOT NOW, WHEN?

NEWS AND COMMENT

The Departments of Justice and Agriculture issued a congressional report on "animal extremism" in September. The report details general information about the ALF in England and the U.S. and gives pie charts and graphs on the location and intensity of attacks. Interestingly, the report claims that direct action for animals is in decline. However, our list of actions in the past few years show far more activity than the report does, and we don't even count phone and and mail threats like they do. Furthermore, action is more widespread than ever before-even in the big years of 1987-88, almost every action was in California and Washington D.C.

Good News: David A., the 19-year old arrested in Bloomington this summer for poultry truck sabotage, apparently was let off with little punishment at his trial in October.

The Sea Shepherds are looking into buying a submarine, as Paul Watson is inspecting Russian and British military subs on sale. The ship will be unarmed, but Watson says he will use sonar to scare whales away from whaling ships and ambush sea turtle killers.

The Memphis Three will most likely receive a suspended sentence soon, as the prosecutor says he will not seek more jail time.

Two hundred activists converged on Wisconsin's state capitol in November, as did two hundred trappers, to argue for the passage of a leghold trap ban proposed by a state legislator from Racine. It won't pass, but the big news was all the action going on in the state. We've listed all that is known in for this year, and in 1992 the McArther Mink Ranch in Janesville was hit, with animals liberated and the building foundations cracked. The farm recently went out of business. We heard that police in the state are looking into all the action there.

In Madison, Wisconsin, activists held a hunt sabotage in late November with lots of media coverage.

Kim Trimiew, an Oregon activist, was briefly imprisoned by the Washington grand jury in October for refusing to testify. The goverment is tyring to link her to the August 1991 ALF raid on Washington State University.

The California Hunt Saboteurs have re-formed, with the first meeting held in Berkeley on December 15. Grassroots activists have been busy in that area as well, producing a newsletter and holding numerous protests.

One thousand five hundred people marched against fur in New York City on November 26.

The Michigan grand jury, supposed to end in December, will go on for 18 more months.

Keith Mann, arrested for numerous arson attacks against the meat trade in England in 1991, escaped from police custody in Liverpool on June 23. Stay free Keith!

Chris Tucker, who was imprisoned in London for throwing a smoke bomb into a McDonalds, was released this summer.

Annette Tibbles, convicted of conspiracy to commit arson against animal abusers, was sentenced to 4 years in jail in England. Send her a letter of support, it costs 52 cents per ounce for airmail: Annette Tibbles/ HMP Holloway, Parkhurst Road/ Holloway, London N7 0NU/ ENGLAND.

The "environmental" Green Party in Chicago called on people to provide information on ALF members after the action there in November. Whose side are the moderates on? Listen, if you don't like ALF tactics, fine, but don't try to pass yourself off as "green" when you suck up to the fascist fur-selling murderers.

Rik Scarce was released from the Spokane jail a few months back, after serving almost 160 days for refusing to talk about Rod Coronado to the Washington grand jury.

A new group to defend people harassed by the grand juries has been set up, with contacts in 35 cities and offices in California and Ohio. Sorry we don't have the addresses...

Vandals Sour on Milk Products — Billboards Defaced in Berkeley

By Janet Wells
Chronicle Correspondent

Yogurt. Creamy and natural, culturally and politically correct, it has been the crowning glory of the health food craze.

But yogurt's good name is curdling in Berkeley, where a slew of billboards promoting dairy products have been defaced, presumably by slogan-wielding vegans — people who have sworn off eggs, milk, cheese and yogurt, as well as meat, fish and poultry.

No one seems to know who has defaced the billboards, part of a statewide campaign aimed at the health and fitness boom by promoting yogurt, cottage cheese, cheese and milk as "Good Fast Food." But it is clearly someone with a grudge against dairy products.

Billboards along San Pablo Avenue and University Avenue now denounce yogurt as "Good Fast Death," and "Go Vegan" is printed in bold letters across an athletic young woman wearing a bathing suit, dipping her spoon into a tub of yogurt.

A dairy billboard along Shattuck Avenue had "mucus" scrawled on it. A billboard advertising eggs used the same theme, suggesting that eggs are "good for death."

At least four billboards have been defaced.

"It seems rather extremist, but funny," said Shalom Ormsby, a vegan who manages the delicatessen at Living Foods in Berkeley. "The vegans are saying that you're bringing products into your body that are not meant for consumption by adult humans".

Vegans think of dairy products as toxic for adults, causing mucus buildup, constipation and diarrhea.

Rather than adhere to the USDA's four food groups of meat, dairy, fruits and vegetables, and grains and legumes, vegans developed their own diet guidelines, restricted to fruits, vegetables, grains and legumes.

"Their point of view is known," said Adri Boudewyn, director of communications for the California Milk Advisory Board, which directed the advertising campaign. "We're not pleased that they chose to attack a billboard as the way of expressing it."

The campaign, which started in July and has included television commercials and 800 billboards across the state, has received "very positive consumer reaction," said Michael Freeman, advertising director for the California Milk Advisory Board. "We're helping consumers understand that dairy foods fit the way we live today. They're healthy and convenient."

The Milk Advisory Board plans to replace the tampered billboards as soon as possible, Boudewyn said.

In the meantime, Berkeley's vegans are getting free publicity.

"I find most of those ads offensive because they're paid for by the dairy industry, which tries to push their products by saying it's healthy to eat," said Michael Bauce, a macrobiotic cook at the Organic Cafe in Oakland. "I think it's great that somebody feels the same way that I do, and to have that message out there."

GO VEGAN
Yogurt.Good Fast death

A roadside billboard making a pitch for yogurt was defaced on San Pablo Avenue in Berkeley

HUNT SABOTEURS: GETTING ORGANIZED

hunt sabs in England blind a murderer with a sheet

The sun was just coming up over the hills of the Cache Creek area of north-central California. There were two teams of three saboteurs in the back of the hatchback pickup, all of us dressed in camouflage and bundled up against the cold. Our team was to get out at the first stop. The night before, we had been given topo maps and a briefing of the situation at hand. Standing around the campfire with a mix of 40 or so camouflaged activists, we discussed our plan to stop the murder of Tule Elk by a small number of licensed trophy hunters. We would split up in teams to cover the area, all equipped with Coast Guard air horns to scare off elk from the hunters. We knew we'd have to be careful; the Fish & Game and BLM cops were patrolling in airplanes, on ATV's and on foot to arrest us, and we'd have to look out for ranchers: most of the the area is private ranchland.

With these thoughts in mind, we jumped out of the back of the truck when the driver told us and headed for cover so that we wouldn't be seen. We had a long day ahead of us....

-From an account of a hunt sab by a West Coast activist

Hunt Sabotage, the active disruption of hunting, has been practiced in England since 1962 and in the U.S. since the mid 80's. As sabbing tactics can vary from region to region, we will discuss methods from around the country in the hope that new hunt sab groups can be formed.

HOW DO I DECIDE WHAT HUNT TO SABOTAGE?

In the West, activists have usually concentrated on trophy hunts for highly visible species such as bison, bighorn sheep, and Tule elk. To find out about trophy hunts in your area, get your state's hunting regulations guide for free from your Department of Fish & Game. These guides list the dates for such hunts as well as lots of other valuable information.

In the East, sabs disrupt the deer hunting which is constant throughout the season. Since many of these hunts take place near town and city limits, they can be made very visible to local media.

An east coast activist we spoke to described sabotage of deer hunts. She said that local activists would gather before sunrise in the area where hunters would be later in the day. They would cover the area, scaring off all the deer. By midday, they would meet back and go home. This is much simpler than the west coast sabs, but the key is that different species, terrain, and human population density will determine what type of sabbing needs to be done.

WHAT TACTICS CAN BE USED TO DISRUPT HUNTS?

The main aim of a hunt sab is to scare away the intended targets of the hunters. This can be done with noisemakers, like whistles and air horns, or by going through areas where hunters will come and leaving human scents.

A second goal is to harass the hunters themselves. Follow them around, block access roads, mislead their hounds, be creative! Even the presence of sabs may anger them to the point that they cannot hunt as well as otherwise.

More specifically, the organization of the sab can vary in tactics. The favored method in the West is to bring together activists from around the region and transport them to the site in vans or trucks. Wildlife and animal liberation groups can be hit up for money to buy gas for the trip and trail food for the duration of the sab. Each activist is instructed to bring camping equipment and dark or camouflage clothing. The sab lasts for days or weeks, and a base camp is made either legally on the land of a sympathizer or illegally on state or federal land. Topography maps are very important, since most of the sabs will not be familiar with the region.

For the actual sabbing, activists split into small groups and are assigned an area of a few square miles to cover. Drivers who know the area well drop the groups off before sunrise when no other traffic is passing by. The groups are out until dusk, and the hard part is being picked up. Each group leaves a few rocks by the side of the road and hides in the bushes. The drivers cruise around the area looking for such signals until all the groups are picked up. This part of the sab is why the drivers have to know the area.

WHAT CAN THE POLICE DO TO HUNT SABOTEURS?

37 states have passed the so-called "hunter harassment" laws banning hunt sabotage. However, every time an activist has been charged with this offense, it has been overturned in court. As happened recently in Montana, the first amendment was cited as to why activists can disrupt hunting and the judge has agreed. As a result, it is unlikely that anyone will be charged with this offense in the future. It is much more likely that police agencies will follow the California example and charge people with trespassing, disorderly conduct, and other minor offenses. Numerous California activists have spent time in jail or paid fines for being caught during hunt sabs.

Obviously, activists caught destroying hunters' vehicles, vandalizing hunt clubs, tearing down blinds and stands and removing salt licks will be charged by the police.

To avoid being caught, activists should lie low when spotter planes fly over, and be on the lookout for police patrols on foot and on ATV's. It is very difficult to be caught in wilderness areas if a group knows what it is doing.

Hunt sabs should avoid situations like a sab in California in 1990 on an island. Activists we spoke to said that the island was small and had little ground cover , so it was a simple matter for the police to arrest almost everyone who went.

WHAT ABOUT THE MEDIA?

You may want to contact the media about the hunt sabotage in order to bring publicity to the hunt itself and the extreme bias of the government towards the hunters. Be absolutely prepared to discuss every ecological and biological question about wildlife mismanagement, wild populations, ecosystem stability, etc. that could come up about the hunt in question. Know what the enemy is going to say ("We're helping these animals by managing their populations," etc.) by reading hunting magazines at your public library.

A FINAL WORD

In England, frequent sabbing around the country has shut down numerous hunts and saves thousands of animals. Get organized and do the same here! It's also a great way to bring the local animal liberation community together to meet and share ideas. Be creative and fight the hunters in your area!

Direct Action Against All Bloodsports

Animal rights group sets fires

CHICAGO — An animal rights group claimed responsibility on Monday for a series of weekend fires that caused minor damage but no injuries in downtown Chicago department stores.

Five of eight incendiary devices ignited, causing small fires in Marshall Field's, Carson Pirie Scott and Saks Fifth Avenue stores late Saturday and early on Sunday when the stores were empty. The Animal Liberation Front said it had planted the devices and would continue to target stores that sell fur.

LOOK TO REAL SCIENCE

Scenes from the University of Arizona after the ALF raid there in April 1989.

ALF fugitive expects to be caught

BY KEN OLSEN

PULLMAN — Although he has eluded federal law enforcement for nearly two years, alleged Animal Liberation Front activist Rodney A., Coronado doesn't expect to be free forever.

"It's inevitable they are going to catch me," Coronado said in an interview several months ago. "I'm not going to leave this country in the hands of the U.S. government and think it will be OK.

"I just hope someone will be ready to take my place as spokesperson for the ALF," he said.

Coronado, 27, was indicted Thursday for destroying two scientists' research and damaging a mink farm at Michigan State University. The charges, announced Friday, include malicious destruction of property, interstate transportation with the intent to commit a crime, setting a fire to end animal research, setting a fire to interfere with commercial fur breeding and transporting stolen goods.

If convicted, he faces a maximum of 50 years in prison, $1.25 million in fines, and 15 years of supervised probation. Other indictments are expected for him and suspected accomplices. Five federal grand juries have subpoenaed more than 40 people in a long-running investigation of Coronado and the ALF that is described as less than half-finished.

While he acknowledges visiting Michigan in February 1992, he says he was miles away when the ALF raid went down. Still, Coronado won't be surprised by the indictments.

"FBI harassment is a compliment," Coronado said. "If you aren't attracting government attention, you should re-examine what you are doing."

Coronado is the key suspect in a series of ALF raids in 1991 and 1992 that hit four universities, a mink food processing operation and a defunct mink farm. He says he faxed a press release to the Spokane Associated Press about the August 1991 Washington State University raid, but denies having anything to do with vandalizing two offices and freeing coyotes, mink and mice in Pullman.

The FBI, Bureau of Alcohol Tobacco and Firearms and a Michigan U.S. attorney announced the charges against Coronado in connection with the MSU incident Friday, though they do not know where he is. That's been the case for more than a year, most of which investigators spent denying Coronado was a suspect. They called him a "person of interest."

Coronado went into hiding because of threats on his life from the fur industry and because federal agents are always heavily armed when they come looking for him, he said. Founder of the Coalition Against Fur Farms, he posed as an aspiring mink rancher and took videos of other ranchers demonstrating mink-killing techniques that later made the TV news program *60 Minutes*.

The National Board of Fur Farm Organizations later posted a $35,000 reward for Coronado.

Federal agents tried to catch him in southern Oregon in June 1992, but missed. They boarded ships belonging to the Sea Shepherd Conservation Society looking for him later that summer. The FBI even tried to persuade family members, who live in California, to initiate a missing persons search for him

Coronado offered to surrender last winter if taxpayer-supported research on mink, coyotes and otter conducted by WSU, MSU, Oregon State University and Utah State University was suspended. He also wanted WSU to return its grizzly bears to the wild and promise to never acquire more endangered species. His offer was declined.

Coronado, an activist whose first well-known act was sinking whaling boats in Iceland in the mid-1980s, says he's not afraid of arrest. "I'm confident enough in my innocence and my ability to defend myself."

But he has been dismayed by the portrayal of ALF. "It's a tactic of (federal officials) to portray us as extreme instead of questioning the scientific validity of what researchers are doing," Coronado said.

Ingrid Newkirk, co-founder of People for the Ethical Treatment of Animals, agrees. "The experiments in Michigan were heinous; animals were left to convulse after being fed toxins," Newkirk said.

She dismisses MSU's defense, that it is doing important work on how Great Lakes contamination is destroying wild mink. "These people were only white-coated pimps for the fur industry," she said.

Coronado defends himself, the ALF and his anti-fur farm coalition as most concerned about the environment and about leaving native wildlife in the wild. The ALF's successes, he says, include helping end mink research at Oregon State.

Setting fire to research facilities is necessary because "as long as you leave the mechanisms of Earth-exploiting industries in place, they will come back."

Top: from the Memphis Commercial Appeal
Middle: from the Moscow-Pullman Daily News
Below: from the San Francisco Chronicle

Bomb Damages Office Of Federal Agency

Reno — A bomb exploded on the roof of the Bureau of Land Management office here yesterday in a blast big enough to be heard at least two miles away.

The building was empty when the bomb exploded around 12:45 a.m., and no one was injured. The bomb apparently was in a satchel or briefcase that was tossed onto the roof of the one-story building.

The bomb ripped a three-foot hole in the building's roof and damaged six work stations. No damage estimate was immediately available.

Anti-fur activists blamed for Chicago store fires

By Sandra Sanchez
USA TODAY

As thousands of shoppers crowded Chicago department stores Monday, federal and local authorities continued searching for matchbox-size devices that are blamed for five weekend store fires.

The Animal Liberation Front, an "underground" animal rights group, says it planted nine incendiary devices in four downtown stores to protest fur sales.

Late Monday, Chicago police and FBI agents had retrieved eight devices from four department stores. Most were hidden in lunch-size paper bags and were made of matches attached to 9-volt batteries that were ignited by a timer.

Agents recovered one device Sunday in the silver and china section of Neiman-Marcus, near crowds of holiday shoppers, says Chicago police Sgt. Edward O'Donnell. The device did not ignite.

"There's possibly one device left," says O'Donnell.

Other devices were found at the Carson Pirie Scott and Marshall Field stores in the Loop, and at trendy Saks Fifth Avenue in the glittery North Michigan Avenue shopping district.

Five minor fires were ignited Saturday and Sunday at Marshall Field, Carson and Saks. Most were in storage areas and were extinguished by in-house sprinklers. None caused extensive damage.

> "While we don't condone (extreme tactics), we don't condemn it."
>
> — Dan Mathews, PETA

As agents scrambled to locate the last device, store officials beefed up security and tried to calm shoppers.

"We're taking every precaution to secure the safety of our shoppers and store associates," says Neiman-Marcus spokeswoman Liz Barrett.

Barrett says merchants often fall victim to animal rights extremists during the holidays. "This is typically when incidents like this likely are to occur because (activists) get a wide audience of attention."

The Animal Liberation Front is known for taking responsibility for such attacks.

Founded in England in the 1970s, it has been declared a terrorist group by the FBI. The agency had been investigating the group's connection to at least 21 incidents in which damages totaled more than $10,000 each.

The Justice and Agriculture departments said in a November report to Congress that the group is comprised of several small clusters of activists who don't know each other, and "there are no formal membership requirements beyond the willingness to inflict damages upon an animal enterprise."

The group claimed responsibility for the weekend fires via a letter sent to People for the Ethical Treatment of Animals.

"And while we don't condone it, we don't condemn it," says PETA spokesman Dan Mathews. "We understand why some activists are driven to more extreme tactics."

WINTER WAR AGAINST THE FUR TRADE

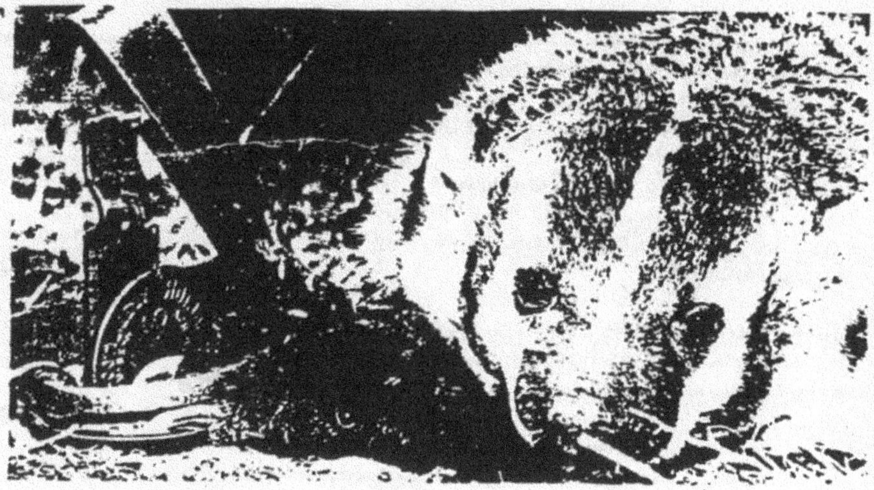

As many activists are aware, the fur industry ıas started a multi-million dollar advertising paign to convince the public to wear fur ıgain. Still, a Los Angeles Times poll on)ecember 25 showed that 50% of the opulation are opposed to wearing fur. The ıdustry in still tottering on the brink, despite ıeir claims of increased sales. To push them ver the edge, we need to redouble our efforts) save furbearing animals.

For many years now, there have been rotests in front of retail fur stores, and these eed to continue. But to expand our ampaign, we need to call public attention to very link in this chain of animal suffering. The following is a st of various businesses who are part of the fur trade in one ay or another. If you live near any of these murderers, set p protests outside their offices over the next few months. tep up the pressure-**THIS CENTURIES-OLD REICH IUST FALL.** For the mink, the marten, the fox, and all ırbearers, **WE WILL REVENGE!**

N THE STREETS-Always confront everyone who ears fur. You have every right to speak out against anyone fur. Let them know that their cruelty will not be tolerated in our city. Don't back down!

NIVERSITY RESEARCH-The fur industry relies on esearch done in labs to increase their profits through ther genetic manipulation of furbearers. Fur farm arch takes place at **Michigan State** in East Lansing till hurting badly from an ALF raid,) **Washington State** in pokane, **Utah State** in Logan, **Idaho State niversity**, **Brigham Young University**, the **niversity of Wisconsin** at Madison and Milwaukee, and **ocky Mountain Laboratories** in Hamilton, Montana.

JR FARM FEED SUPPLIERS-The unnatural state of e pelts of murdered fur farm prisoners is partly due to the oes of special feeds developed by feed suppliers. The ain ones are:

eger Co./ 545 Hardman Ave./ South St. Paul, MN
ational Fur Foods/ Box 220/ New Holstein, WI 53061 crucial feed supplier for the industry)
isco Fur Foods/ Box 10/ Abbotsford, WI 54405
eartand Blends/ Route 1/ Scribner, NE 68057
orthwest Fur Feeds Cooperative/ Edmonds, WA

JR PROCESSORS: These are the scum who clean up e pelts for their future use as vanity items.

&W Pelt Processing/ Rte. 2/ Oranton, WI 54436
atinum Co-op Processing/ 113 Whiteside/ olumbia, IL 62236
ational Superior/ 4447 West Cortland St./ Chicago, IL 634
bari Ltd./ 3 Rosol Ln./ Saddle Brook, NJ 07662

R FARM EQUIPMENT SUPPLIERS:

s Fur Farm Supply/ Box 348/ Eden Valley, MN 329
verdale Mills (cage wire)/ 130 Riverdale St./ rthbridge, MA 01534
own of Minnesota/ 1200 Central Ave. NE/ nneapolis, MN 55413
Illinois Mink Wire Co./ 38614 N. Fairfield Rd./ Lake Villa, IL 60046
Utah Fur Breeds Agricultural Co-op/ 8700 South 700 W./ Sandy, UT 84070
Friesens Inc./ Box 889/ Detroit Lakes, MN 56502
Continental Fur Farm Supplies/ Box C/ Delavan, WI 53115
Valentine Equipment Co./ 4259 S. Western Blvd./ Chicago, IL 60609

FUR AUCTION HOUSES: This is where trappers and fur farmers sell the skins to retailers. A weak point in the industry as only a few remain open.

Seattle Fur Exchange/ 240 Andover Park West/ Seattle, WA 948138
North American Fur Auctions/ 1275 Valley Brook/ Lyndhurst, NJ or 65 Skyway/ Rexdale, Ontario, M9W 6C7 CANADA

TRAPPING SUPPLIERS:

Northern Fur and Sport/ 9191 Leavitt Rd./ Elyria, OH 44035 This is the largest trapping supplier.
Krufick Outdoor Supplies/ 30 Lightcap Rd./ Latrobe, PA 15650
Verleeng Trappers Supply/ Smithville, OH
Rocky Mountain Fur Co./ 1507 Willis Rd./ Caldwell, ID 83605
Montgomery Fur Co./ Ogden, Utah.
Russ Carmen (a real scumbag)/ New Milford, PA
Duke Traps/ West Point, Mississippi
Woodstream Traps/ Lititz, PA

FUR FARM ORGANIZATIONS: These are small groups of fur farmers who meet to produce propaganda, lobby state legislators, and manage sales of skins. This is only a small sample.

American Fox Assn./ Max, North Dakota
Canada Mink Breeders Assn./ 65 Skyway Ave. Suite B/ Rexdale, Ontario M9W 6C7
Fur Breeders Agricultural Cooperative/ 8700 S. 700 W./ Sandy, UT 84070
Fur Farm "Animal Welfare" Coalition/ 225 E. 6th St. #230/ St. Paul, MN 55101 **This are the biggest and most evil-they must be confronted! See the latest Earth First! Journal for an article about the lies they are spreading.**

CHINCHILLA FUR FARMS-There are 6 or 7 chinchilla farms left which imprison over 1000 animals, and a few smaller ones. There are only four buyers for chinchilla pelts in North America:
Rosenfelt in New York, Canchilla in Canada, Princeton in New York, and the largest, Jerry Fullingham, who handles over 200,000 pelts worldwide and is located just outside of Denver, Colorado.

MINK FUR FARMS-As of last year, there were 571 mink farms left in the U.S., down from 2,000 a few years ago. 57 of these farms also imprison fox. Wisconsin "produces" the most mink pelts but Utah has the most mink farms.
Utah-150 mink farms. Wisconsin-114. Minnesota-72. Oregon-29. Washington-28. Idaho-27. Iowa-25. Pennsylvania-21. Illinois-15. New York-12. Ohio-11. South Dakota-7. Other states-45.

Here are some addresses for fur farms around the country. Some of these may be out of business, since this comes from a 1992 Fur Farm "Animal Welfare" Coalition listing. We have tried to list farms from around the country, but if you live in the Midwest or Utah, try local phone books for a lot more. Imagine how mad these murderers would be if they woke up to see protestors outside their farms!

Crider Furs, Inc./ Route 2, Box 150/ Nicholls, Georgia 31554
This is the largest fur farm in the nation, with 82,000 mink imprisoned there. Most mink farms are much smaller.

Franklin, Idaho has 3 mink farms: Jeffrey Hobbs, Boyd T. Hobbs, and Larry D. Kingsford.

Gengel Mink Farm/ 38614 North Fairfield Road/ Lake Villa, IL 60046

Hoosier Hills Fur Farm/ RFD 1/ Lawrenceburg, IN 47025

Webster City, Iowa, has 2 mink farms: Twilight Mink Farm/ RF 2, Box 119/ 50595 and Hillpipre Mink Farm/ 136 Parkview Dr./ 50595

Carmel's Mink Ranch/ Route 143/ Hinsdale, MA 01235

Channing, Michigan has two mink farms: Robert Roell/ Sta Route, Box 92/ 49815 and Jim & Vince Roell/ Box 88 49815

Minnesota activists: Check your phone books!

Cary Mink Farm/ Route 1, Box 98-A/ California, Missour 65018

Crowell Mink Farm/ 1109 Church Ave./ Bozeman, Montana 59715

Kirkpatrick Fur Farm/ 2304 South Memorial park Rd./ Granc Island, Nebraska 68803

Merle Main Mink Ranch/ Route 60/ Gerry, New York 14740

Mohoric Mink Ranch/ 7035 Chatham Rd./ Medina, Ohic 44256

There are 3 mink farms in Astoria, Oregon: Trails End Fu Farm/ Route 3, Box 546/ 97103, Bill & Nancy Tynkila/ Route 6, Box 118/ 97103, and Ray & Verna Tynkila/ same address

Burns Mink Ranch/ Box 377, RD3 Bend Rd./ N Wilmington, Pennsylvania 16142

Utah and Wisconsin activists: check phone books fron around your state.

ABS A TARGET OF RIGHTS ACTIVISTS

nimal Researchers Feel Hunted

By Janet Wells
Chronicle Correspondent

nclosed by bulletproof Dr. Roy Henrickson sits inside his University of s at Berkeley office, someone standing ue his windows. He knows the thick panes should a slug of metal, but he says wonders how quickly a or rock could come his when he leaves his office.

e tall, imposing researcher less wary when he walks to asement labs, the elevator remaining motionless until he clears the security block with a magnetic card. When he works at a field station up the hill, he has to remember to deactivate the motion sensors before entering.

At private companies researching high-energy physics or defense weapons, such security measures are common. But Henrickson is a university veterinarian, not a nuclear engineer — and as head of Berkeley's animal research program, he has been cast, along with thousands of researchers nationwide, in a war against animal rights advocates.

"The whole climate is one of living under harassment and apprehension," said Henrickson. "This is terrorism."

Now, in a signal of the increasing polarization over the animal research issue, universities and medical centers are dramatically tightening security to keep animal advocates at bay. Video cameras, surveillance teams and digital door codes are all part of the high-tech array,

LABS: Page A10 Col. 1

BS: Tight Security for Animal Researchers

ge 1

ry employees are trained alert for suspicious pack-

versities and research in- s are into the multimil- dollars in increasing secu- d O. W. Sweat, director of for the National Institutes h, the country's biggest of funds for biomedical

een 1991 and 1992, the of incidents attributed to ights advocates increased nt, to a total of 569 crimi- protests and boycotts. The sed an estimated $9.6 mil- roperty damage and lost , according to the Lee Virginia-based organiza- tracks the animal rights nt.

lifornia alone, an estimat- illion in damages has oc- animal research records, nt and facilities since officials of the California Research Association, tes the use of animals

animal rights movement gain momentum in the 70s, when advocates ob- sily evidence of cruelty to y animals and helped jor changes in state and egislation to ensure the reatment of animals used ch.

umane treatment is no nough for many advo- o now call for the com- ssation of invasive re- animals.

e old days, people used to cs and let them get syphi- experiment and not treat rgued Elliott Katz, presi- Defense of Animals, the cal and visible animal oup in the Bay Area.

ur ethics and morals im- e decided that before do- nvasive research on a pa- have to have the pa- nsent," he added. "Work- animals, we haven't d to that stage."

Humans

rchers, in turn, feel that ghts advocates promote s of cats, dogs and mon- e expense of human safe- ychological well-being.

John Young, primary veterinarian at Cedars-Sinai Medical Center in Los Angeles, was forced to move after demonstrators held four protests in front of his Playa del Rey home last year. "They would stand out in front of the house with gruesome photographs, talk to the neighbors and pass out leaflets," said Young, who is trying to keep his new address a secret. "I'd like to believe that these people are incapable of doing harm, but when you see incidents in abortion, with people being shot and killed, you have to wonder if it could happen with the anti-research movement, too."

Indeed, harm seems to be on the minds of at least some animal rights advocates. At UC Berkeley, researchers receive dozens of telephone calls and letters each week containing violent messages.

Russell De Valois, a UC Berkeley optometry professor who uses cats and monkeys to study the neurology of vision, has been a frequent target of Katz and other animal rights advocates. In recent weeks, flyers with his home phone number and the message "Die, De Valois" were circulated on campus. His wife and children also have been the targets of threats and taunts.

In Defense of Animals does not advocate violence or illegal acts. Nonetheless, the group does not strongly condemn such tactics, either.

"We have never given out any researcher's phone number or address," Katz said. "But if people are upset and want to tell someone like Russell De Valois that he's an irresponsible, cruel person, they should have the right to do that."

Death Threat

In 1988, De Valois' colleague, ophthalmology professor Richard Van Sluyters, received a death threat from an anti-vivisectionist who died while rigging a powerful homemade bomb.

"The police told me, 'Drive a basic-colored car, don't park in the same place and look under your car every day,'" said Van Sluyters, who uses kittens in his research on blindness. "I didn't know whether to hide or never go to my office again."

At Stanford University, animal research was housed at the medical center until administrators began to fear that a bomb or fire set by animal rights advocates would endanger patients as well as animals. In 1989 Stanford moved researchers to its $30 million animal facilities, which are equipped with more than the standard high-tech lock and surveillance systems.

One lab area, for example, is accessible only after researchers pass by an optical scanner that identifies users by their eyes.

"You can give your key card away, but you can't give your eye away," said Joanne Blum, Stanford's associate director of laboratory animal medicine.

For his part, Henrickson insisted that UC Berkeley spend $58,000 to install bulletproof windows in his offices in the Northwest Animal Facility, the headquarters for much of the animal research at the university. During construction of the $14 million facility, which was heavily protested by animal rights advocates, the university posted 24-hour security guards and spent $500 a day on a dog squad to sniff for bombs.

Animal rights advocate Elliott Katz countered that the university's focus on security is "paranoid."

Ethics Gap

The ethics gap does not appear to be narrowing from either side.

"We want to keep pressure on people like De Valois and encourage students to go into fields that don't use animal research," said Bill Boeger, spokesman for UC Berkeley's student animal rights group. "It's so controversial, they will be constantly harassed."

But although the controversy and violence have motivated some scientists to abandon biomedical research, the stream of grant money has remained steady. As of May, the National Institutes of Health were financing 19,377 grants, totaling $4.2 billion, for research that in some way involved animals.

"We have a long history of using animals in biology to figure out the principles of nature," said UC Berkeley's Van Sluyters. "Humankind exists on the backs of animals for the food chain, for clothes, conveyance, pets. To (change that) would be to overturn modern living."

Vegan vandals tell all about dairy billboards

Pair did it 'for the animals'

By Faith S. Raider
Contributing Writer

Two Bay Area vegans have come forward, on condition of anonymity, to explain their reasons for covering dairy industry billboards in Berkeley with spray paint and poster paper two weeks ago.

At least two Berkeley billboards bearing the slogan "yogurt, good fast food," briefly read "yogurt, good fast death" and "go vegan!" after alterations by two vegans — hard-core vegetarians who do not eat dairy products or eggs.

A billboard on Shattuck Avenue advertising eggs now bears the one-word addition "mucus."

One "billboard vegan," who spoke on the condition of anonymity, said political not nutritional convictions spurred the pair to action.

"The reason we do it is for the animals. The meat and dairy industries torture millions of animals every day," he said.

"Animals are kept in small cages, pumped with drugs, attached to machines, and as soon as they can't give anymore, they are slaughtered and consumed."

While ads for burger-oriented fast food would seem like a more obvious vegan target, the activists say the Milk Advisory Board's health and fitness campaign, which began in July, is "just as offensive as the meat ads."

"The meat and dairy industry are the same industry. They reap huge profits and have almost unlimited access to the media," said the "billboard vegan."

Adri Boudewyn, Director of Communications for the California Milk Advisory Board, said, "We wish that when people have a beef, they would start a dialogue instead of defacing property."

Boudewyn said the labor costs of replacing the billboards is a few hundred dollars.

"They should get their own board," the director said.

The vegan activists said health concerns are reason enough to become vegan. Vegans avoid meat and dairy products in order to steer clear of toxins and dairy-eating after-effects such as mucus buildup.

The two activists are not part of an organization, but say they were inspired by other vegan billboard

SEE PAGE 13

Manchester Times
AN INDEPENDENT HOME TOWN NEWSPAPER
WEDNESDAY, AUGUST 11, 1993 MANCHESTER, TN 37355

Livestock Barn Fire Termed 'Highly Suspicious' by Police

By JOHN HENSON
Staff Writer

Tennessee State Arson Investigator Larry Dauberman has arrived a fire at the Coffee County Livestock Company's barn on the Old Tullahoma Highway as highly suspicious. The fire, which was discovered ... [illegible]

Michael Boyd of Hillsboro ... damaged the arena and about 25 percent of the cattle pen area ... [illegible]

(See FIRE, Page 5A)

OFFICERS INVESTIGATE BLAZE
Fire Lt. ... (left) and state arson investigator Larry Dauberman investigate a fire at the Coffee County Livestock Company's stockyard on the Old Tullahoma Highway. The livestock barn suffered extensive damage in the arena and about 25 percent of the cattle pen area. STAFF PHOTO BY JOHN HENSON

Vegan vandals

FROM FRONT PAGE

vandalism exploits they saw in the Bay Area.

They said their "community beautification program" is also an attempt to make veganism as "mainstream" as vegetarianism.

DIARY OF ACTIONS

Every single night, the women and men of the Animal Liberation Front carry out direct action to stop animal cruelty at its sources somewhere in the world. England sees thousands of attacks a year, and ALF units are active across the industrialized world. Whether it's the Black Ravens in Russia, the DBF in Sweden, Animal Rescue in Japan, or the ALF in New Zealand, Canada, Israel, Poland, Italy, Spain, France, etc., the goal is the same: to liberate the suffering and destroy the property of those who kill for profit.

INTERNATIONAL ACTIONS

Unfortunately, there is no good source for international actions outside Britain, so we have only read of a few actions. In **Germany**, 3 shooting towers used by hunters were brought to the ground on consecutive nights. The towers are made of metal and concrete, so it was no easy job. In **Norway**, red paint was splattered all over a vivisection office of some sort in May. In **Singapore**, cats were liberated from some sort of government-owned station. In **Canada**, a butcher shop had its locks jammed in January in Victoria, the Paint Panthers hit a fur store in Montreal in May, and fur stores have had windows smashed in Ottawa.

In **England**, actions occur on a nightly basis, so it would be impossible to list even a few hundred of them. Some highlights include: 150 hens liberated from a slaughterhouse in London in February and the place was sabotaged, the same night saw a vivisection company in Brighton suffer heavy damage from 30 ALF activists, 80 rabbits were liberated in Lymm in May, 19 empty chicken rearing sheds were destroyed by fire in May in Whitchurch, a broiler shed in West Hadham was burned down in July, a slaughterhouse near Manchester was wrecked in August, 83 hens were liberated near Kent the same month, 2 pigs were liberated from Wye College, 10 beagles were liberated from a Cheshire hunt club, 6 dogs were liberated in Lincolnshire, and literally thousands of animal abusing businesses suffered attacks in the usual manner. Also, the Animal Rights Militia planted an "intricate explosive device" at Birmingham University in February.

UNITED STATES: JANUARY-NOVEMBER 1993

These reports are taken from various sources, so see our previous issues for sources for the actions before September. Probably a lot more has happened in the U.S. that has not been reported or that we haven't read about. We only print actions that have been previously reported by mainstream media or activist and enemy publications; again, we are not an ALFSG, only a news magazine, so activists can send action claims to the Edmonton group.

New York State (and elsewhere?)-In an article in *GQ* magazine on PETA, the existence of an ALF-style pet rescue group was mentioned. The group supposedly warns owners of abused animals to treat them better, and if they do not, the pets are taken from yards and sometimes homes. They are then placed in decent homes.

San Francisco, CA-ALFSG had word of actions as of May 1993 but no details.

Chicago, IL-same as above.

Seattle, WA-same as above.

Los Angeles, CA-same as above.

Madison, WI-A Fur store has been attacked repeatedly.

January 13-Cleveland, Ohio-Ciska Furs spray painted and splattered with paint. *Paint Panthers.*

February 8-New York, New York-The Fur Vault, Ritz Thrift Shop, Elizabeth Arden, Bloomingdale's, Fendi Bergdorf Goodman, and Harold J. Rubin Furs damaged with paint bombs and spray painted slogans like "Fur Shame," "Blood $," "Scum," "P.P.," and "Murderers." *Paint Panthers*

March 26-Oakland, CA-Butcher shop spray painted. *ALF Golden Gate Unit*

April-Berkeley and Oakland, CA-A large number of animal abuse billboards were spray painted with slogans such as "Go Vegan!" "Vegan Power!" and "Animal Torture."

April 14-Bethesda, MD-Three McDonald's, two Kentucky Fried Chickens, and Honey Baked Ham were spray painted with slogans. *Meat Free Mission*

April 27-Montgomery County, MD-Five vivisectors had their homes spray painted with slogans like "Animal Torturer," etc. *Animal Avengers*

May-Berkeley and Oakland, CA-More animal abuse billboards spray painted.

May 26-San Francisco, CA-3 chicken restaurants, 2 butchers, and 2 leather shops had slogans painted and locks glued shut. *ALF Golden Gate Unit*

June 10-Memphis, TN-The owner of Gilbert Kay Furs had his home spray painted and its locks glued. A taxidermy was spray painted and its windows were broken and door locks glued. A me shop was spray painted. *ALF*

mid-June-San Francisco, CA-3 fur shops had locks glued. *ALF Golden Gate Unit*

July-Memphis, TN-An unsuccessful arson attack was made on Jack Lewis Furs, and the store was spray painted. The store had a new $3,000 security camera, but it proved worthless as the attackers were well disguised. It did record the time the attack was made.

July 6-Montgomery County, MD-Fake bombs were left on the front steps of 4 vivisectors' homes. The bomb squad found that the packages contained a brick, a plastic mouse with fake blood, and a threatening note.

July 9-Albany, CA-A KFC had all its locks glued, slogans painted on 3 walls, and all windows etched with acid. *ALF Golden Gate Unit*

July 16-San Francisco, CA-City Meats (sells veal) had its front lock glued and slogans painted. A Burger King had its front lock glued. *ALF Golden Gate Unit*

July 23-Berkeley, CA-An article on the harassment of a University of California vivisector mentioned that the campus had been spray painted with slogans calling him a "killer."

late July-Manchester, TN-A fire was lit with files in the office of the Coffey County Stockyard and was quickly put out. ALF slogans were spray painted on the walls. *ALF*

July 30-Bloomington, IN-After 4 delivery trucks at Sims Poultry had their refrigeration units unplugged and were spray painted, police arrived and arrested one of the two men they saw. (See the news section.)

July 31-San Francisco, CA-2 trucks at Robert's Corned Beef had all locks glued and slogans painted all over them. At United Meats, a back fence was cut through, and 3 trucks had all locks glued and slogans painted such as "Meat is Murder." *ALF Golden Gate Unit*

August 6-Manchester, TN-The Coffey County Stockyard was burned to the ground, with $100,000 in total damages. Local police and media wanted to deny that it was an ALF action, and even went as far as detaining a local man for questioning. However, a meat market was apparently painted with "ALF" the same night or at least recently, and the Tennessee Bureau of Investigation is treating it as an ALF action. *ALF*

August 6-Memphis, TN-On the night before an anti-fur protest, an attempt was made to tear out the phone lines for Jack Lewis . Unfortunately, the lines for the whole building were taken out well, so store owners yelled at demonstrators, blaming them. [local media]

August-Madison, WI-At the University of Wisconsin, the ALF broke through a door at the building housing all the campus vivisection offices and set files on fire. We don't know the intended target, but the University does fur farm and farm animal research, among other things. *ALF*

August-Milwaukee, WI-A meat delivery van was set on fire. *ALF*

August-Milwaukee, WI-On the outskirts of town, a chicken restaurant was set on fire. *ALF*

August-Memphis, TN-A KFC and a hunting store were attacked and the Ashford Meat Market was hit several times.

September-Delavan, WI-An article in a local newspaper featured a butcher whose shop was going out of business due to numerous attacks.

September 15-Alameda County, CA-Alameda County butcher shop and meat jobber hit with sprayed slogans and several windows broken. *ALF* [NY Transfer News Collective]

September 20-Alameda County, CA-Alameda County butcher shop and poultry shop had locks glued and slogans etched on the windows with acid. *ALF* [NY Transfer News Collective]

October-Sacramento, CA-A fur store was spray painted with stenciled slogans. [from Up Front 'zine]

October-Milwaukee, WI-8 puppies were liberated from a pet store. *ALF* [reported at WI trap hearing by many activists, sorry we don't have the media source. We hope to have news clippings of WI actions for our next issue.]

October-Berkeley and Oakland, CA-Over the course of the month, at least 30 dairy industry billboards were altered or spray ted. At least $5,000 damages for the California Milk Advisory rd, which claimed that each one cost several hundred dollars to replace. [numerous media reports]

October 17-Walnut Creek, CA-Fur store in Walnut Creek had locks glued and slogans painted on walls. *ALF* [NY Transfer News Collective]

October 28-Alameda County, CA-Pumpkin with "Happy Halloween from the ALF" written on it thrown through the window of an Alameda County chicken restaurant and the locks were glued as well. *ALF* [NY Transfer News Collective]

October 31-Alameda County, CA-Alameda County butcher shop had locks glued, windows etched with acid, and slogans painted on the walls. Ham retailer had locks glued, windows etched with acid, and a large front window broken. McDonald's had a window broken. Fur store had locks glued, slogans painted on walls, and windows etched with acid. *ALF* [NY Transfer News Collective]

October 31-Reno, NV-The office of the Bureau of Land Management was bombed at night, with heavy damage to the roof and six work stations. Nobody that we know of has claimed the attack, but since it happened on Halloween, when the *EF! Journal* had listed the Earth Liberation Front's call for a Night of Action, we assume it was done either for the wildlife displaced by BLM policies or for the cows and sheep bred for slaughter on BLM lands. [mainstream media]

November-Madison, WI-A fur billboard was paint bombed. [eyewitness account at WI capitol]

November-San Jose, CA-Animal abuse billboards were spray painted. [from Up Front 'zine]

November-Orlando, FL-A slaughterhouse was attacked with tires slashed on vans, painted slogans, locks glued, and maybe more. [source-see below.]

[Nov]ember 22-Alameda County, CA? (not sure)-Van for veal distributor had windshield etched with acid and tires slashed. Ham retailer had windows broken, slogans painted, and locks glued. Two butcher shops had locks glued, slogans painted on walls, and windows etched. McDonald's had "#1 killer in the world" painted on the walls and locks glued. *ALF* [NY Transfer News Collective]

November 24?-Orlando, FL-The same slaughterhouse was attacked again. [A Florida 'zine describes this action, and it seemed clear that the editor knew about the action. We'd like to say that while the police probably can't read every tiny 'zine that comes out, the fact that we came across the account shows that the issue could just as easily wind up with them. So we won't list the name of the 'zine and we encourage the editor to be more careful in the future (note-that doesn't mean that we condemn or condone the action itself.)]

November 26-San Francisco, CA-Local TV news reported red paint thrown on fur stores. —San Francisco region, CA-Z Furman Fur Service (private home) paint bombed, Bernard's Fine Furs (private home) had front windows smashed and paint bombs thrown. Saga Fur and Leather was paint bombed and had its locks glued and most windows etched. Herbert's Furs had locks glued. Michelle's Furs had locks to building glued. Sheepskin store was paint bombed. Kane's Furs had locks glued, slogans painted and front windows broken. JE Harl fur store had locks glued, windows etched, slogans painted, and expensive light fixture destroyed. Mіddent's Furs had locks glued, windows etched, and slogans sprayed. California Fur Industry skyscraper had locks glued and windows etched. *ALF* [NY Transfer News Collective]

November 27-28-Chicago, IL-8 or 9 incendiary devices were left in 4 department stores which sell fur, and six went off in Marshall Fields, Carson Pirie Scott, and Saks Fifth Avenue. None ignited in Neiman Marcus. The devices went off at night, and set off sprinklers after small fires ignited. Police recovered 2 whole devices, which were described as a matchbook and timer in a brown paper bag, and the FBI says it thinks that people crossed state lines for the action. The ALF sent a press release to PETA, saying that the action signalled a "more intense" campaign of "economic sabotage against stores which sell fur." *ALF* [NY Transfer News Collective and mass media]

Dial-a-Degenerate

As promised last issue, here are more toll free phone numbers for the animal abusers who sell furs, imprison fur-bearing animals, or supply or support the fur trade in one way or another. Call them and tell them what you think of their crimes against innocent animals. Calls from pay phones are still toll free. Remember to be polite. In some areas, these numbers are cut off because people harass them from pay phones.

Fin Fur......1 800 4USIMAGE
Mr. Chips......1 800 343-2447
Pollacks......1 800 635-4417
Furs and Leather......1 800 872-6465
Bizakis Furs......1 800 541-2114
Max Zeller......1 800 336-FURS
Rhomburg...... 800 762-7310
LJ Freeman......1-800 424-0002
Ron Lee Apparel......1 800 759-FURS
Sof Tex......1 800 635-2504
Pollack Furrier Supply Co.......1 800 422-7467
Diamond Furrier Supply Co.....1 800 242-1924
Samuel Bauer & Son......1 800 SMBAUER
RP Outdoors......1 800 458-6608
Tubari Ltd. Fur Processors......1 800 332-0037
Dean Parrison (a trapper)......1 800 999-6498
King of Sports Fox Food......1 800 223-8581

LET THE MORONS BE HEARD......

To Beef or Not to Beef

According to the latest issue of the Beef Brief, a publication of the National Cattlemen's Association and Beef Board:

Vegetarian diets can pose health risks. Eating meat is good for the economy. Eating meat is good for the environment.

Besides, says the board, real Americans eat meat.

☐ Estimated number of cows it takes to supply the 22,000 footballs the National Football League uses each season: 3,000

People will tell you with pride that Wyoming is hard on women and horses. How plain do you need it said?

HUNGRY HUNTER. PRIME RIB · CHOICE STEAKS

NORTH AMERICAN SPORTSMAN

"Drinks like a fish, snores like a chainsaw, sleeps like a log, wakes up like a bear!"

WYOMING

Go all the Way!

"One cowboy with commitment is worth more than a hundred who are only concerned"

REAL MEAT STEAKS FOR ITSELF ... THERE'S ONLY ONE MEAT FOR A MAN-
C.E.C. REAL BEEF

If you are one of those folks who think Wisconsin hunters are safe from the "East Coast Nuts" and "West Coast Fruit Cakes", then I suggest you talk to Mansavage. AWARE has been battling one attack after another, fighting our own local brand of animal rights extremists.

Dear Editor,

Enclosed is a photo of my daughter Leisann Stolz, the new Miss Wyoming, USA. She loves the red fox coat given to her by the Wyoming Trappers Association, and is pictured wearing the garment at the Miss USA Coronation Ball. Leisann asked me to hurry this photo to you so it can be shared with readers of the American Trapper magazine. We really appreciate the kindness of the Wyoming trappers.

Women were put on earth to reproduce, and are close to animals. Women's liberation is on an equal to gay liberation – they are both ridiculous.

--Wyoming steer wrestler

If we kick ranchers off the public lands, what are people going to eat? People need meat.

–Colorado public lands rancher

Cow Palace

COWBOY CHURCH

Sun., Oct. 31, 10:00 a.m.

Stockyard Club

Good news of Christ taught by Coy Huffman. Bring your friends. Stay for rodeo!

The author has an eighth-grade education, but a lifetime of learning about animals and nature as a world-renowned hunter and trapper.

REAL BEEF

There's only one meat for a man.

JESUS LOVES COWBOYS

Some Ideas for Aggressive Tactics

Most animal liberation events consist only of marching and perhaps a little civil disobedience. But hasn't CD become an expected ritual of protest in this country? What was once radical and new is now routine to the point that protest "leaders" often negotiate the CD with the police in advance! Clearly, fresh street tactics are needed to bring animal suffering to the attention of the public.

In England, there is a group called the Animal Liberation Investigation Unit which practices a unique form of public direct action. 20 to 30 members of the group will march into a slaughterhouse, factory farm, or laboratory in broad daylight with video cameras. They try to gain as much photographic evidence of cruelty and torture as possible, and then get it out to the local media. Many of them are arrested for trespassing in the process, the same charge that many CD arrestees receive. But notice the difference between the two types of action-one is staid, boring, and predictable, while the other is exciting, confrontational, and brings graphic evidence of torture to the public eye.

We think that the movement to save animals could benefit immensely from a wave of ACT-UP style tactics. Disruptive, confrontational, and media-savvy actions are often angry and unpleasant, but in the long run they bring results. What if a U.S. version of the ALIU existed? What if scores of rowdy activists disrupted meat industry meetings or fur auctions? What if cities across the country had local groups using such tactics?

Maybe within a couple of years we can work towards these types of actions. This means that we radicalize the grassroots animal/environmental movement, stop playing polite games and stop engaging in the "same old, same old..." FOR ALL THE ANIMALS BEING TORTURED RIGHT NOW-LET'S GET AT IT!

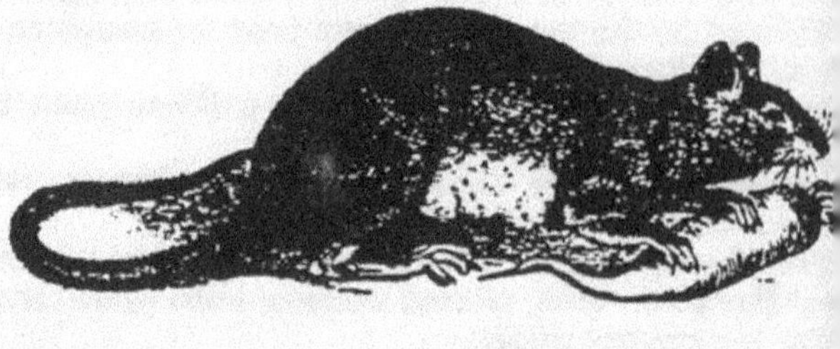

THE MILITANT VEGAN

Issue #5

April 1994

FUR STORE TORCHED IN WISCONSIN

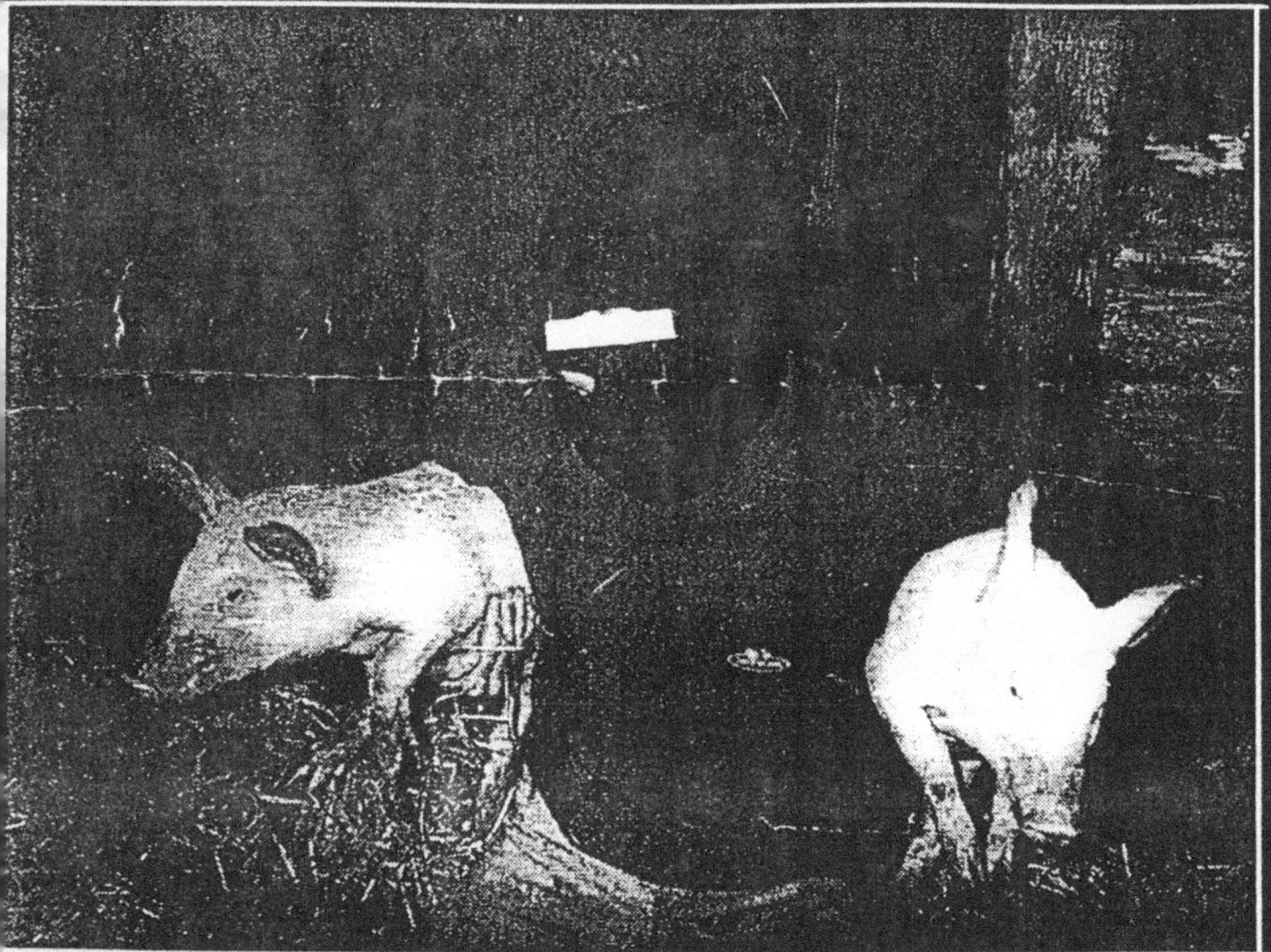

ACTION FOR ANIMALS ACROSS THE COUNTRY

Inside this issue:

Undercover Report from Mink Conference

Sea Shepherds Sabotage Whaling Ship

Major Designers Drop Fur after Protest

and More!

THE MILITANT VEGAN- ISSUE # 5

APRIL 1994

Welcome to our fifth issue! We've got the latest news of grassroots animal liberation action, and a special undercover report from the International Mink Show in Wisconsin this January. As always, activists around North America will receive free copies, but we encourage people to xerox this magazine and distribute it in your area. With people in several states making copies of each issue now, the circulation of this information is in the thousands.

As we've mentioned in the last two issues, the vegan movement is rapidly growing, especially in the Midwest. Things are still growing, and with protests every day somewhere in North America and more than 20 acts of sabotage and liberation in just the first 2 months of the year, it seems clear that 1994 will be the most successful year ever for the movement. With enthusiasm, creativity, and a commitment to grassroots organizing, we will save thousands of animals and shut down more and more animal abusers.

If you are new to vegan ideas and want to save animals, we recommend reading Diet for A New America by John Robbins for starters, and contacting PETA at PO Box 42516/ Washington, DC 20015 for recipes and information about animal abuse. Avoid all the overpriced health food stores, as Asian and Indian groceries have better food at cheaper prices. Copy recipes out of cookbooks at libraries and bookstores.

While this magazine focuses on the fight for animal liberation, we fully support and take part in campaigns for human rights and non-animal environmental issues. We don't stand for any particular ideology, just values like compassion, responsibility, justice, and so on. We encourage the movement to attract people from many different backgrounds and we encourage individual activists to keep in shape and remain drug free for the better advancement of our ideas.

The Militant Vegan is not an ALF support group, and we make no contact with illegal units. This is to ensure that we can continue publishing the good news of animal liberation. So if you see articles about direct action or are a member of an ALF cell, send the clipping or a report of your actions to the North American ALF Support Group/ Box 75029, Ritchie P.O./ Edmonton, AB/ T6E 6K1/ CANADA.

In England, the ALFSG is at BCM 1160/ London, WC1N 3XX/ ENGLAND, and they print a quarterly magazine for prisoner support (20$ a year for a subscription,) sell t-shirts and other items and take donations for ALF prisoners. A separate ALF Press Office takes action claims and acts as media spokesperson after raids. They can be reached at ALF Press Office/ BM 4400/ London/ WC1N 3XX/ ENGLAND. The Swedish ALF is at DBF/ Box 2051/ S-265 02/ Astorp 2/ SWEDEN. The Spanish ALF Supporters Group is at / APDO: 50390/ 28080 Madrid/ SPAIN. The Israeli ALF Supporters Group is at / PO Box 6023/ Tel Aviv 61060/ ISRAEL.

War over animals

Activists blamed for arson attacks

To keep up with the movement, subscribe to Out of the Cages (14$ a year) at PO Box 2960/ Santa Cruz, CA/ 95063. The best animal liberation magazine anywhere is Arkangel (15$ a year, they take U.S. cash) at BCM 9240/ London/ WC1N 3XX/ ENGLAND. The Earth First! Journal is also useful, write them at PO Box 1415/ Eugene, OR/ 97440. All activists should read Free the Animals! by Ingrid Newkirk, Eco Warriors by Rik Scarce, and the new third edition of Ecodefense, which is available for 18$ from the Earth First! Journal.

Outside the smelly, blackened ruins of her fur shop, spray painted on the side with "ALF" and the words, "No More," Eva Del Conte said she wouldn't talk about the Animal Liberation Front.

We hope you enjoy this issue-keep building up the movement, and we get closer and closer to a victory for the animals. It will take long years and hard work, but in the end, our efforts will pay off. We can wipe out the fur trade soon, and start really taking on the meat and dairy industries, the source of almost all human-caused animal suffering.

The Militant Vegan is a newsmagazine only, and we do not intend to encourage crime against animal killers. This magazine is for informational purposes only.

On the cover: ALF activist liberating pigs from Wye College in England, August 1993.

NEWS AND COMMENT

Kim Trimiew and Deb Stout were jailed by the Spokane grand jury for refusing to testify on February 18. Please send support letters to each of them at: Spokane County Jail/ W. 1100 Mallon/ Spokane, WA 99260. With four of the grand juries reconvened after they were supposed to end for 18 more months, it is clear that their main purpose is long-term intimidation of the movement.

Peaceful protest against hunting was banned on federal lands in December, after S.187 passed the Senate as part of the anti-crime bill. The "hunter rights" bill endorses hunting as a "right," and bans speech and protest against it on the one third of this country which is federal land. We warn the 182 members of Congress who hunt that we will not accept their "law" which, as always, upholds the powerful against the weak.

Alabama and Nebraska are considering "hunter harassment" laws. These laws typically ban hunt sabbing and passive protest at hunts, and are on the books in 47 other states. While more than 60 people have been arrested under such charges, few have been convicted due to the blatant suppression of speech and assembly that the laws represent.

The Bear Defense Action Network is organizing "poach patrols" against the barbaric practice of killing black bears for their paws and gall bladders in southern Oregon. To get involved, call (503) 482-6429.

Fashion designers Calvin Klein and Ann Klein dropped fur after considering "the humane treatment of animals" after PETA occupied their main office in January. This is a major blow to the fur trade, and the Fur Farm "Animal Welfare" Coalition will have to withdraw their new brochures which tell of Calvin Klein proudly using fur.

Animal abusers suffered another blow soon afterwards, as the Nevada Supreme Court unanimously rejected the lower court ruling that PETA had slandered the vicious baboon beater Bobby Berosini in 1989. Long played up by our enemies as a case of animal liberationists' "lies," a lot of murderers will now be eating their words.

Anti-fur demonstrations were held in cities across Canada on February 12, that nation's day of protest against the fur trade. Other demos against fur have been held in Vancouver, Memphis, Seattle, and at the opening of the Seattle Fur Exchange Fur Auction on February 22.

Protests against pet theft were held in about 25 cities around the U.S. on February 14.

PRISONER SUPPORT: The following activists risked their lives and their freedom to save defenseless animals. They would all love to get letters, and it costs 52 cents per ounce airmail to England.
Vivien Smith was jailed in England in 1991 for conspiracy to burn scores of meat trucks. Write her at: Vivien Smith TT2743/ A4 Unit/ HMP Holloway/ Parkhurst Road/ Holloway/ London N7 ONU/ ENGLAND.

Terry Helsby was recently convicted in Liverpool for causing tens of thousands of dollars damage to butchers' shops and a zoo. Write him at: Terry Helsby EF0761/ HMP Risley/ Warrington Road/ Risley/ Warrington/ Cheshire/ WA3 6BP/ ENGLAND.

Allison McKeon was sentenced for the same offense. Write her at: Allison McKeon RE2370/ HMP Askham Grange/ Askham Richard/ York/ YO2 3PT/ ENGLAND.

Max Watson was also sentenced for the same "crime." Write him at: Max Watson BJ2477/ HMP Haverigg/ Haverigg Camp/ Millom/ Cumbria/ LA18 4NA/ ENGLAND.

Mark Power is also in jail for animal liberation activities. Write him at: Mark Power HP0606/ HMP Foston Hall/ Foston/ Derbyshire/ DE6 5DN/ ENGLAND.

Anthony Miller was jailed in New Mexico in 1990 for freeing horses and destroying the trailers used to transport them away from their natural range under abusive conditions. He was a government employee, and was sentenced to 10 years in jail for his act of kindness! At the time, he knew nothing of the animal liberation movement, but has since made contact with a number of groups. Please write Anthony because he gets little support because his action was unknown to the movement for so long: Anthony Miller 40351/ PO Box 1059/ Santa Fe, NM 87504-1059

Court rejects grand jury witness' appeal

BY KEN OLSEN
Staff Writer

Investigators throughout the country will probably find out what Kim Trimiew says to a federal grand jury in Spokane investigating the Animal Liberation Front.

But that doesn't mean she is entitled to immunity from prosecution across the nation, a three-judge panel from the 9th U.S. Circuit Court of Appeals ruled Friday.

If Trimiew is indicted by one of the four other grand juries investigating the ALF, she can request a hearing where the government has to prove it didn't use any of her testimony against her, the judges ruled.

That finding could mean Trimiew returns to the Spokane County Jail, where she was held on contempt charges for two weeks in October for refusing to testify before the grand jury. Her attorney, Stephen Houze of Portland, could not be reached for comment Friday.

In an earlier interview, Houze said if the three-judge panel rejected the appeal, he would ask the full appeals court to reconsider.

Trimiew, 21, is an Oregon activist and a target of grand jury investigations in Washington, Oregon and probably Michigan. She was subpoenaed to Spokane to testify before the grand jury investigating the 1991 ALF raid at Washington State University in August.

Trimiew only has immunity from prosecution in Washington. Her attorney argues that since there are so many jurisdictions investigating the ALF raids, she will never be able to tell whether her testimony helped bring about her indictment other places. The federal government rejected his request for extra safeguards for her, like broader immunity.

U.S. District Judge W. Fremming Nielsen jailed her Oct. 5 for contempt after she twice refused to testify. The appeals court freed her on bail Oct. 20, pending its decision.

SEA SHEPHERDS SABOTAGE WHALER

On January 24, the Sea Shepherds attempted to sink a whaling ship in Norway in retaliation for Norway's continued killing of Minke whales. Below are the Sea Shepherd communique (issued before they realized that the ship only partially sank) and an article from the Norwegian media.

Sea Shepherd Strikes Again in Norway-Second Outlaw Whaling Ship Sunk
January 24th, 1994 Santa Monica, California (Sea Shepherd HQ)

The Sea Shepherd Conservation Society is responsible for the sinking this morning of the pirate whaler Senet in the port of Gressvik, Norway at 0145 hrs. The Senet, registered in Gressvik, killed five Minke whales illegally during the summer of 1993. The ship is owned by Martin Slevik.

This is the second Norwegian whaler sunk by the Sea Shepherd Conservation Society since the withdrawal of Norway from the International Whaling Commission in July 1992. Sea Shepherd agents sunk the whaler Nybroena on December 27, 1992.

This second sinking is in retaliation for the illegal slaughter of some 300 Minke whales in 1993.

The attack was organized by Lisa Distefano, 30, the director of Sea Shepherd's Oceanic Research and Conservation Action Force (ORCAFORCE.) The Senet was scuttled by ORCAFORCE field agents trained in underwater demolition. The ship was sunk at dockside. There were no crew members on board. The agents left a Sea Shepherd calling card on the ship to verify our actions.

Captain Paul Watson, 42, the founder and international director of the Sea Shepherd Conservation Society, informed the Norwegian authorities of the sinking and called on the government of Prime Minister Gro Harlem Brundtland to recognize the worldwide moratorium on commercial whaling.

"It is with great reluctance that we must initiate these actions," said Captain Watson. "However, when nations do not heed the law, it is the duty of concerned citizens to enforce the law against the offending nation. Norway is a pirate whaling nation. Our actions were an enforcement of international conservation regulations against illegal whaling activity."

Captain Watson added, "I think that Lisa Distefano and her crew acted very responsibly. There were no injuries. The future for the world's whales is a little more secure today with the loss of this pirate whaling vessel."

The Sea Shepherd Conservation Society has sunk seven whaling ships and shut down operations on three others since 1979. None of the strikings resulted in injuries and no criminal charges have been filed against the Sea Shepherd Conservation Society for the attacks. The Society only targets whaling operations that are in violation of the conservation regulations of the International Whaling Commission.

The following is a translation of an article that appeared in the Norwegian newspaper <u>Stavanger Aftenblad</u> on January 25:

NORWEGIAN AUTHORITIES REACT STRONGLY TO WHALE BOAT SABOTAGE

OSLO (NTB): Norwegian authorities reacted strongly to the action on the whaling boat "Senet" outside of Fredrikstad, Sunday night. State Department will ask the authorities in the USA for cooperation to stop the organization Sea Shepherd from using their base in California for sabotage abroad.

"We disassociate completely from Sea Shepherd's attempt to sink the whaling boat outside Fredrikstad. It's sabotage that borders on terrorism and is of course totally unacceptable," said press spokesperson Ingvard Havnen in the State Department. Also, the international environmental organization Greenpeace condemned the sabotage action against the "Senet."

Secretary Jan Odin Olavsen from the Norwegian Small Whale Hunting Association characterized the sabotage in Fredrikstad as the absolute bottom from the controversial conservation society. "The attack has only one purpose, to create international fame for Sea Shepherd. For us whalers, the attacks on Norwegian whaling vessels have no effect, except that we become more insistent on working for our cause, " Olavsen said to NTB.

It was around 01.45 Sunday night that people from Sea Shepherds cut two cooling water intakes to the flush pumps in the "Senet," so that the water flooded into the boat. Only quick reaction from the Fire Department in Fredrikstad, when skipper Arvid Enghaugen discovered the sabotage around nine Monday morning, stopped the boat from going under.

According to a press release from Sea Shepherd, the sinking attempt was led by the leader of the organization's action group, Lisa Distefano. The activists put Sea Shepherd's visiting card on the door to the engine room. They also locked the door with a large padlock to hinder the salvage work.

The "Senet" last year had a quota for five Minke whales, which were shot in 11 days. The rest of the year, the boat does regular fishing. The crew on the "Senet" had been told earlier that the boat could be targeted for actions by Sea Shepherd because it is so close to the Swedish border. As late as the New Year weekend, a message came from the police in Lofoten that something might be up. The crew had therefore in the last weeks kept the "Senet" hidden around Onsoy. But Sunday night, it again moored at at the Slevik pier after a three day long trip to Denmark. The fact that activists struck so quickly points to them keeping the boat under surveillance.

Sea Shepherd leader Paul Watson says that the organization is planning several similar actions. The purpose, according to Watson, is to increase the whaling boats' expenses through higher insurance costs, and other costs, so that it will not be economically profitable to participate in the whaling.

Animal rights group suspected in arson

y MIKE MULVEY
ukesha County Bureau

Radical activists linked to blaze at Brookfield furrier

Brookfield — The under-
und Animal Liberation Front
uspected of starting a fire at a
ll known fur shop in what au-
rities say would be the radical
oup's first arson in Wisconsin,
as learned Thursday.
Investigators found the letters "ALF" and the words "We skin you alive" painted on an exterior of a wall at Chudiks' West Inc., 4120 N. Calhoun Rd., which was the site of a Sunday morning fire.

ALF is the acronym of the Animal Liberation Front, which took credit last month for several arson fires at Chicago department stores.

Chudiks, a fur retailer, suffered at least $125,000 in damage to its building and furs, said Deputy Fire Chief Richard J. Ronan.

No one was injured in the blaze.

"These ALF people are animal activists who are against animal laboratory testing and the selling of furs," Ronan said. "The fire remains under investigation, and it's being investigated as an arson.

"Our arson team, the Brookfield police, the state fire marshals office and the U.S. Bureau of Alcohol, Tobacco and Firearms are all working on the case.

"The writing would lead us to believe someone wanted to take credit for it. This is believed to be the first fire started by ALF in

See Fire 6A

Anti-fur group takes fire blame

By Penny Roberts
Tribune Staff Writer

Chicago police are investigating whether a radical animal-rights organization planted fire-starting devices in four of the city's largest department stores over the weekend.

The Animal Liberation Front is claiming responsibility for leaving the devices, which started small fires in Saks Fifth Avenue, Marshall Field's and Carson Pirie Scott, and forced the evacuation of the top floor of Neiman Marcus.

In a news release dated Sunday that was faxed to the Washington, D.C.-based People for the Ethical Treatment of Animals, the organization said it targeted stores that sell fur products. PETA released the statement Monday.

"This action signals the start of a new, more intense campaign of economic sabotage against stores which sell fur," the statement said. "Any store selling fur items will be considered a legitimate target. No fur will be tolerated—fur hats, fur gloves or fur-trimmed coats are enough to put a store on the ALF hit list."

The statement also said the organization planted nine devices in four stores, but police have reported finding just eight. The incendiary devices consist of a matchbook and a timer attached to a 9-volt battery, and are designed to "flash" and start a fire. They were left at the sites in lunch-size paper bags.

Bomb and Arson Section Sgt. Edward O'Donnell would say only that police are seriously investigating possible involvement of the Animal Liberation Front and that it is the only organization that has claimed it placed the devices.

Other police sources said the statement was also faxed to Women's Wear Daily in New York City. Recipients of the fax message contacted the Federal Bureau of Investigation, which in turn notified local law-enforcement officials Monday morning.

The Animal Liberation Front is a radical branch of the animal-rights movement that has been linked to several terroristlike activities. Their first actions were documented in March of 1979, when they released five animals from New York University Medical Center in New York City.

Over the years, they have claimed responsibility or been blamed for vandalizing facilities, disrupting research, threatening scientists and setting afire at least eight

See Fires, Page 8

Fires

Continued From Page 1

buildings as well as several meat trucks, according to PETA.

In Chicago, the Animal Liberation Front claimed responsibility in January 1991 for "liberating" 11 rabbits and 10 guinea pigs from Hektoen Lab on South Wood Street—a Cook County Hospital research laboratory.

The organization has no national headquarters or direct contact with the public. It disseminates its messages through anonymous telephone calls or by sending information to PETA, a non-violent, educational organization of animal-rights activists. Workers discovered the latest fax Monday morning.

"It appears they sent it that night [Saturday]," said PETA spokesperson Jenny Woods. "They never contact anyone directly. They're very careful."

The devices started fires in three of the stores, causing minimal damage and no injuries. One was discovered at the fourth store before it could ignite. Investigators found no evidence of break-ins or forced entry, leading them to surmise the devices were planted Saturday as shoppers flocked to the stores.

Police said they now believe more than one person was involved.

Spokespersons for the department stores declined to comment on the organization's possible involvement.

The president of the Associated Fur Industries of Chicagoland questioned whether an animal-rights organization was really responsible.

"It doesn't make any sense. If they were targeting fur sales, why did they set the bedding department on fire?" said Hal Waitz. "I think they're just claiming they did it so they can get publicity and attention."

Radical group linked to arson at fur shop

Fire

From 1A

the state, but ATF has said the group has been more active elsewhere in the country."

An angry Barth W. Chudik, store owner, said the blaze was the latest in a series of incidents at his store.

"It's them (ALF), all right. I've had vandalism committed by animal rights' organizations in the past. I've had acid thrown on my van. I've had slogans written on my building. I've had my store's locks glued shut. I've received threatening phone calls.

Chudik: Will stay in business

"But no one has ever tried to burn my place. And no one has ever tried to kill me. Now, I've been a victim of the former. I hope the same isn't true of the latter."

Chudik said he doesn't know what he can do to protect himself or his business.

"When people are this far off the edge, there isn't much you can do," he said. "I'm going to stay in business and be around for a long time. We're not going to run and hide. I'll take whatever security measures I can."

The Chudik family has been in the fur business in Brookfield since 1916 and has run its store on Calhoun Road for 24 years.

Ronan said it appears the fire was started with some type of flammable liquid on the northeast corner of the building. He said authorities are unaware of a local ALF organization.

Last month, ALF took cre
for placing eight fire-starting
vices outside of four downto
Chicago department stores t
sell furs. The devices star
three small fires that were qui
ly extinguished. No one was
jured.

In taking credit for the Chi
go fires, ALF vowed to intens
its sabotage against busines
dealing in animal furs.

ALF also is suspected in
1992 torching of several delive
trucks at a Minneapolis m
wholesaler.

Fur store arson

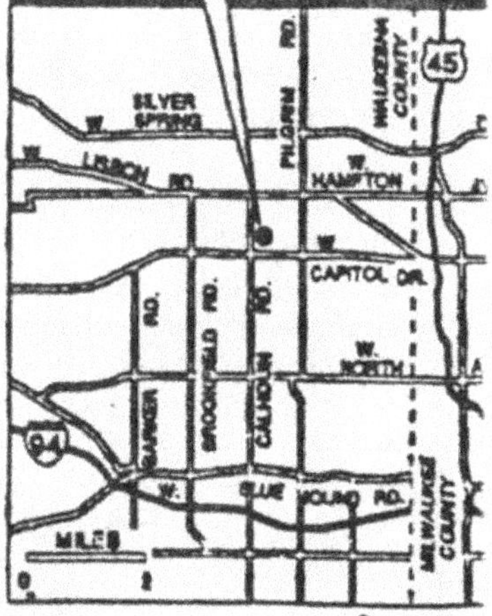

SILVER SPRING
W.
W. LISBON RD.
PILGRIM RD.
WAUKESHA COUNTY
45
W. HAMPTON
W. CAPITOL DR.
BARKER RD.
BROOKFIELD RD.
CALHOUN RD.
W. NORTH
94
W. BLUE MOUND RD.
MILWAUKEE COUNTY
MILES
0
1

Sentinel gra

Arson Hotline

The Arson Hotline, 1-800-362-3005, is offering a $5,000 reward for tips leading to the arrest and conviction of anyone involved in the Brookfield fire. Authorities said all tips are kept confidential.

Top: Milwaukee Sentinel, December 31, 1993
Above: Chicago Tribune, November 30, 1993

UNDERCOVER REPORT ON THE FUR FARM INDUSTRY

To effectively fight the industries of animal abuse, we must understand the way they wo and know their weak points. We are publishing this article to give our readers importa information that can be used to destroy the fur trade as well as to show the animal kille that we can and will infiltrate them at every step of the way. In the future, we hope to ha more articles of this nature on various animal abusing businesses.

On January 8, 1994, the fur farm industry had their annual International Mink Show in Madison, Wisconsin. I went to this event as an investigator for the Coalition to Abolish the Fur Trade. I discovered many things that confirm the need for the animal rights movement to continue to focus as much energy as possible on this issue.

Before I discuss the findings from this investigation, I would like to thank D'Arcy Kinmetz and the Alliance for Animals for conducting an excellent protest and civil disobedience at this event. Five members of the group raided the conference, with several of them wearing bloody fur coats. Two of them chained themselves to the podium while the other three were physically pushed out of the building. Eventually, security had to remove the entire podium that the protesters were chained to! This received news coverage on three TV stations.

I began my investigation by talking to the organizer of the event, a fur farmer named Gene Cooper from Wisconsin. He claimed that China has just opened its first fur stores and is a new market for the industry. The industry is also exploring the possibilities of opening fur markets in South America. Korea is the biggest fur consuming nation, and national groups should take note of this as they are in a position to do something about it. Koreans could consume all of the mink pelts produced in North America and then some! There is so little mink produced these days, 18 million a year compared to 45 million annually in the late 80's, that supply is below demand and fur farmers are starting to make money again. They estimate that is will take ten years to meet this demand. Of course, this estimate does not take the animal liberation movement into consideration! An anti-fur effort in Korea and all the Far East is imperative to our success.

The first workshop was on Aleutian Disease (AD.) This is a disease that has wiped out several fur farms in the last year. Farmers dread AD and believe that a cure will never be developed. They believe that is ,must be prevented by testing all breeding mink and killing those infected. Several researchers are experimenting with mink in an effort to find ways to curb this disease and save the industry money. They include Rocky Mountain Laboratories in Hamilton, Montana with Dr. Marshal Bloom and Utah State University in Logan, Utah with Dr. Gary Durrant.

Evidently, AD has become a big problem in Utah. Raccoons are not native to the state, but were introduced for hunting purposes. The raccoons approach mink in fur farms and transmit the disease to them. Utah activists take note, efforts are underway to eradicate the raccoons.

One speaker, Kent Disse from Minnesota, claimed that formaldogen gas can be used to disinfect the cages and prevent AD. The fur farmers recognize that this chemical is currently illegal, but they still went into detail on how to make it. It was recommended that this chemical be made without employee help in order to avoid criminal prosecution.

There were two other things that I noticed during this workshop. One is that researcher John Gorham of Washington State University developed an iodine program to help detect AD. The fur farmers claim that this test is ineffective. This is just one more example of minks and other animals being tortured in labs for results that are of no use. Fortunately, the ALF has virtually crippled Dr. Gorham's mink research. The other thing will be of no surprise to anyone. The fur farmers talked about ways to keep other wildlife away from their mink to eliminate the possibilities of disease transmission. One said that starlings were a problem at his farm so he placed a bowl of feed at the edge of his farm. They would then flock to this feed and became used to it. He then added salt so that it was 30% salt and 70% feed. He claimed that the starlings ate this mixture once and never came back. When asked if this killed the birds, he proclaimed "Who cares?" to a roomful of laughter.

The next workshop dealt with melatonin implants. After a ten year process, the FDA is about to approve this product (which is now available.) Melatonin causes the mink to fur out sooner. To explain, each winter fur bearing animals develop a thicker, prime coat. It is at this point that they are skinned and killed. By injecting mink, fox, chinchilla, or Finnish raccoon with melatonin, the animals fur out in October instead of December.

The advantage to this is the savings in terms of labor and feed. The average mink consumes 64 pounds of feed before being killed. Mink who have been injected with melatonin consume an average of 52 pounds of feed before slaughter. Feed costs are cut by 18.8%.

One mink farmer claimed that in tests, melatonin implanted mink had heavier leather and were harder to flesh. This is undesirable to the fur farmers. The manufacturer said that an early pelting out process avoids this problem. He added that this implant will not reduce fighting or self mutilation. He also pointed out that melatonin is already available in Canada and one fur farm using the product was receiving two to four dollars more per pelt than the average mink farmer.

This is the first FDA-approved chemical ever produced for mink besides antibiotics and vaccines. The sole purpose of this product is to save the fur farmer money. It costs about 40 cents per dose and is injected into the loose skin between the shoulder blades. The manufacturer, Terry Cairns of Wildlife Pharmaceuticals, said, "Mink don't seem to mind it too much. I think they mind being handled more than being injected."

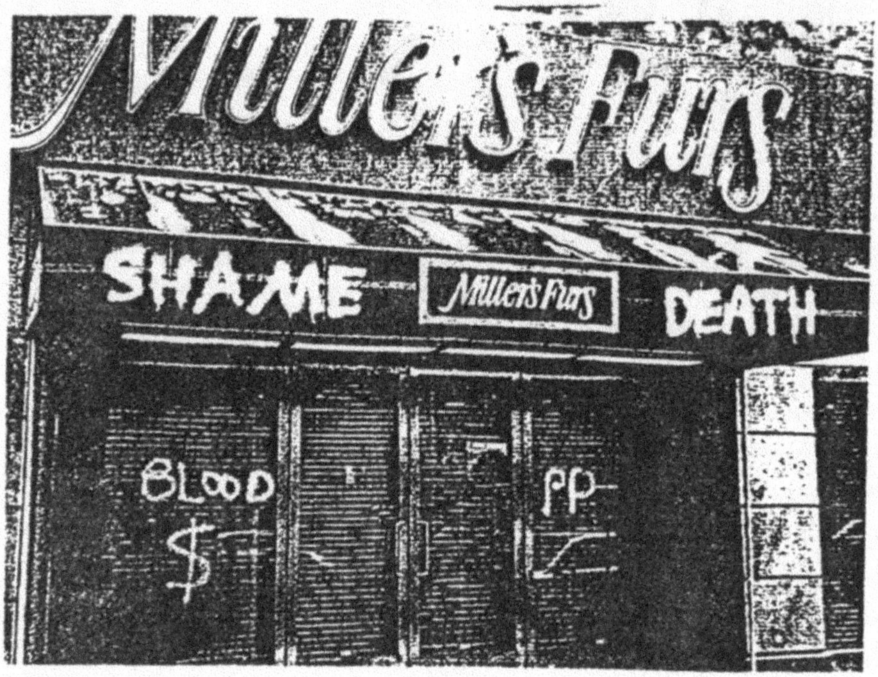
Miller's Furs
SHAME
Miller's Furs
DEATH
BLOOD
$

Wildlife Pharmaceuticals is the only company that makes this product, since four others could not afford the FDA approval process. They are located at 1401 Duff Drive, Suite 600, Fort Collins, CO 80524, 1-800-222-WILD. Terry Cairns is a fox farmer as well.

The next discussion was about how to increase breeder reproduction. The fur farmers have decided to expose the mink to one and a half hour of lighting each morning or evening in addition to sunlight hours. This tricks the minks' biological systems and pushes breeding success up from about 85% to 93%.

The real key to their success, however, is through scientifically formulated mink feed. Perhaps the main mink research center at this point is the National Fur Foods Experimental Mink Ranch. The other big players were crippled by the ALF, but this one is, at this point, untouched. They have developed feed which, when added to the standard wet feed (ground. up slaughterhouse by-products and grain,) cuts disease rates in half by reducing bacteria counts in the feed. This product also helps develop minks with lighter leather, silkier fur, uniform pelt size, and breeders with better milking and bigger kits. This is a major asset to the fur farm industry.

The National Fur Foods Co., which is a subsidiary of National Milk Specialities, is located in New Holstein, Wisconsin. The experimental fur farm may be located in nearby Oshkosh. They can be reached at 1-800-558-5803. This company needs to be shut down!

The spread of Aleutian Disease is of great concern to the fur farm industry. The development of high quality pelts while cutting costs at the same time may be their only greater concern. Furriers feel that U.S. mink quality is getting worse. Once again, National Fur Foods is working to solve this problem. They claim that their feed is specially formulated to produce lighter leather, silkier fur, etc. I cannot emphasize more how evil, and how crucial, this company is.

The next workshop covered management, pelt prices, and the future. With pelt prices up, due to lack of supply, the fur farmers plan to upgrade their equipment and buy new breeding stock to eliminate some of the inbreeding that was going on. It was again mentioned that using National Fur Foods crumlets would save them money. One mink farmer warned against expanding the mink herds as this would lead to lower prices. An updated water system has been produced by Aqua Cir-Clean of Green Bay, Wisconsin. It was promoted as a real money saver in terms of labor costs.

The mink industry has a problem with animals dying shortly after birth. It was recommended that they watch kits closely during April and May as this is the time when they are born. National Fur Foods claims that they have people at their experimental fur farm during all hours of the night during this time period. They are watching the kits to correct any problems that will lead to an early death.

The next discussion covered the use of antibiotics in mink to help keep them alive until pelting time. I overheard someone say that only 3 antibiotics are approved for use in mink. The speaker mentioned this but continued to list 10 or 15 different antibiotics that could be used along with the correct dosages.

Mike Savidusky of Savidusky Furs in Madison, Wisconsin spoke next. Due to a lack of competition, he is once again on stable ground. his focus is on youth and he is experiencing his best times since 1986. It is apparent that overconfident activists are ignoring the fur issue because they believe that we've already won. The battle isn't even half over and we must continue to hit the furriers hard.

The ecology issue is something that the furriers are now focusing on. They say that fur is a "natural" product. They ignore the fact that 66 times more energy goes into the production of a fur coat than a synthetic one. The Coalition To Abolish the Fur Trade has information to counter every one of their claims of this issue.

Due to higher pelt prices, wholesale rates will be higher next year. They won't be able to sell their coats at near nothing prices during the '94-'95 season. In response to this, Savidusky claims that 40-45% of his profits are now coming from cleaning, restyling, remodeling, etc., so even if he sells low, he can make more money when more fur is on the street. There is a small group of furriers, all at least 300 miles apart, who are unloading tons of merchandise at extremely low prices to capitalize on this. They all schedule their sales around each other and get the merchandise on consignment.

It is the fur industry's belief that the movement against them is weakening because our protests have been less confrontational and shorter. What does this tell you? We must have large, long, loud protests. This summer we will begin our "Summer Heat" campaign. Up to 10% of the mink on fur farms die from heat related diseases and this will be the basis for the campaign. It would be great if other groups joined us in this new, angry campaign that aims to truly educate the public. We can destroy the furriers' morale by showing them that we're stronger than ever-we've just been putting our energies elsewhere for the past two years. We must focus on the fur trade and win!

(The next workshop, given by the Fur Farm "Animal Welfare" Coalition, described a new propaganda video to be shown to Michigan schoolchildren that promotes animal abuse.)

It is clear that we must embark on a new, confrontational campaign that embraces new tactics as well as old ideas that have proven to be effective. We suggest that activists push for city ordinances that ban the sale of wild fur. This will be the first step in our efforts to completely abolish the fur trade. All stores that still sell fur must be boycotted and they need to know why they lost your business. Fur wearers must be made to feel uncomfortable. They see fur as a status symbol and when they are frowned upon, their coat will lose its appeal. Posters can be put up with a paste made from a flour/water mixture. Stickers and leaflets must be everywhere. Consider investigating fur farms and documenting the conditions the animals are in. We have a small fur farm list and your state department of agriculture may help you as well. If a group of activists conducted a civil disobedience on a fur farm, the media would get shots of the small, filthy cages the mink are kept in. This should be considered. Other activists have sabotaged fur stores and fur farms. This causes the furriers' insurance premiums to skyrocket. I know of a fur store in Memphis that was attacked repeatedly and lost their lease and their insurance.

In conclusion, the fur trade is hurt but still kicking. Grassroots groups must continue to fight in the streets while the national groups need to work on shrinking the fur markets in Korea and the Far East. Let's stop these murderers once and for all!

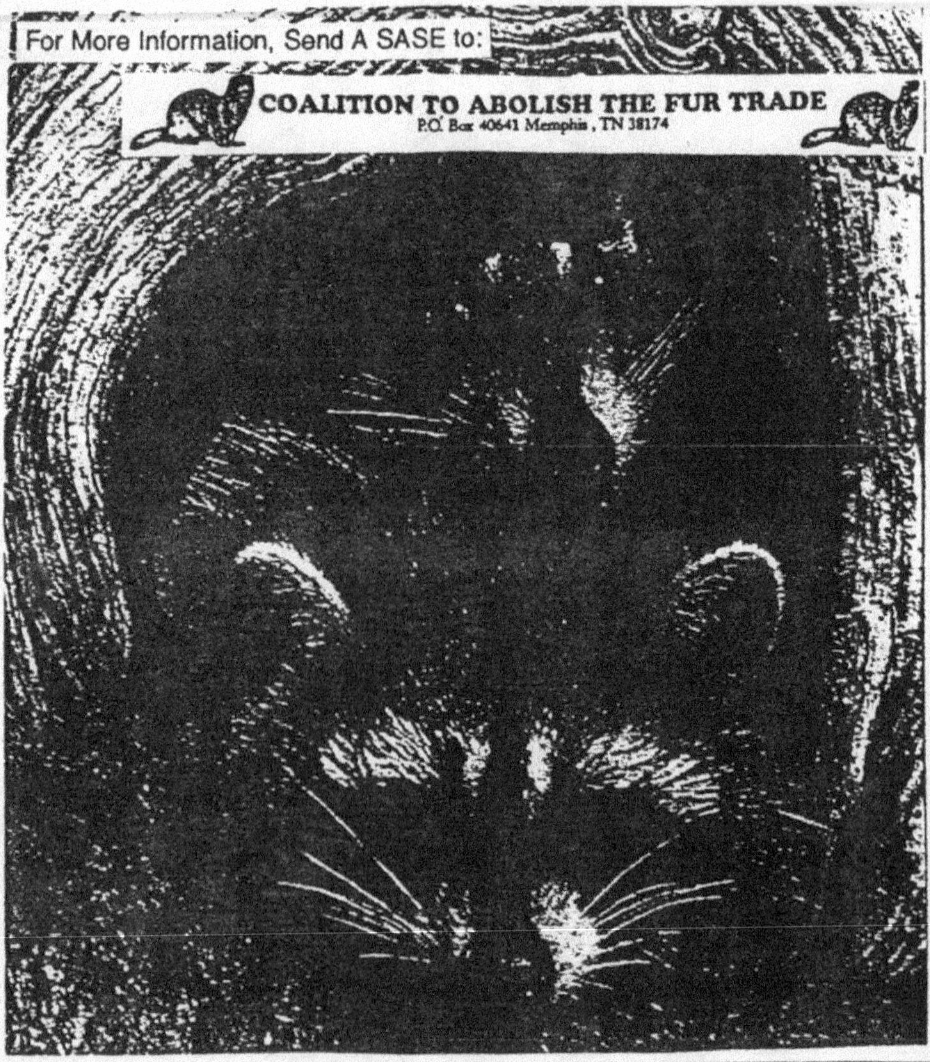
For More Information, Send A SASE to:
COALITION TO ABOLISH THE FUR TRADE
P.O. Box 40641 Memphis, TN 38174

The Silent Treatment

An author draws hard time for clamming up about the Animal Liberation Front

WHEN STUDENTS turned out for the first day of Rik Scarce's class in sociology research methods at Washington State University this fall, they were told that their assigned instructor wouldn't be coming—and probably wouldn't make it the rest of the semester. Scarce, the author of the 1990 book *Eco-Warriors: Understanding the Radical Environmental Movement*, was still cooling his heels in the Spokane County Jail; in May he was ordered behind bars for refusing to discuss his research on the Animal Liberation Front with a federal grand jury.

Scarce was released in October (the presiding judge, who could have detained him until December, decided that coercive confinement was not working). But some environmental activists have taken his long incarceration as a clear message that the government is keeping the heat on in a two-year-old investigation of Operation Bite Back, a series of attacks against fur farms and research laboratories carried out in 1991 and 1992 by the ALF. And some are concerned that the government will take up similar investigations of other groups on the extreme fringes of the environmental movement. "First it was the ALF," says Robert Amon, an Idaho-based member of the radical group Earth First! who expects to be investigated by a federal grand jury this fall. "Next it will be Earth First! again. Then maybe the Lewiston [Idaho] Rotary Club for considering inviting us to come as guest speakers."

For the 35-year-old Scarce, the trouble began in 1992, when a federal grand jury investigating vandalism of U.S. Department of Agriculture research offices at Washington State University subpoenaed him to testify. Among other things, the grand jury wanted to know whether Scarce had interviewed three ALF members who were suspects. Arguing that as a writer he had a First Amendment right not to divulge anonymous sources and a professional obligation not to break promises of confidentiality, Scarce refused to talk. Some state and federal courts do grant writers, reporters, and academics professional privilege, but many—including the Ninth Circuit Court of Appeals, which heard Scarce's case—do not. On May 1- Scarce was ordered to jail for contempt of court.

"I'm not a suspect": Scarce

"I'm not a suspect," said Scarce from his cell. "I have not been charged with a crime."

A sticking point in Scarce's argument involves the company he keeps. Several suspected ALF members are allegedly close friends of his, and Rodney A. Coronado, a key suspect in ALF raids in four states, was staying at Scarce's house in Pullman, Washington, on August 1- 1991, the day of the raid at the university (Scarce says he was out of town). Coronado was indicted in July on five federal charges in connection with a February 1992 raid at a Michigan State University lab; he's been in hiding since the fall of 1992.

Meanwhile, the government continues its investigations of the ALF. A new grand jury will likely convene in Grand Rapids, Michigan, and in Spokane, another person has been jailed for not talking about the ALF case. "This proves you don't have to be a Molotov-cocktail-throwing subversive to gain the government's attention," says Scarce. "People should look at my case and think about the other possibilities." —KEN OLSEN

In her case, Powers believes her crime was walking downtown wearing a parka that had a fake fur collar, which she had bought at an outlet store. She doesn't have any other explanation for the 2-foot-long splotch of red paint that somebody squirted on the back of her coat.

After she found the paint, she went over the previous hour. What stood out was seeing two men walking by her, one of them carrying a sign that read "FUR IS DEAD."

That Saturday, Jan. 8, there was an animal-rights demonstration downtown. That Saturday, too, the Eddie Bauer store downtown reported that $5,000 in merchandise had been slashed, including down-filled parkas and leather chairs.

It was the second such incident. The store's manager told police that Eddie Bauer had received several letters telling it to stop selling items made from animal material.

STEP UP SECURITY, USE CAUTION, RETAILERS WARNED

Fur retailers should exercise extreme caution when they spot an unmarked or unusual package as part of stepped-up security measures in 1994, federal law enforcement authorities have advised the Fur Farm Animal Welfare Coalition.

Marsha Kelly, executive director of the St. Paul, MN-based Coalition, said federal authorities have encouraged fur retailers to beef up security following the planting of nine incendiary devices by the Animal Liberation Front (ALF) in Chicago-area retail stores over the Thanksgiving weekend. Federal law enforcement officials have told the Coalition that precautions are advisable to protect people and property from further ALF violence.

"There is no need for alarm, but the FBI does urge retailers and all industry members to take steps to ensure that they and their operations are safe and secure," said Kelly. "A well-prepared industry will not only increase physical security, it will help deter further incidents."

As previously reported here, devices used in the Chicago incidents consisted of a nine-volt battery attached to a timer and a matchbook, placed in a paper bag. Six of nine devices ignited, setting off small fires. Despite a statement by People for the Ethical Treatment of Animals (PeTA) saying that ALF's intention was to set off sprinklers and inflict only water damage, according to the Coalition the devices were placed under shelves and in other locations chosen to avoid being extinguished by sprinklers.

Similar incidents have occurred recently in Europe. Two members of the British fur trade recently received letter bombs, according to European sources. Danny Sawrij of the Swalesmoor Mink Farm in Halifax/Yorkshire, England, called police when he became suspicious of a video cassette-holder that arrived in the mail. The holder contained a bomb, which was removed before detonating. In a related incident, the owner of a London fur shop and his three-year-old daughter were hurt when a flare exploded after he opened an envelope. Both were treated at St. Mary's hospital for injuries.

The British ALF is thought to have connections to American cells of the ALF.

Federal authorities are in the process of informing local law enforcement agencies about ALF activities and tactics. To reduce the chance of damage or injuries due to ALF actions, they have offered the following advice to fur industry members:

-Contact local law enforcement officials to brief them about the potential for ALF action against your business. Ask them to help you conduct a security review of your operation.

-Conduct a thorough inspection of your facility every day before closing, keeping a special lookout for packages or paper bags left under shelves, displays or furniture.

-If unidentified parcels or packages are found, use extreme caution. DO NOT ATTEMPT TO HANDLE OR REMOVE THEM YOURSELF. Contact enforcement authorities immediately.

"The animal-rights movement must learn that terrorism and violence do not pay," said Kelly. "In addition to protecting ourselves, we can help send that message by exercising good judgment and working cooperatively with authorities who will put these criminals behind bars."

---

p: Outside, December 1993
ove: Seattle Times,
anuary 14, 1994
ght: Fur Age Weekly,
ebruary 10, 1994

DIARY OF ACTIONS

Every single night, the women and men of the Animal Liberation Front carry out direct action to stop animal cruelty at its sources somewhere in the world. England sees thousands of attacks a year, and ALF units are active across the industrialized world. Whether it's the Black Ravens in Russia, the DBF in Sweden, Animal Rescue in Japan, or the ALF in New Zealand, Canada, Israel, Poland, Italy, Spain, France, etc., the goal is the same: to liberate the suffering and destroy the property of those who kill for profit.

Note: The Diary of Actions is intended to report news of "illegal" actions to save animals, not to encourage crime. All reports listed come from movement and opposition publications, internet bulletin boards, mainstream media, and local 'zines. There is probably a lot we missed, since we obviously cannot read every little 'zine out there. To help get out the news of direct action, send reports and clippings to Out of the Cages/ PO Box 2960/ Santa Cruz, CA 95063.

INTERNATIONAL ACTIONS

In Whitehorse, Yukon Territory, **Canada**, the *ALF* slashed 54 tires and glued the locks of 17 trucks belonging to the Department of Renewable Resources on December 14. The DRR is carrying out a wolf kill program. The activists cut barbed wire topping a security fence to get in.

In **Croatia**, the *ALF* has been glueing the locks of meat and leather shops while actively opposing the war there. In Hamar, **Norway**, the *ALF* has sabotaged the building that almost all furs there go through, as well as fur stores in the city. In **Finland**, the ALF carried out an "Operation Bite Back," in which locks were glued and windows smashed at numerous fur stores from October to December.

In **England**, *ALF* attacks happen every day and it would be impossible to list them all. Some highlights include: over 100 wild birds released from captivity in Surrey, two chinchillas liberated in London on November 14, 50 hens liberated from a farm in Yatton on November 21, 30 turkeys liberated and vehicles sabotaged in Ringmer a week earlier, 100 battery hens liberated in East Sussex on December 13, the attempted burning of a slaughterhouse in Spon End, and arson attacks on a meat truck and a vivisection company in West London.

A new group called *The Justice Department* sent a large number of letter bombs to animal abusers, some of which went off, and firebombed chain stores which test on animals. This has caused quite a bit of controversy in the movement in England.

In **Northern Ireland**, a McDonald's had its windows smashed on December 4 by the *ALF*. In **Sweden**, the *Djurens Hamnars* (Animal Avengers) attacked fur stores, butchers, and vivisectors in Stockholm during the summer with paint and glued locks, and liberated 9 guinea pigs and 2 rabbits from an animal breeder outside the city on November 8.

UNITED STATES

In our last issue, we listed actions from January 1 through the end of November 1993. Since then, we have learned of a few more during those months:

May 31-Baltimore, MD- At the Johns Hopkins University School of Public Health, 10 rats, 5 dogs, and 3 cats were liberated. *Students Against In Vivo Experiments and Dissection (SAVED)*

Summer-Fon du Lac, WI-A large number of attacks against animal abusers took place. *ALF*

June 24-Grosse Pointe, IL- Lee's Fashion and Furs and two other fur shops were spray painted with slogans, had posters glued to windows, and locks glued. *Vegan Action League*

August-Eaton, OH- At least three beef promotion billboards were spray painted with slogans such as "ALF." *ALF*

August-Dayton, OH- A butcher shop was spray painted with slogans like "Meat is Murder." *ALF*

November-Los Angeles, CA- Two cars belonging to fur store owners had their windows broken. *ALF*

November 27- Marietta, OH- Leather shoe store had slogans such as "Blood Money," "Cow Killers," "Don't Wear Animals," and "Murderers" painted on the walls. *ALF*

DECEMBER 1993-FEBRUARY 1994

December 11-Fond du Lac, WI-A McDonald's received 4 holes in its windows and a display on the roof was deflated. *ALF*

December 23-San Francisco, CA- Activists damaged 25-30 fur garments in 5 department stores and on the streets with super glue, razor blades, and scissors. *ALF*

December 26-Brookfield, WI- Chudik's West fur store was set on fire, with $125,000 in damages. The store and the owner's van had previously been attacked repeatedly with acid, painted slogans, and glued locks. *ALF*

January-Ohio- Unspecified action against animal abusers.

January 5-San Jose, CA- Tarlow's Furs had several windows smeared with etching fluid. *ALF*

January 7-Stockton, CA- Mansoor Furs, the only furrier in the city, had its lock glued and slogans spray-painted. A Chuck E. Cheese restaurant received similar treatment. *ALF*

January 8-Seattle, WA- In the second such incident, an Eddie Bauer store received $5,000 damage from slashed merchandise after refusing to stop selling clothing with fur trim.

January 13-Tillamook County, OR- Survey stakes were pulled up at a clear-cut site in an action to sabotage those who destroy wildlife habitat. *ALF*

January 15-Beverly Hills, CA- Display window of American Express smashed to protest promotion of fur. *ALF Nov. 26 Cell*

January 16-San Francisco, CA- Activists not part of ALF threw red paint on Robert's Furs.

January 17-Oakland, CA- Middent's Furs had windows etched, locks glued, slogans painted, and canvas awning torn to shreds. *ALF*

January 22-San Francisco, CA- Kane's Furs had a lock glued, slogans painted, and holes put in the windows. *ALF*

January 27-Beverly Hills and Santa Monica, CA- Display window of Somper Furs smashed. Display window of Adrienne (furs) smashed. An escalation in actions is planned for the succeeding months. *ALF Nov. 26 Cell*

January 27-San Francisco, CA- Nagano Furs had windows etched. *ALF*

January 29-San Francisco, CA- Kane's Furs had holes put through its windows. *ALF*

January-February- San Diego, CA- Several attacks on meat companies have been reported in local media, with at least one arson attack in which a refrigerated meat truck was burned and the building was spray painted with "Meat is Murder." Mike Brown, the president of a targeted meat company, said, "The more this is publicized, the worse it makes it....I wish I sold produce in San Diego instead of meat." The actions were claimed in a phone call to a local tv station by the *Farm Animal Revenge Militia*.

February-Oakland, CA- At least 2 Hormel meat chili billboards spray painted with slogans like "Go Vegan."

February-Detroit area, MI- Locks are glued at fur stores week after week.

February-Philadelphia area, PA- Paint-filled ornaments were thrown at Ham Sweet Ham and the lock was glued. Other animal abusers have also been attacked.

February 5-San Francisco, CA- Kane's Furs had locks glued, slogans painted, and neon sign smashed. Herbert's Furs had its door etched and lock glued. A veal restaurant had its windows etched. *ALF*

February 8-Pittsburgh, PA- *Paint Panthers* hit Abraville Furriers.

February 9-Columbus, OH- *Paint Panthers* hit at least one fur store.

February 9-Cincinnati, OH- *Paint Panthers* hit at least one fur store.

February 10-Chicago, IL- The *Paint Panthers* hit the American Fur Mart and the Chicago Fur Outlet.

February 11-Omaha, NE-The Julia Talent Fur Store was hit by the *Paint Panthers*.

February 14-Denver, CO- The *Paint Panthers* hit Koslough Furs.

February 14-Colorado Springs, CO- Lay Limited Furs was hit by the *Paint Panthers*.

February 15-Kansas City, MO- The *Paint Panthers* hit Genhardt Furs and Sident Furs.

February 16-St. Louis, MO- The St. Louis Fur and Leather Gallery was hit by the *Paint Panthers*.

February 19- Pleasant Hill, CA- The ALF liberated 6 rabbits from Diablo Valley College. Students told the ALF of a professor who killed a rabbit by snapping its neck, and bragged about it. The animals were taken from the Horticulture garden and placed in a caring, permanent home to guarantee that they will live out their lives in safety. *ALF*

February 20- Oakland and Walnut Creek, CA- Middent's Furs had locks glued, windows smashed, and paint bombs thrown inside. J.E. Hart Furs had locks glued and exterior painted. *ALF*

February 21-New York, NY- *Paint Panthers* hit Elizabeth Arden Furs and Fendi Furs.

Late February-Louisville, KY- At a bowhunting trade show, an elaborate fake bomb was left that contained a note saying that a real bomb was hidden in the building. Five thousand convention goers had to be evacuated for hours.

Beef signs spray-painted

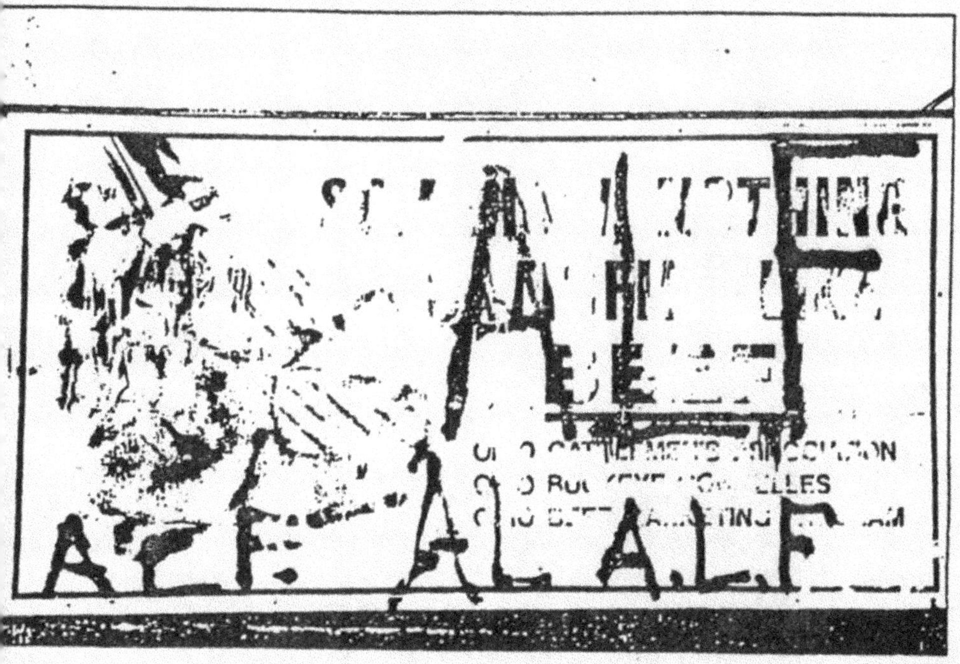
A.L.F

Photo supplied

...he letters "A.L.F." were painted repeatedly on several ...ef promotion signs in Preble County, Ohio. Officials believe the letters stand for the Animal Liberation Front, an underground animal rights group.

...arm bureau offering reward for vandals of pro-beef signs

JIMMY JOHNSON
Palladium-Item

...EATON, Ohio — The Preble ...unty Farm Bureau is offering ...reward for information on ...ndals who defaced signs that ...mote the sale of beef.

...t least three signs have been ...ay-painted in the last three ...nths.

...n early August, vandals ...nted signs on U.S. 35 and U.S. ... near Eaton that read, ...omehow Nothing Satisfies ...e Beef."

...sing black and white paint, ... letters "A.L.F." were paint... repeatedly on the signs.

...fficials believe the letters ...nd for the Animal Liberation ...nt, but they do not know if ... underground animal rights ...up really had anything to do ... the vandalism.

The ALF has claimed responsibility for 60 percent of animal rights terrorist acts, such as arson and bombing, in the United States since 1977, said Jim Hill, of the Preble County Farm Bureau.

A butcher shop in Dayton was recently spray-painted. A trademark of ALF is the phrase "Meat is Murder," which was left on the shop's wall.

Hill said there's no way to prove ALF is involved, but the vandals clearly know something about the organization, he said.

"That's basically the symbol that they leave," he said.

"You could go out today and ask 100 people on the street..."What does ALF stand for? And they'd say ... the TV show," he said, referring to a TV sitcom that featured a creature from outer space named Alf.

"It's tough to think it's kids playing around," he said.

He said the incidents in Preble County and the one incident in Dayton are the only ones he's heard of in Ohio.

Though ALF is an underground organization, Hill said the People for the Ethical Treatment of Animals (PETA) group often defends ALF's acts. Hill noted that PETA's director, Ingrid Newkirk, recently toured laboratories that used animals for testing at Miami University and Wright State University.

Asked about the vandalism of the signs around Eaton, Jenny Woods, a representative of PETA, said, "We don't condone the action but we can understand the frustration of people who see what's going on in a slaughterhouse."

Terrorist acts by ALF include the arson of a University of California veterinary diagnostic laboratory, which caused $4.5 million damage, and the destruction of 32 years of research at a Michigan State University laboratory.

Hill quoted a U.S. Departments of Justice and Agriculture study about the growing trend: "It appears the willingness of animal right extremists to employ destructive and violent methods remains strong."

Hill said anyone with information about the sign vandals should call the sheriff's office at (513) 456-4111.

Palladium-Item reporter Larry Price contributed to this story.

FOND DU LAC • WISCONSIN

Officer discovers damage

A police officer on patrol found four plate glass windows broken at the McDonald's restaurant, 929 E. Johnson St., early Dec. 11. The windows were possibly hit with ball bearings. An inflatable figure on the roof of the restaurant was also deflated.

THE MILITANT VEGAN
Issue #6 out in July

The Militant Vegan

#6

August 1994

THE MILITANT VEGAN - ISSUE NUMBER SI[illegible]

AUGUST 1994

Welcome to Militant Vegan #6! In this issue we bring you reports from sev[illegible] of direct action for anima[illegible] clippings and updates of news affecting us and the animals, and more! Pramiering [illegible] a direct action comic w[illegible] tactical and safety information. We hope you enjoy everything and please rememb[illegible] distribute! We are happy [illegible] say that circulation of this magazine has now reached many countries all over the [illegible] the people who have ma[illegible] copies. So, for the animals, let's get the word out!

If you are new to vegan ideas and want to save animals, we recommend reading [illegible] America by John Robbins [illegible] starters, and contacting PETA at PO Box 42516 / Washington DC 20015 for recip[illegible] about animal abuse. Av[illegible] all the overpriced health food stores, as Asian and Indian groceries have better [illegible] prices. Copy recipes out [illegible] cookbooks at libraries and bookstores.

While this magazine focuses on the fight for animal liberation, we fully suppor[illegible] campaigns for human rig[illegible] and non-animal environmental issues. We don't stand for any particular ideology [illegible] compassion, responsibil[illegible] justice, and so on. We encourage the movement to attract people from many d[illegible] grounds. Also, though we are [illegible] direct action magazine, we believe there is room for many different types of activis[illegible] rights movement, and supp[illegible] *all* those who are working towards a cruelty-free world in whatever way they can.

The Militant Vegan is not an ALF support group, and we make no contact wit[illegible]. This is to ensure that we c[illegible] continue publishing the good news of animal liberation. So if you see articles abou[illegible] a member of an ALF c[illegible] send the clipping or an anonymous, untraceable report of your actions to the N[illegible] Support Group / PO B[illegible] 8673 / Victoria, BC / V86 3S2 Canada. The Coalition to Abolish the Fur Trade [illegible] announced that they are a[illegible] interested in knowing about actions. You can send reports to C.A.F.T. / PO Box 40[illegible] / 38174.

In England, the ALFSG is at BCM 1160 / London, WC1N 3XX / England, and [illegible] magazine for prison[illegible] support (20$ a year for a subscription,) sell t-shirts and other items and take donat[illegible] prisoners. A separate ALF Pre[illegible] Office takes action claims and acts as a media spokesperson after raids. They can [illegible] ALF Press Office/ BM 44[illegible] London WC1N 3[illegible]. The Swedish ALF is at: DBF-[illegible] Animal Avengers [illegible] 02/ Astorp 2/ Sweden. T[illegible] Spanish ALF S[illegible] APDO: 50390/ 28080 Mad[illegible] SPAIN. The Isra[illegible] Group is at/ PO Box 6023/ [illegible] Aviv 6 1060/ ISR[illegible] ALF Supporters Group is at/ [illegible] Box 223/ 86-300 [illegible].

ANIMAL LIBERATION
BY ANY MEANS NECESSARY

To keep up w[illegible] subscribe to Out of the Ca[illegible] (14$ a year) at [illegible] Cruz, CA 95063. The b[illegible] animal liberation [illegible] is Arkangel ($15 a year, th[illegible] take U.S. cash) a[illegible] WC1N 3XX/ ENGLAND.

We hope you [illegible] remember that you can ma[illegible] difference!

The Militant Veg[illegible] that reports the known fa[illegible] about direct acti[illegible] do not intend to encoura[illegible] crime against an[illegible]. This magazine is for informatio[illegible] purposes only.

NEWS AND COMMENT

Two protesters were arrested July 2nd in Memphis after they locked themselves to the door of a Goldsmith's department store at a demo organized by the Coalition to Abolish the Fur Trade. Activists in Memphis are also publishing an inspiring newsletter.

The Memphis Three are still awaiting the result of their appeal of their conviction on four counts of attacking fur stores in 1992. They served three weeks of a yearlong sentence before being released on appeal last summer.

David Barbarash, wanted in Canada for ALF actions in Edmonton in 1991 and 1992, was arrested in Scotts Valley, California on May 9. He was driving along a road with activist Johnathan Paul following in another car when they were stopped at a roadblock by 30 local police and FBI agents. David was jailed and sent back to Canada, where he is awaiting trial for allegedly liberating cats from the Univeristy of Alberta and setting fish company trucks on fire. He can recieve letters at: David Barbarash/ Edmonton Remand Centre/ 9660-104 Ave./ Edmonton, Alberta/ T5H 4B5/ CANADA.

Darren Thurston, convicted of the same charges, was sent back to jail in May. He can receive letters at: Darren Thurston/ A-E #13/ Calgary Correctional Ctr./ Box 3250, Station B/ Calgary, AB/ T2M 4L9/ CANADA.

Kim Trimiew and Deb Stout are still in jail for refusing to testify to the Washington grand jury investigating the ALF. Write them separately at: Spokane County Jail/ West 1100 Mallon/ Spokane, WA 99260.

Vivien Smith, sentenced to six years in jail for burning scores of meat trucks in England, escaped a few months ago. Let's hope she stays free!

English Animal Liberation Prisoners would love to get letters from supporters in North America. Airmail costs 52 cents per ounce. Activists currently in prison are:

Terry Helsby EFO 761/ HMP Risley/ Warrington Road/ Risley, Warrington, Cheshire/ WA3 6BP/ ENGLAND.

Annette Tibbles TT2215/ HMP Holloway/ Parkhurst Road/ Holloway, London/ N7ONU ENGLAND.

Angie Hamp/ HMP Holloway/ Parkhust Road/ Holloway, London/ N7ONU ENGLAND.

Allison McKeon RE2370/ HMP Askham Grange/ Askham, Richard, York/ Y02 3PT/ ENGLAND.

Max Watson BJ2477/ HMP Haverigg/ Haverigg Camp/ Millom, Cumbria/ LA18 4NA/ ENGLAND.

SPATTER MATTER

Paint-filled balloons or ornaments have been used to "bloody" this huge sign in Woodbridge, N.J. On the third redecoration, rain drizzled the "blood" all over the coat. Surely Mother Nature doesn't appreciate the way furriers are harming her citizens.

Animal rights activist gets jail sentence

'Crimes of urban intimidation'

KATHLEEN ENGMAN
Legal Affairs Writer

Edmonton

An animal rights activist who kidnapped cats and fire-bombed fish company trucks had his suspended sentence replaced Thursday with two years less a day in jail.

"A free society cannot survive when zealots . . . deliberately break the law in an effort to impose their will on others by dangerous and unlawful intimidation," three Alberta Court of Appeal justices said in sentencing Darren Todd Thurston.

No matter how laudable their motives or how passionate their beliefs, such zealots undermine a free society, the justices said in a written judgment.

The justices said it's important to "indicate in the clearest possible terms that crimes of urban intimidation are totally inconsistent with the freedoms . . . of a democratic Canada.

"Those freedoms depend upon the recognition by every citizen of the rule of law."

Thurston pleaded guilty to arson, and break and enter with intent to commit an indictable offence. On Sept. 3, 1993, a Court of Queen's Bench justice gave him a suspended sentence, noting that he'd already spent 15 months in pre-trial custody. Other mitigating factors included Thurston's relative youth of 23 years, his guilty pleas, and no prior criminal record.

"The suspended sentence does not reflect the seriousness of the circumstances in which the offences were committed . . . The crimes had an element of urban intimidation to them," the justices said.

They also upheld the trial judge's order that Thurston pay $73,725 for property damage he caused.

Bryan Fallwell, owner of Billingsgate Fish Company Ltd., said he was pleased that Thurston's sentence had been increased. "I thought he got off much too lightly the first time."

If Thurston had picketed his store, he said he could have accepted it. "But to take it into a terrorist situation, it is criminal."

Thurston, a leader of the Animal Liberation Front, and accomplices had set fire to three Billingsgate trucks on Dec. 15, 1991. The fire spread. Ironically, about a dozen lobsters died because the fire caused a short in the water circulation system in their tanks.

Lives of firefighters were endangered because one of the trucks was fuelled with highly explosive propane. Total damage was $54,940. Scrawled on the walls were the words: "murder" "revenge" and "ALF."

Six months later, Thurston and accomplices broke into the University of Alberta's Bio Animal Kennel. Phone cords were cut, paint was splashed and files were strewn about. Twenty-nine cats valued at $44,350 were stolen. Scrawled on the walls were the messages: "We'll be back for the mice" and "No more." Damage there was $22,375.

On June 8, 1992, Thurston and others sent a communique to the media, along with pictures of two people holding cats and a banner reading "Free ALF." The communique to *The Edmonton Journal* said the group intended to set fire to a university building, but "unfortunately we ran out of time." It also said "Shut down your labs and re-introduce the prisoners to their native habitat. We won't stop until they do."

The justices added that Thurston's new sentence is not "by any means the maximum sentence which the court is prepared to impose in cases of dangerous and unlawful public intimidation."

IN THE HOME

When police searched Darren Todd Thurston's home on June 19, 1991, they found:

- **a 9-mm handgun loaded with 15 rounds of ammunition**
- **150 rounds of 9-mm ammunition**
- **128 rounds of 6.72-mm ammunition**
- **a gas mask**
- **two training grenades**
- **two bayonets**
- **police scanners**
- **an Animal Liberation Front publication on how to make incendiary bombs**
- **an Animal Liberation Front primer with an article on fire-bombing and delayed arson devices and another article on improvised weapons**

FBI joins probe into attacks on meat firms

Fires claimed to be work of animal-rights group

By PAT FLYNN
Staff Writer

The FBI has joined the investigation into a series of arson attacks, ostensibly committed by an animal-rights organization, against meat wholesalers in San Diego.

FBI spokeswoman Jan Caldwell said yesterday that she could not confirm the agency's involvement, but sources familiar with the investigation said the bureau has taken up the matter.

FBI agents yesterday interviewed John Cummins, owner of San Diego Meat Co. on C Street downtown, one source said.

Cummins' company was hit in the predawn hours Sunday by a fire that did $75,000 worth of damage to a building and its contents. The business also was attacked late Thursday night, when two of its refrigerated trucks were ignited with a flammable liquid.

Investigators looking into the Thursday-night incident found the slogan "Meat is Murder" spray-painted on the company's building as well as the acronym "f.a.r.m." Less than half an hour after the Thursday fire was set, a man claiming to represent an organization called the Farm Animal Revenge Militia called television station KUSI and claimed to have started the blaze.

The "Meat is Murder" slogan also was found in the aftermath of an Oct. 7 arson in Clairemont in which a van belonging to City Meat Co. was torched.

"We don't know of any organizatio
that name," said San Diego Fire Dep
ment Capt. Bob Landis of the Metro A
Strike Team. "We don't know whether
is one person with some problems or
hopes there is an organization.

"We're still in an investigation mo
Landis said, "trying to find out who
group is, what it stands for or whe
there's any credibility to the thought th
is a group."

Cummins, owner of San Diego M
said he senses that authorities beli
some sort of organization is responsible

"I feel it is (a group)," he said. "I d
think it's a nut, but they may be having
of their nuts working on it. To me, it's
organized group against eating farm
mals. The people who are working o
seem to think so."

Cummins said he has taken exten
security precautions at his site since
second attack and doesn't expect that
business will be struck again, but he sai
fears that other businesses may bec
targets.

"Anyone who's that violent or persis
is liable to pop up again," he said.

Mike Brown, president of City Meat
declined to discuss the Oct. 7 arson o
company's van and previous vandalism
volving the van.

"I really don't have any comme
Brown said. "The more this is public
the worse it makes it. My feeling is I w
sold produce in San Diego instead of m

Meanwhile, two animal-rights acti
disavowed violence in the name of
cause.

"Certainly personally, and as an org
zation, we don't feel those tactics are
propriate," said Florence Lambert o
Jolla. "I guess I would not consider
person being a true animal-rights per
We really are responsible people."

Lambert is founder and director o
Elephant Alliance and is active in o
animal-rights organizations here.

Lambert said the person or people
sponsible for the fires most likely are
the way-out fringe if they are involve
any animal group."

Wayne Pacelle, national director o
Fund for Animals, stressed that author
cannot take for granted that the arson
involved in animal-rights issues despite
slogans.

"We're all very skeptical of the clai
individuals involved in something like t
Pacelle said from his organization's o
in the Washington, D.C., area. "I n
heard of such a group before this. N
wish I'd never heard of them at all.

"We use legitimate means to pu
what we think are legitimate issues —
courts, legislatures and peaceful pro
Arson or that sort of thing are just ta
that shouldn't even be considered," he

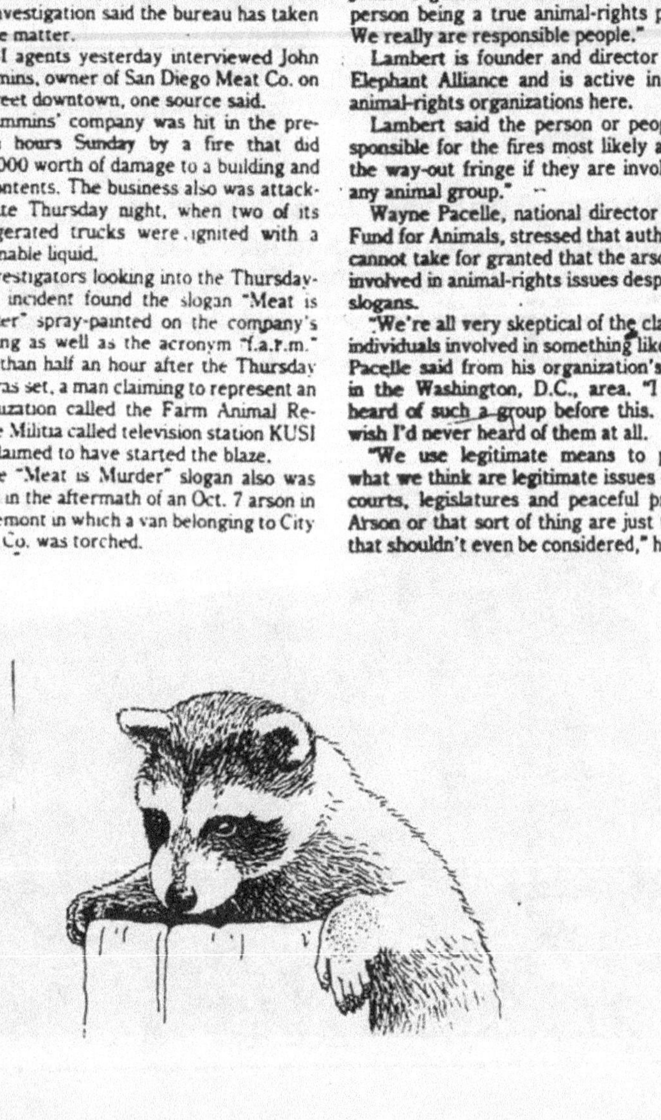

DIRECT ACTION FOR ANIMALS! PART 1
starring
Wendy & Ramona
This comic is for entertainment only. It is not intended to encourage crime.
It all Started at the World National Factory Farm Animal Rememberance Day Rally...
And so, fellow compassionate individuals, the time has come to speak out against inhumane treatment of animals. Against abusive farming procedures. blah blah blah blah blah...
Wendy! I haven't seen you all summer!
Hey Ramona! I might have expected to run into you here!
WHAT DO WE WANT?
WHEN DO WE WANT IT?
STOP THE MADNESS
I ♡ COWS
I HEAR THEIR SCREAMS
ZZZZ
ZZZ
Actually, I kind-of wonder what I'm doing here. These demos make me feel so hopeless.
Me too! I guess demonstrations are important, but why do they waste so much time on speeches, when everyone here already cares about animals?
Sign this petition?
STOP EATING ANIMA
Yeah - I'm sick of talk, talk, talk! The animal abusers don't even notice our rallys!
I wish someone would do something that would really have an effect on those monsters!
HUMANE FARMING NOW
Sign this petition
Anyone could hear what we're talking about... want to come over to my house?
Sure! Let's skip the candlelight vigil.
Get me out of here!
Sign this petition?
I hear the moos... I hear the clucks... I hear the gobbles... All together now!
END the HORROR
HUMANE FARMING NOW
WHAT DO WE WANT?
STOP THE MADNESS
GO VEGAN
Somehow I don't think we'll be missed.
Nope.

A few hours later...
So now we know what needs to be done... How do we locate good targets?
Since neither of us have cars, we can't really go out to the country where the factory farms are...
But we can hit the butcher shops!
Yeah! Do you have a yellow pages?
Meat 58
THE STEAK STORE
McGerris's Meat Co. -Our Specialty- ★ Veal ★
J&J Meats
SAUSAGE-R-US
Hey! This one is near my old high school!
Would it be a good target?
Well, there's an alley on one side of it where kids from school used to smoke...
VIS MEATS
That sounds good...
Oh, and it has big windows! About four of them!
Great. We'll smash the
It's a quiet neighborhood though. We'd wake up everybody.
Hmm. That's a problem. Wait! We could ruin the windows with glass-etching fluid.
What's that?
Artists and decorators use it to stencil designs on glass-but we can use it to ruin the butchers' windows with slogans! I'll just have to find a stained-glass supply store that has it, or maybe an art-supply or crafts store.
Perfect. I guess everything else we need - super glue for their locks, spray paint, heavy rubbe gloves, and a paint brush for the etching fluid - I can get a hardware store.
Great. Let's plan this for Sunday night, then, and if we have t change our plans, just remember to say nothing explicit over the phone...
That Sunday night...
We're almost there. Let's park our bikes and walk the rest of the way so we have another chance to check things out.
Good Idea.
I'm so glad we waited till 3AM! There's no-one out! I don't even see any lights on!
Shh! We have to whisper now!
Now... you look-out while I put superglue in the lock...

so far, so good...
IS MUR
Put the etcher and paintbrush away in my pack so you don't have to take off your own. Then you can take my spray-paint out at the same time.
Okay. Good idea!
MURDE
GLASS
mustn't forget to alter my printing...
Meat is Murder ALF
Now what?
Look out for me while I slash up this awning. Then let's go!
A few minutes later...
whew!
Weeks go by and the attacks continue...
Sheriff, what can you tell us about this wave of butcher-store vandalisms? Do the police have any leads?
Uh, we have reason to believe the attacks are perpetrated by people who do not eat meat!
This is an obviouslyattempt to discredit us! Mayhem and property destruction do nothing to help animals! Our "Sing Along for Animals" fundraising campaign, on the other hand...
SPOKESPERSON FOR LOCAL ANIMAL WELFARE GROUP
The vandalism has cost local butcher stores over $30,000! Insurance rates for meat shops in the area have skyrocketed!
Yeah!
Ha!
A few days later
Thanks for coming over! We can make plans for our next "party" and I wanted to show you a drawing I made... for a possible incendiary device.
Wow, really?
EARTH FIRST!
You know that big meat distribution place we checked out last week? Instead of our usual tactics, why not burn out one of their trucks?
Great? How?
AUGU
EARTH FIRST!
Look! We fill two plastic bottles - the cheap, thin kind - with kerosene, and tape them together with a kerosene soaked sponge between them. Then, we stick two incense sticks in the sponge and leave the whole thing in the cab of the truck!
BURNING INSENCE
PLASTIC BOTTLES WITH KEROSENE
SPONGE
TAPE
So, what we need to buy, preferably without touching them, are: insence, some bottled water, tape, a sponge, kerosene from the camping store, and a few lighters--in case one doesn't work.
I'll get a glass-cutter too. Then maybe we can cut the truck's window and avoid the noise of breaking it!

But Wendy, let's be extra careful this time. Let's buy secondhand shoes that are too big, and stuff the toes--just in case we leave footprints. Then we can just throw the shoes away afterwards.
Yeah. Let's buy some old clothes, too, so we don't leave anything--even a thread of carpet or a cathair, that could be traced back to us!
And don't forget to burn that drawing!
The following night...
ALLIED MEAT DISTRIBUTION, IN
ALLIED MEATS
ALLIED MEATS
Okay! The coast is clear! Go ahead and cut that window!
Right!
SKREEK
Good thing I wrapped the end of this hammer in tape... it's much quieter... Hey! This worked!
TAP
Okay! It's unlocke now!
click
So... now that the incense is lit, we should have about three minutes to get away before the real fire starts...
Wait a minute! Do you hear Singing?! It sounds like a bunch of people are coming!
My God! You're right! What could it be?!
Oh no! It's a candle light vigi And they're headed this way! What the heck are they doing out so late?
Those must've been some really long speeches beforehand!
ANIMA
Come on! We'd better just get out of here!
All we are saying... is give humane farming practices a chance...
ANIMAL PALS
A few minutes later... Here we are at the very site from which our slaughtered brothers and sisters are sent all over the city, and we must ask the question...
EEK! FIRE!
Aaak! We'll be discredited!
They'll think we started it! RUN!
EEK!
FACTORY FARMING STINKS
ALLI MEA
Get out of here!
HISS
To be Continued.

In the past couple of years as the vegan movement has rapidly grown, we have noticed an unfortunate trend among some younger segments of the movement. Using veganism as a way to appear tougher or better than other people may be helpful to those who are trying to determine their identities and their views, but in the end this hurts the movement as well as those individual activists. This article, then, is directed at these activists in the hope that they will learn from the larger movement and consider a more effective form of behavior.

It has become too commonplace for militant animal rights activists and vegans in general to scorn others who don't subscribe to their views, or even to snub vegetarians who aren't vegan [yet].
This article isn't meant as an attack on anyone who may be guilty of such behavior, and certainly isn't meant to promote harmful infighting, but is rather an attempt to bring up something which all of us as part of a growing movement need to think about.

We were all probably meat eaters once; and at some point of course we concluded that meat eating was wrong. Chances are, however, it wasn't an unfriendly and ridiculing vegan who convinced us of that. If any of us was influenced by another into making the switch, most likely it was by an exemplary, kind person with an open enough mind that they were not above explaining themselves to us. And of course, even if one of us was never influenced by anyone and was vegan his/her whole life, it wouldn't hurt him/her to try to be that kind of person. If we say that we respect all life (this is the basic tennant of animal rights philosophy) then we should show it in how we treat *everyone*. Let your personality be an affirmation of your beliefs!

Of course, all of us deal with frustration when encountering apathy and antagonism. And no, we probably shouldn't all just smile and nod when somebody starts bugging us about murdering lettuce (we've all heard that one, right?) We can make sure to always know the facts so that we can explain ourselves articulately and convincingly. But we must never assume that everyone is opposed to our ideals or is simply not worth our time. And Seeing all non-vegans as an ignorant mass awaiting conversion to a superior way of life is just as bad. Go about

with the intent to learn something new from another person every day, and you'll be surprised how soon people start wanting to hear what you have to say!

For the few of us for whom shyness or distrust *still* prevent from friendliness, here's a couple of reasons why personality makes a difference, from a strategic point of view:

1) **People are more likely to listen to you.** A friend used to joke that people she dated always went vegan after meeting her. True, perhaps they'd just never heard of veganism before that, but more likely it was because they admired her, and grew to admire her lifestyle. This just goes to show that people are more likely to be influenced enough by someone to make a serious change in their own lives if they *like* that person.

2) **Security.** What 's the oldest stereotype of the militant extremist? Cold, hard, and lacking in social skills or interest in anything besides their cause, right? Setting oneself apart as an extremist will not only make you stand out to the police but will aid them in their investigations. You will seem like an "obvious" direct activist in their eyes. Also, if you take the trouble to make lots of different types of friends, it won't seem so strange to your roommates or neighbors if you go out at all hours: they will assume you're attending social functions.

3) **You are the movement.** Our community is ever growing but still small enough that many people are still unknowlegable of what we stand for. We have no manifesto, so what it ultimately comes down to is that every militant animal rights activist is representative of the entire movement. What kind of movement that is depends on what kind of people we are. It's up to us whether our movement is a hateful, alienating, arrogant one, or an open-minded, caring, articulate, impressive one. Insuring the latter over the former does not make one less radical. It is nothing less than an important tactic on the path to a cruelty-free society.

DIARY OF ACTIONS

Every single night, the women and men of the Animal Liberation Front carry out direct action to stop animal cruelty at its sources somewhere in the world. England sees thousands of attacks a year, and ALF units are active across the industrialized world. Whether it's the Black Ravens in Russia, the DBF in Sweden, Animal Rescue in Japan, or the ALF in New Zealand, Canada, Israel, Poland, Italy, Spain, France, etc., the goal is the same: to liberate the suffering and destroy the property of those who kill for profit.

Note: The Diary of Actions is intended to report news of "illegal" actions to save animals, not to encourage crime. All reports listed come from movement and opposition publications, internet bulletin boards, mainstream media, and local 'zines. There is probably a lot we missed, since we obviously cannot read every small 'zine out there. To help get out the news of direct action, send reports and clippings to Out of the Cages/ PO Box 2960/ Santa Cruz, CA 95063

INTERNATIONAL ACTIONS

In **Sweden**, the *Animal Avengers* set three meat trucks on fire. In **England**, several actions happen every day and it would be impossible to list them all. Some highlights from the *ALF* include the burning of a meat truck in London, an arson attack on a vivisection company in London, arson attacks in three cities on a chain store that tests on animals, a stallion liberated in Swale, 58 hens liberated in London, 10 puppies liberated in Hants, and numerous vehicles trashed. The *Justice Department* sent more real and hoax letter bombs to animal abusers, all of which were disarmed by the police. The *Poultry Liberation Organization* carried out a contamination hoax that cleared eggs off store shelves in Brighton and left a device that exploded at night in an egg store in Bexhill. The *Hunt Retribution Squad* placed incendiary devices in the offices of a hunting magazine in Windsor. In **Northern Ireland**, letter bombs were mailed to hunting magazines and hunting clubs, all of which were disarmed by the police.

UNITED STATES

Here are a few more actions from the past few months that we did not know about for #4 or #5:

October 7, 1993-Clairemont, CA- A van belonging to the City Meat Co., which had been previously attacked, was set on fire. "Meat is Murder" was painted at the scene. *Farm Animal Revenge Militia*

January 28-San Diego, CA- Two vans belonging to the San Diego Meat Company were set on fire. *Farm Animal Revenge Militia*

January 30-San Diego, CA- The *Farm Animal Revenge Militia* broke into the San Diego Meat Company through a boarded-over window and set the building on fire. Damages were $75,000, and "F.A.R.M." and "Meat is Murder" were painted on the walls.

February 12-Syracuse, NY- A bucket of paint was thrown on the front of a fur store.

MARCH 1994-MAY 1994

March-New Jersey- Unspecified actions against animal abusers.

March?-Woodbridge, NJ- A fur billboard was splattered with red paint three times.

March-San Francisco Bay Area, CA- Hanes Furs received glued locks, a sign partially smashed, and slogans painted in front of the store. A Honey Baked Hams received a glued front door lock, glass etch on the windows, and slogans all over the store front. A butcher shop received glass etch on the windows and spray painted slogans. A milk ad on the street was smashed. A McDonalds received a smashed window. A sheep skin store received two broken windows. Robert's Furs received a glued lock and painted slogans. The Harris Steak House received glued locks, painted slogans, and etched windows. Two trucks at Robert's Corned Beef received slashed tires, painted slogans, etched or broken windows, and one had its locks glued. *ALF*

late March-Cleveland, OH- The ALF broke into a meat packing plant and caused serious damage to equipment and supplies. Security cameras filmed the masked activists, and the footage was shown on local tv stations. Apparently, the police have questioned local animal rights supporters, but no arrests have been made. *ALF*

April-Pueblo, CO- Animal abuse billboards were spray painted.

April 5-San Francisco, CA- A McDonalds had slogans spray painted on its walls and smeared onto its windows with etching cream. *ALF*

April-23? (Earth Day)- San Jose and San Francisco, CA- Durham's Meat in San Jose and Columbus Sausage and Meat were hit by the ALF in an effort to radicalize Earth Day. Four trucks were severely damaged at Durham's. *ALF*

April 28-San Francisco, CA- A restaurant is hit because it serves live lobster. Windows etched, locks glued. *Crustacean Liberation Front*

May 1-West Hollywood, CA- Display window of Contemporary Hides smashed. Increased police patrols and surveillance have limited our number of actions. *ALF November 26 Cell*

May-Oakland, CA- Butchers and fish shops are attacked. *ALF*

May-Newtown, PA- Ham Sweet Ham had its windows shot out. *ALF*

May-Southhampton, PA- A fur store had its windows shot out. *ALF*

May-Washington D.C.- A fur store had a ball bearing shot through their display window. *U.S. Congressional Cell*

the diary of actions is continued on page 11...

Under fire: *San Diego Meat Co. saw $75,000 in damage from yesterday morning's arson, the second there since Thursday*

Anti-fur protesters targeted Goldsmith's Department Store Saturday. About 30 protesters showed up, including this pa who chained themselves to doors before being hauled off b store security personnel.

Meat firm arson sets off search for group

UNION-TRIBUNE

City fire investigators are probing whether a radical animal rights group is linked to arson early yesterday that caused $75,000 damage to the San Diego Meat Co. in downtown San Diego.

The fire came just three days after another blaze at the same location destroyed two refrigeration trucks for delivering meat to restaurants.

Fire Capt. Bill Middleton of the Metro Arson Strike Team said someone broke into the meat business early yesterday by pulling boards off a window. A flammable liquid was splashed around and a fire started in two rooms.

Investigators discovered graffiti that read "Meat is Murder" and "f.a.r.m." spray-painted on the building. The same phrases were painted on a Clairemont meat company van that was torched Oct. 7, authorities said.

After the Clairemont fire, a man who claimed to be part of the Farm Animal Revenge Militia called a San Diego TV station to claim responsibility for the crime, said fire investigators.

"We're looking at a group ... that is apparently trying to have a movement or have some presence in the community by advocating that the purchase and serving of meat is somehow related to murdering animals," Middleton said.

The fire was reported at 1:14 a.m. and under control within a half-hour, a dispatcher said. The fire caused $60,000 in damage to the C Street building and $15,000 to its contents.

McDonalds vandalized

Someone shot six windows at McDonalds, 699 S. Military Road, with a BB gun between midnight and 3:35 a.m. June 1. The vandals also spray painted "meat is murder" on the side of the restaurant.

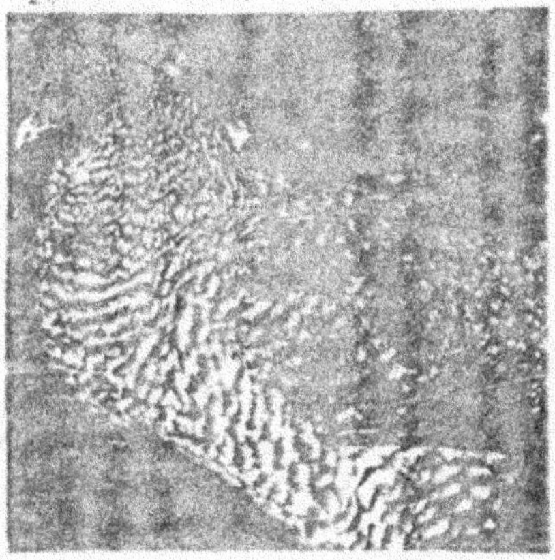

Reward offered for information about vandalism

The Fond du Lac Police Department, and McDonald's are offering a $700 reward for information leading to the arrest of the person or persons responsible for vandalism to the restaurant at 699 S. Military Road.

Between 11:30 p.m. May 31 and 3:30 a.m. June 1 someone shattered seven windows and spray painted an exterior wall, according to the police report. The windows were shattered by ball bearings which apparently were fired at the building with a sling shot.

Fur boycotters at store charged

Two 19-year-old members local animal rights group cuffed themselves to the doors of Goldsmith's de ment store in Oak Court Ma urday while urging custome boycott the store because it fur coats.

Forrest Bobbitt and Matt lard were detained by smith's security officers an er charged with vandalism disorderly conduct. They are banned from all Goldsm locations, officers said.

Security officers said th alition to Abolish the Fur T which has about 100 membe Memphis, has protested a store twice before but "Th never gone this far."

Nearly 30 people particip in the two-hour protest. bers of the group say they continue to stage protests a store until it is "fur-free."

—*Audrey Will*

DIARY OF ACTIONS CONTINUED

May-Silver Spring, MD- A Gillette billboard was spray painted with "Gillette Kills Animals" for their continued use of animals in product testing. *U.S. Congressional Cell*

May 25- Santa Cruz, CA- Buildings where vivisection takes place on the UC campus were spray painted with slogans including "ALF." *ALF*

May 31- Fond Du Lac, WI- A McDonald's had six windows shattered and "Meat is Murder" spray painted on a wall. The local paper reported that there was a $700 reward offered for the attackers. *ALF*

June-Kensington, MD- A Roy Rogers/ Hardees fast food restaurant had "Meat is Murder" spray painted on their wall and a brick delivered through their window. More to come... *U.S. Congressional Cell*

June-Oakland, CA- A butcher shop had "ALF" etched on its windows in very large letters. The shop, located in a crowded shopping district, has visible damage from previous attacks. *ALF*

AND NOW A FEW WORDS FROM THE ANIMAL ABUSERS...

A WORD ABOUT THE ENDANGERED SPECIES ACT.

THE ENDANGERED SPECIES ACT IS COMING UP THIS SPRING FOR REAUTHURIZATION IN THE UNITED STATES CONGRESS. THIS LAW HAS BEEN USED BY THE ANIMAL RIGHTS NUTS TO HAMPER THE SALES OF BOBCAT & OTTER PELTS IN SHIPMENTS OUT OF THE USA. THEY ALSO WANT TO PUT BUGS, BEATLES, WORMS & GOD KNOWS WHAT NEXT. IF ANY OF THESE THINGS ARE FOUND ON YOUR LAND OR WHERE YOU FISH, TRAP OR HUNT, YOU WILL BE BARRED FROM USING THAT LAND. TELL YOUR CONGRESSMAN YOUR FEELINGS ON THIS NUTTY ISSUE. ASK HIM TO VOTE FOR THE COMMON SENSE AMMENDMENT ON THE ENDANGERED SPECIES ACT.

XIII. CREATION AND VIEW OF HUNTING

We believe God created the cosmos, and planet earth as a beautiful habitation for mankind. We believe man, God's special creation, was given dominion over the earth, to partake of, and govern all its resources wisely. We further believe that the art of hunting with bow and arrow is a time proven means of human survival and resource management and that it is in harmony with the divine plan.

Gen. 1:1-31; Gen 9:2,3; Gen. 10:9; Gen. 27:3

JOIN TODAY!

For more information call or write:

ABUNDANT WILDLIFE SOCIETY OF NORTH AMERICA
12665 Hwy 59 N • Gillette, WY 82716
(307) 682-2826

CHRISTIAN
BOWHUNTERS
OF
AMERICA
JOHN 3:16

Then along came Environmentalism, a view that nature and natural forces should be the dominating force of change. It is a concept that Nature is "god", and man is no more or less than any other living creature in the natural flow of events. This new philosophy was based upon several tenets:

4. Man must reject all of modern technology and call for a return to a simple, pastoral life free of fumes, artificial chemicals, and any noise but the chirping of birds and the croaking of frogs

6. Most environmental groups, with no regard for truth, use misinformation to further their agendas and are anti-God, anti-American and anti-gun (in the hands of law-abiding citizens). ABUNDANT WILDLIFE SOCIETY believes America is the greatest nation on earth, that its greatness is due to its Christian heritage, and that guns in the hands of law-abiding citizens are the best means of restraint against the tyranny of government.

6. To share the common joy and experience of bowhunting with other Christian bowhunters.

Send to: Christian Bowhunters of America, Treasurer
351 West North St., Carlisle, PA 17013

THE MILITANT VEGAN-NEXT ISSUE OUT IN OCTOBER

animal liberation

the militant vegan

november 1994

issue# 7

OPEN SEASON ON THE FUR TRADE

rod coronado arrested * 1994's record year of actions * action report from finland * prisoner support, press clippings, news, and more!

The Militant Vegan - Issue Seven
November 1994

We're proud to say that the Militant Vegan has reached issue seven; it has far surpassed anyone's initial expectations. At the outset, only twenty-five copies were produced. Now the Militant Vegan is distributed to a number of countries around the world, well beyond the scope of its humble beginnings. The far reaching circulation of this magazine is due not to the comparatively small mailing we give it following production, but because of the amount of recirculation you give it. Keep up the good work! By xeroxing the Militant Vegan and distributing it at demos, shows, and through the mail, you get the word out to thousands of people. Feel free to sell copies as a fundraiser for your group, as many people have done. As long as more people know about the plight of the animals and know that there is something they can do about it, the better off the animals will be!

If you want to take the most important step to save animals and are wondering about veganism, we suggest you pick up Diet for a New America by John Robbins and contact any one of a number of groups devoted to the issue of veganism. One such group is PETA (P.O. Box 42516 Washington DC 90015,) which is more than willing to send you recipes and information on veganism. Literature on vegan cooking and nutrition can be found, and easily copied, at most bookstores and nearly all health food stores. You can avoid the high prices at health food stores by shopping at Asian and Indian groceries.

When the Militant Vegan was started there was a void in terms of magazines focusing on direct action on behalf of animals. Now, however, there are other good sources of this information available. If you are interested in the active defence of animals we recommend you look at the newsletter of the North American ALF supporters group, "Underground," which you can get for $3 from the NA-ALFSG (P.O. Box 8673, Victoria, BC, Canada V8W 3S2, e-mail: un028@freenet.victoria.bc.ca). They also run a literature distribution from which you can order lots of great booklets and magazines (including back issues of the Militant Vegan.) The

> **Note**: The Militant Vegan is a news magazine that reports the known facts about direct action for animals. We do not intend to encourage crime against animal torturers and killers. Thismagazine is for information only.

He Knows If You've Been Bad or Good

ALFSG also badly needs donations for prisoner support.

The Militant Vegan is not an ALF support group, so w make no contact with illegal units. This is to guarantee that w are able to continue reporting the good news of animal liber tion. If you see any articles about direct action or are a memb of an ALF cell, send clippings or an untraceable report of yo actions to the NA-ALFSG. You might also want to send info mation to the Coalition to Abolish the Fur Trade (CAFT, P.C Box 40641, Memphis, TN, 38174.)

The English ALFSG is at BCM 1160, London, WC1 3XX, England, and they print a quarterly magazine for prison support ($20 a year), sell t-shirts and other items, and take d nations for ALF prisoners. A separate ALF Press Office tak action reports and acts as a media spokesperson after raids. Th can be contacted at ALF Press Office, BM 4400, London WC1 3XX, England. The Swedish ALFSG is at DBF - Animal Aven ers, P.O. Box 2051, S-265 02, Astorp2, Sweden. The Spanis APDO, 50390, 28080 Madrid, Spain. The Israeli: P.O. Box 602 Tel Aviv 6 1060, Israel. The Polish: P.O. Box 223, 86- Grudziadz 1, Poland.

A good way to keep up with the movement is to su scribe to "Arkangel," the best animal liberation magazine aroun at BCM 9240, London, WC1N 3XX, England ($15 a year, th take U.S. cash). Don't forget "Underground" for keeping abrea as well (address above).

If this issue of the Militant Vegan is as enjoyable as t last please pass it along to your friends. Remember, you c make a difference!

NEWS AND COMMENT

od Coronado, perhaps the North American movement's best known spokes-rson, was arrested on the Pascua Yaqui reservation on September 28th. Rod s charged on connection with fires set at Michigan State in 1992, and has aded capture for the fourteen months since the issue of a warrant for his est. Please refer to page 4 for more information on Rod, and write him at: d Coronado F4445, Newaygo County Jail, PO Box 845,White Cloud, MI 349. A group has formed to support him at :Rod Coronado Support Com-ttee, PO Box 1891, Tucson, AZ 85702.

se Olsen, accused of attempting to burn a fur billboard in July of 1992 in icago, was recently convicted and sentenced to two years in jail. Because suffers from chronic fatigue syndrome, there is an appeal to have her clas-ed as minimum security. Anyone wishing to write on her behalf should d letters to Howard Peters III, Director, Illinois Department of Correc-ns, 1301 Concordia Court PO x 19277, Springfield, IL 62794 77. Letters to Lise should be t to: Lise Olsen, B48426, PO x 5001, Dwight, IL 60420, or ite to the NA-ALFSG (address facing page).

rren Thurston, convicted for F actions in Edmonton in 1991 l 1992, is serving a four year tence following a March appeal the Crown. Write to him at: rren Thurston, Fort katchewan Correctional Facil- Bag 10, 7802-101 St., Fort skatchewan, AB, T8L 2P3, nada.

vid Barbarash has been re-sed after being arrested on the ne charges.

n Trimiew and Deb Stout e also been released after be- held for refusing to testify be- a Washington grand jury.

rjeet Aujla was charged in ly June with "conspiracy to se explosions." Write him at: jeet Aujla, HMP Birmingham, nston Green Road, Birming-n, B18 4AS, England; 011-44- -554-3838.

ry Helsby, Allison Mckeon, and Max Watson have been convicted ear- this year for vandalizing butchers' shops and a zoo. Write them at, respec-ely: Terry Helsby EF0761, HMP Risley, Warrington Road, Risley, rrington, Cheshire, WA3 6BP, England; Allison Mckeon RE2370, HMP ham Grange, Askham, Richard York, Y02 3PT, England; and Max Watson 477, HMP Haverigg, Haverigg Camp, Millom, Cumbria, LA18 4NA, En-d.

nette Tibbles is serving four years on a "conspiracy to commit arson" con-ion. Write her at: Annette Tibbles TT2215, HMP Holloway, Parkhurst Road, loway, London, N7 0NU, England.

Angie Hamp and Keith Mann, underground ALF activists, were arrested at an animal sanctuary in the spring of 1994. They can receive mail at, respectively: Angie Hamp TW1687, HMP Holloway, Parkhurst Road, Holloway, London, N7 0NU, England; and Keith Mann, HMP Manchester, 1 Southall Street, Manchester, M60 9 AH, England.

Vivien Smith, the longtime English ALF activist who escaped from prison earlier this year, remains underground.

Six Hunt Sabs were arrested in England in early November. The arrests have occurred under section 68 of the new Criminal Justice Act of 1994, which aims to stop the success of hunt sabbing in shutting down hunts across the U.K. For more information, write: Hunt Saboteurs Association, PO Box 1, Carlton, Nottingham, NG4 2JY, England.

Two *legal* blows to the fur industry. The November 9th elections in Arizona saw the banning of commercial trapping on public land through the passage of Proposition 201. Voters in Oregon approved Ballot Measure 18 which bans the hunting of bearsover bait and the hunting of bears and cougars with hounds. Hopefully we'll soon see propositions to ban fur farming!

Pressure pays off, judging by the number of businesses that have decided not to handle fur any more. In Memphis, Tennessee, Jack Lewis Furs has gone out of business after years of actions. In New York, the Limited, Fontana, and Campaign have decided not to line the collars of their coats with fur following ALF activity in that city. Think of what could be accomplished if more people got out there and did something about these animal exploiters!

Fur Free Friday is November 25th, and the National Activist Network and Coalition to Abolish the Fur Trade plan to turn up the pressure with CD actions in at least 15 cities.

The North American ALFSG office in Victoria was recently broken into, with their computer and other equipment stolen. Fortunately, they had backup discs and no information was lost. However, they are more than ever in need of large donations, so please send them whatever you can.

California Hunt Sabs will be back in action November 18-20 in the northern part of the state to stop black bear hunting.

Canadian hunt sabs recently stopped a goose hunt by using air horn to scare the flock from the hunters.

This summer, five activists in Syracuse, New York were arrested in a CD outside a fur store, and a CD was held outside a fur store in Minneapolis as well. Arkansas saw its first radical protests ever as well this summer, with fur store owners having to lock their doors to keep out the demonstrators.

Hunt sab support is going on right now in Minneapolis for fifteen activists recently arrested in a sab. They're scheduled to go to trial on December 5th and are in need of donations for their legal defense. Anyone interested in contributing should contact SOAR 235 CMU, 300 Washington Ave. SE, Minneapolis, MN, 55455. SOAR has also had several members arrested at recent CD's at fur stores and a McDonalds.

ROD CORONADO ARRESTED

On September 28, 1994, longtime activist Rod Coronado was arrested in Tucson, Arizona, where he was living under an assumed name on the Yaqui tribal reservation. Charged with the February 28, 1992 ALF raid on Michigan State University fur farm researcher Richard Aulerich, Coronado was extradited to Michigan and will be held under charges that could put him in jail for 50 years. As the target of a nationwide manhunt by the FBI and the BATF and five federal grad juries, Rod's arrest will undoubtedly be held as a victory by those who slaughter animals and destroy the environment.

But how did the 28 year old activist come to be such an important figure in the movement? As many are aware, his long years of hard work and seemingly heroic deeds have been an inspiration to fight harder and longer for animals and the earth. Rod Coronado grew up in Morgan Hill, California, just south of San Jose. Even as a child, he loved animals, sculpting whales and "taking special care of the family pets," according to his father. A 1986 San Francisco Chronicle article described how he sent $150, "his entire savings account," to Greenpeace and other environmental groups. After graduating from high school, he joined the Sea Shepherds in Vancouver, Canada and was soon sailing on missions in defense of whales. In a spectacular attack in November 1986, Coronado and a friend went to Iceland undercover and on one night sunk two whaling ships, half the nation's fleet, and smashed the whale processing plant's equipment and computers to the tune of two million dollars damage. Iceland has never resumed whaling since that day.

After another Sea Shepherd anti-whaling campaign which got him banned from the Faroe Islands, Rod and two fellow activists formed an ALF cell to hit fur stores in Vancouver. Smashing windows and throwing paint all over the furs, the numerous attacks forced two stores out of business. Unfortunately, a passerby one night saw the ALF activists' van and they were arrested. Coronado jumped bail, and there is still a Canadian warrant for his arrest for this incident. His dedication at this time period can be shown in a March 1988 article in the Santa Clara Valley Metro, where he describes the animal liberation and environmental movements as the same and explains, "It's war," to a reporter's question about ALF actions. For the next two years, he continued to serve on Sea Shepherd campaigns, but decided to quit mainstream groups in 1990 for a new project.

In a front cover article for the EF! Journal in 1991, "Freedom for Fur Farm Prisoners," Rod described his campaign with his Coalition Against Fur Farms where he infiltrated the fur farm industry, giving the movement valuable information on that filthy trade. Posing as someone interested in learning the ways of the industry, he filmed a fur farmer breaking a mink's neck; this footage was used by CBS's 60 Minutes program and was seen by millions of viewers. After buying a fur farm ranch from a farmer, he and fellow activists spent long months rehabilitating the fur farm animals, and successfully re-introduced them into the wild. This action was an important step in the growing cooperation between the radical environmental and animal liberation movements.

In June 1991, the ALF began a devastating campaign against the fur farm industry, beginning with an arson attack on the Experimental Fur Farm at Oregon State University. The farm closed forever and records on fur farmers were taken. Five days later, a million dollar blaze hit a mink foods cooperative in Edmonds, Washington, a major player in the ability of fur farmers to increase their yields and genetically alter the wildlife they imprison and slaughter. Two months later, Washington State was raided by the ALF, with numerous animals liberated and a fur farm researcher's data destroyed in a pool of acid on his office floor. In December, a $119,000 blaze destroyed the mink processing plant of a fur farm in Yamhill, Oregon. Then in February, over $100,000 damage was done at Michigan State and 30 years of research was destroyed. Aulerich is a major ally of the fur trade, and at this point the FBI and BATF stepped up their efforts to defeat the ALF. In May, the BATF sent a helicopter with an armed squad to Coronado's cabin in southern Oregon, but Rod went underground and was not found for over two years despite the manhunt. He was targeted for the raids because he wrote the press release for the WSU attack; Rod says he was acting only as spokesperson for the ALF. Despite the grand juries impaneled to stop the ALF, Utah State's Animal Damage Control Program research lab was hit in October 1992, with coyotes liberated, the field station set on fire, the head researcher's office bombed, and proof of illegal dumping of radioactive animal corpses revealed to the public. The government blamed Rod for this raid as well.

When he was caught, Coronado was acting as a guide for troubled Native American youth on the reservation, taking them on trips to the wilderness. During his years underground, his many press releases and articles inspired many activists and were partly responsible for the new animal liberation/environmental activism around the country. Rod needs all the support he can get during his trial, so we encourage everyone out there to write him c/o the North American ALFSG with letters of support and donations for his trial. As far as we at the Militant Vegan are concerned, Rod Coronado is as great an American hero as Martin Luther King Jr. and he deserves as much support as possible.

Up in smoke. *Aulerich surveys the damage.*

Rod Coronado #F4445
Newaygo County Jail
PO Box 845
White Cloud, MI 49349

Boots

BOMB SCENE: A policeman guards the wrecked Boots shop

Militants' terror trail

By KATHRYN LISTER

NIMAL rights campaigners have been re active in the past 12 months than y other time in their 18-year history. And none more so than the Animal eration Front, which caused £15 mil- n worth of damage last year.

Scotland Yard says the group has de more than 400 incendiary attacks ce the late 80s.

The ALF has even produced a manual scribing how to make timed incendi- devices and petrol bombs, and how t to damage vehicles, locks and tele- one lines.

The 2,000-strong group was founded Ronnie Lee in 1976 after he was eased from a three-year jail sentence arson. Lee — freed again from prison years ago for plotting fire-raising acks on department stores — described animal laboratories and factory farms as "the concentration camps of the human Reich".

The group's toll of havoc includes £20,000 of damage when members attacked vehicles at a Bristol dairy.

Firebombs also caused £65,000 damage at a meat depot in Bournemouth and £100,000-worth at a pork pie factory in Reading. In the West Midlands a meat company lost 10 refrigerated lorries worth £500,000.

Ten years ago the ALF claimed to have poisoned Mars bars in protest at tooth-decay experiments on monkeys — a hoax which cost the manufacturers more than £3 million.

Police find three shop fire bombs

By Colin Wright

POLICE investigating five early morning fires at stores and shops in Harrogate and York recovered three incendiary devices which, it is believed, were planted by animal rights militants.

Two Boots stores and an outlet of Fads — DIY subsidiary of the company — were damaged along with a gun shop and an Imperial Cancer Research shop between 1 am and 4 am yesterday.

Devices were recovered from the Boots and Fads out- ... York and from the Imperial Cancer Research shop in Harrogate. They were being examined last night.

North Yorkshire police have contacted Scotland Yard's anti-terrorist branch, which maintains a database of animal rights groups. The force was also liaising with police in Hampshire, Thames Valley and Cambridge, where in recent months there have been similar fires for which animal rights groups have admitted responsibility.

A police spokesman said last night that no group had admitted blame for the five fires which caused considerable damage to two outlets.

The Boots store in Harrogate suffered significant damage to its first floor although the outlet in York was not badly affected and opened for business.

The most serious threat was posed by the fire at Fads where hundreds of gallons of paint and inflammable material are kept. The store was badly damaged.

Boots has been a target of several animal rights attacks since last year and incendiary devices have been recovered from fire-damaged outlets throughout the country.

A company spokesman said: "We have suffered attacks recently for which animal rights activists have claimed responsibility."

NEWS photo Cindy Goodman

RED PAINT is cleaned from the exterior of a North Vancouver house. A business selling furs was the target of anti-fur forces. The vandalism resulted in extensive cleaning work.

Animal protesters send five bombs

MARY BRAID

MAL rights extremists are be- d to be responsible for parcel b attacks yesterday on four panies associated with the trade. Three people suffered or injuries.

ter the incidents in Kent, cestershire, Oxfordshire and burgh, a fifth bomb was made at a London branch of Boots, chemist. The attacks all oc- d within two hours.

otland Yard said anti-terrorist ers were involved in investiga- . Robin Webb, spokesman for nimal Liberation Front, said lieved the bombings were the of the Justice Department, ewest and most violent ani rights group, which has ed responsibility for 32 bombs sent to laboratories, meat trade employees and hunt supporters since October. Before Christmas, the group sent 13 parcel bombs to scientists and suppliers of animals to laboratories. Two exploded and 11 were made safe.

In the first explosion yesterday a 12-inch cylindrical package blew up at Graham Gilder, a haulage firm, in Elmstone Hardwicke, near Cheltenham, Gloucestershire. A second parcel bomb was found at Peter Gilder Haulage, 16 miles away at Bourton-on-the-Water. Later, a device exploded at the headquarters of the ferry operators Stena Sealink, in Ashford, Kent. A secretary suffered minor cuts. The companies are involved in the transportation of animals.

A man suffered injuries at the Pig Improvement Company, Fyfield Wick, near Abingdon, when a poster tube exploded, and another man received hospital treatment after a package exploded at Ross Breeders, a chicken breeding plant at Newbridge, Edinburgh.

£2m animal fire attacks

Detectives are probing the involvement of activists in the series of blazes, Hampshire police said today.

Portsmouth animal rights campaigner Lin Sandell said today the attacks would continue.

"The reason it is done is because we are all against vivisection," she said.

"We want it to stop and we have to take direct action because the government is doing nothing."

Oxford disrupted by firebombers

ANIMAL rights activists disrupted the centre of Oxford yesterday when two incendiary devices they planted in city centre stores went off. Three others failed to ignite.

Detectives confirmed that the attacks on stores selling leather and woollen goods had the hallmarks of animal rights activists. They came after three similar attacks in Cambridge recently where the Animal Rights Militia attacked a leather shop, Boots the Chemist and a woollens shop. The first floor of Boots was severely damaged by a device believed to be the size of an audio cassette.

A spokesman for the Animal Liberation Front said yesterday: "The Animal Rights Militia claimed responsibility for the Cambridge attacks and said it was the beginning of a campaign in towns and cities across England against all forms of animal abuse. This could be the second wave of a new campaign." Police were alerted early yesterday when a blast was heard at C H Brown and Son, a leather shop in Oxford's covered market.

The explosion started a fire in the ground floor of the shop and caused heavy smoke in nearby stores. The workshop was flooded, causing thousands of pounds of damage, after a sprinkler system was activated. Two more devices were later discovered, at a furrier and a leather shop.

Shortly before 8am another device was found at West World and two hours later staff at the Edinburgh Wool Shop raised the alarm after a fire broke out. At one stage a large area of the city centre was sealed off but was re-opened during the rush hour.

Chief Inspector Laurie Fray, of Thames Valley Police, said: "All the indications are that some animal rights activist group are behind this. We do not know who because no-one has claimed responsibility."

Activist pledges attacks will be continued

BACKGROUND

By CLIVE SIMPSON

The News

Firebombs on the Isle of Wight last night are the latest in a series of terror campaign attacks by animal rights campaigners to hit the south.

Arsonist sought in horse buggy blazes

Carriage firm out of business

Darryl Fears

WRITER

Fire officials are still search- for the arsonist who torched horse-drawn carriages at a hwest Atlanta company day.

re Department spokesman Szymanski declined to ulate on whether the 4:51 blaze at Capitol City Car- Co. at 319 Walker St. was omly set, or the work of ani- rights activists, or compet-

tlanta's controversial e-and-buggy industry has been under fire from area al protectionists, who say orses are treated poorly.

ve white carriages were oyed under the tin roof at Capitol City Carriages, h sits on the same block as nshirah Horse Drawn Carriage Co. at 313 Walker St. The fire put Capitol City owners Edward Gates and Will Johnson out of business.

"There was a diversion created to occupy the guard dogs," Szymanski said. "A fire was set in each carriage." No horses were injured.

Four years ago, the Atlanta Equestrian Society reported that horse-and-buggy owners feed, train and maintain their horses poorly, prompting legislation that placed carriage horses under the authority of veterinarians in the state Department of Agriculture.

Five buggy companies operate about 25 carriages in the city, according to Atlanta's Bureau of Taxicabs and Vehicles for Hire, which regulates the trade for the city.

Capitol City Carriages, started 10 years ago by Gates and Johnson, accounted for a fifth of the 10 buggies that operate on Downtown streets and hotels each weekend.

Animal Lib attack on lab

Vandals daub red paint on workers' homes

Rabbit farm shutdown forced by rights groups

'You can't keep looking for bombs under cars'

By David Banks

Daily Post Staff

A CHESHIRE rabbit farm is ceasing trading because of the activities of animal rights groups.

Hylyne Rabbits is going into voluntary liquidation following a series of actions by the Animal Liberation Front and other animal rights groups.

The farm at Statham, Lymm, recently suffered £25,000 worth of damage in an arson attack, a parcel bomb has been sent to it and rabbits have been stolen in raids.

Hylyne director Edwin Sutton said: "You can't carry on when you've got to keep looking under your car to see if there's a bomb.

"We haven't gone bankrupt," said Mr Sutton. "We've got plenty of money. I'm just not prepared to put my staff through all this.

"It is an absolute disaster, but we can't carry on."

It was the continuing threats of ALF action and the spiralling insurance costs which prompted Mr Sutton's decision to go into liquidation.

Animal rights groups are jubilant.

A spokesman for the ALF called it a "victory for the rabbits".

The ALF claimed responsibility for the raids last May and September and for the arson attack last month.

Responsibility for the parcel bomb was claimed by the Justice Department, a very extreme group which, unlike the ALF, says it does not care about the risk of injury to people through its actions.

ALF spokesman Robin Webb said: "I'm delighted for the rabbits.

"We've had butchers and fur shops put out of business before, but this is the first time I can recall a venture of this type going into liquidation.

"I'm sure this will encourage activists everywhere."

Mr Webb said he had no sympathy for those who would lose their jobs as a result of the decision.

For the newly formed Hylyne Action Group, a Manchester-based organisation which was planning a series of demonstrations against the farm, yesterday's news was a victory before they had even started their campaign.

Its spokesman said: "This is really a victory for the ALF."

The rabbit farm, a family business, was started in 1955 with an initial capital of only six shillings.

It grew rapidly to become known world-wide for its breeding techniques and breeders from all over the world came to study its methods.

Mr Sutton worked in the business with his wife and eight part-time staff.

Local councillor Sheila Woodyatt said: "My impression has always been that this was a well-run and well respected company."

DIRECT ACTION FOR ANIMALS Part 2
fighting the fur industry!
with
Wendy & Ramona
This comic is for entertainment only. It is not intended to encourage crime.
One Saturday in December...
Hey! You got plans today?
No, why?
Let's go downtown!
Yeah!
DEMO
CHORES
AMEBIX
Gosh Ramona! No-one would recognize you! It's perfect
Let's Go!
GLOVES
METROPOLITAN VIGILANTE TIP #1: Try to avoid wearing anything that would make you stand out from a crowd
We fit right in!
Ha!
Merry
Tis The Season...
#2: Pick the busiest shopping day possible.
Spare some change for food, ma'm?
Milton! Make this...vermin stop harassing me!
This makes my day...
PAINT
In Here!
Grencher's
DEPARTMENT STORE
VEGAN
FUR!
Act nonchalant, but keep both eyes open! Check (maybe on a separate trip) for security cameras!
Is this on sale?
SEDUCE HER WITH THE GIFT OF FUR
Razor blade
Umm... what luxury!
I know! Did you see this one, "Sandra?"
We'll smash them oneday...
Tiny pocket scissors hidden in sleeve
SNIP!
Don't drop bits of fur on the floor! Put them in a bag & flush them down the ladies room toilet!
Uh... didn't you want to look for a necktie to give your dad...?
Stay Aware! Leave before you draw too much attention to yourself!
Many stores later...
We got so much accomplished today! It was worth having to touch those gruesome coats!
And I've got one last sticker. I'll put it on this payphone
While we're here, let's call some fur business's 800 numbers!
CAROL DEC 20-25
20¢
Back at Ramona's...
Well, you two sure are dressed up! Where the heck did you go, a funeral?
CHORES
MELVINS
ALF Strikes Again
Don't tell anyone how you spent the day, except to anonymously and safely claim your actions!
Oh, we went downtown, saw glamourous people, went to glamourous stores, tried on glamourous clothes...
Good God-what's got into you?
Must be holiday spirit
Huh! Sounds dangerous.
Let's just say it's not for the faint of heart
ALF Strikes Again
Stay tuned for more adventures!
♥ Happy Holidays

REPORTS FROM FINLAND

Fighting the Finnish Fur Trade

Finland is widely known from its strong fur industry. While there are around 500 fur farms in the US, the number is 2000 in Finland. Over half of the fox pelts in the world are produced here and the number of minks murdered is 1.5 million annually.

Another sad fact is that while the fur industry is on the decline in almost every western country, it's getting stronger here. During the summer, furriers announced that 1993 was the first profit making year in a long time. Their newest report claims that the increasing demand for Finnish fur pelts gives them the opportunity to raise fox farming by twenty percent and mink farming by three.

One of the biggest fur auction houses is located here in Helsinki. There are several international pelt auctions held every year. The auction houses are considered the weakest link of the fur industry as only a few of them remain here in Europe. Others are located in Copenhagen, Denmark and Oslo, Norway.

So far, activism against the furriers has been quite low due mainly to the policy of our only national group, Animalia. But there's light at the end of the tunnel- radicalism and the general will to do more than ever before are definitely on the increase. In the latest fur trade publication, they mention their fears of the growing movement in Finland, saying, "we have to be prepared for immoral attacks from anti-fur groups."

This has created a need for a new group, a new group which is totally uncompromising and which supports any type of action for furbearing animals. This group will organize aggressive protests (the kind of activity we haven't seen in Finland yet,) and maybe even Civil Disobedience protests aginst the fur auctions. The group will serve as a mouthpiece for illegal direct actions and explain to the public why this type of activity occurs.

This new group will only concentrate on the issue of fur, simply because it is a cruel form of animal abuse which can be defeated. For far too long, the Finnish furriers have collected obscene profits without interference from animal rights activists. The time has come to put an end to this.

Please write care of Vegan Resistance.

Vegan Resistance

During the past couple of years, the Finnish animal rights movement has seen a dramatic growth of radicalism. Twenty years of legal work by the only Finnish national group, Animalia, has accomplished no real change in the fur trade for which Finland is famous as one of the world's biggest producers. Animalia's work, although important, is best known for it's moderate stance.

The failure of legal campaigning and lobbying has contributed to increased sales of furs. New fur consuming counrtries (like South Korea, China, and especially Hong Kong) have driven the growth of fur farming. The anger and frustration of seeing that happen led to the first direct actions a couple of years ago in Helsinki. After the first hit, windows have been smashed, locks glued and walls spraypainted with slogans several times a year. Slowly the actions have begun in other cities as well. Turku, Tampere, Lahti, Mikkeli and others saw their first actions this year. The first animal rights related arrest happened this summer, when a man, not part of the ALF was arrested at the scene after vandalizing a fur store with paint.

Animalia's policy of *totally* non-radical and non-confrontational work has resulted in the the formation of the first radical and uncompromising animal rights group, Vegan Resistance. The group's purpose is to spread veganism / radical direct action for animals on the grassroots level.

Usually Finland tends to trail a few years behind Sweden, but looking at the radical actions in Sweden now, the furure looks promising...

Vegan Resistance, PO Box 1, 00691, Helsinki, Finland

WHO'S BEHIND THE MASK?

A letter from Darren Thurston, written September 5.

.....Early one morning I lay very still; I was under a pine tree, my whole body pressed into the earth. I'd been there for six hours already, watching the Ellerslie Research Station, a University of Alberta animal laboratory. All of a sudden a field mouse ran over my hand and stopped to stare at me, this strange one lying under a tree with binoculars and a radio to his ear. It talked but a short moment and went back on its way; needless to say I didn't understand what it said but it moved me. It made me think again of my commitment to the earth and just why I'd been lying under a pine tree eight hours a night for seven days straight. Later that week I helped liberate 29 cats and damage equipment at that laboratory.

Unfortunately not all stories end up happy-nineteen days later I was arrested by the RCMP. Fortunately 29 cats are still out there, living their lives in loving and caring homes. I spent 15 months locked up awaiting trial, and finally in September 1993, I was given a suspended sentence, two years probation, and ordered to pay $73,725 restitution. The state was not impressed. They wanted blood-oops, I mean three more years' prison time, and immediately appealed the judge's sentence. On May 12, 1994, after I was free for a very short eight months, the Alberta Court of Appeals issued a written decision sentencing me to an additional two years less a day. On Friday the 13th, after saying many tearful goodbyes, I took the long walk and turned myself in.

I'm well into my government vacation now and I've just recently been transferred to "the fort," which is definitely nicer than the last two government resorts. Not to say it's been all fun; I'm not too happy to be back inside after only eight months out, but I've gotten used to my temporary home. I think of it as a strengthening process, one where we can harden ourselves in our struggle. For the battle has begun and it is not going to be easy. More people will go underground. And more people will go to prison-in England activists are serving four, six, ten year sentences. Yet actions continue there unabated. Sisters and brothers (mothers, fathers, uncles, aunts, and even second removed cousins,) earth and animal warriors, we must join hands with others fighting for their own liberation. You must realize that we all have tremendous power-it takes but one person to cost them millions. When you see the pictures of a masked liberator, stop asking who's behind the mask and look in the mirror!

Many thanks to all those who have written me during my time inside. It sure helps me survive. And to the few people who have traveled thousands of miles and put hundreds of hours into my support, a huge thank you. To those on the front lines, stay strong, stay free, and keep fighting the good fight.

Clenched Fist Salutations,
Darren Thurston

Diary of Actions 1994

Please Note: The Diary of Actions is intended to report news of illegal actions to save animals, not to encourage crime. All reports come from movement and opposition publications, internet bulletin boards, mainstream media, and local 'zines. There is probably a lot that we've missed, and probably more actions that were never reported in the press. We have more info for the early months of the year than this fall because it takes us months to find about reported actions. To help get out the news of direct action, please send news clippings or reports to the North American ALF Support Group at PO Box 8673/ Victoria, BC/ CANADA V8W 3S2.

1994: A Record Year For Direct Action

Both here in the U.S. and across Europe, 1994 so far has seen record levels of direct action. During the 1980's, U.S. actions peaked in 1987-88 with a record of 52 actions in one year, according to the *Report to Congress on the ALF*. These years were characterized by high-profile lab raids and were mostly limited to California and the east coast.

Starting in mid-1993, ALF actions saw a furious increase across the country, including many states which have never seen action before. The patterns of the past year seem to suggest that the ALF has changed course from the 80's and is now concentrating on widespread but low-level attacks and firebombings of fur and meat industry targets. Ironically, the increase in action happened right after the 1993 *Report to Congress* portrayed the ALF as in decline and the federal grand juries starting in 1992 were supposed to break the back of direct action in the U.S. The following report lists the major actions in Europe this year and every report we've found for the U.S.

International Actions

In **England,** thousand of actions happen every year, and it would be impossible to list them all, especially as this year has been the biggest ever in the 22 year history of direct action for animals. The **ALF** scored a big victory against the major rabbit breeder Hyline and its marketing company, forcing them out of business with rabbit liberations and effective firebomb attacks. A lab raid in Surrey in April liberated over 200 animals, just a few days after a dairy was trashed in Fareham. Another dairy was severely damaged in Torquay in August. Just some of the live liberations this year include six cats in the North West, ten puppies in Garetmar, three sheep at Leeds University, 100 guinea pigs in Essex, eleven cats in Cheshire, 100 hens in West Sussex, 82 hens in Long Buckby, and so on... **The Animal Rights Militia** caused over two million pounds of damage in Cambridge on July 6 with incendiary attacks at leather and wool shops, and in August both Oxford and the Isle of Wight saw similar multiple firebomb attacks with many animal abusers burnt out and many more millions of pounds of damage done. The **Justice Department** continues their controversial and violent campaign, sending a spate of letter bombs to meat packers and other animal abusers, injuring several animal abusers. They have also bombed a livestock company with 12 powerful incendiaries, and firebombed several other animal abusing businesses. Other letters primed with booby traps or explosives have been sent out, making the total of **JD** actions close to 100 over the last year. The **Poultry Liberation Organization** continued their campaign with another major contamination hoax, and the **Hunt Retribution Squad** has been active this year as well. We don't even have space to list all the English arson attacks and liberations, much less the thousands of glued locks, smashed windows, etc...

Sweden has seen a major increase in action this year, with animals liberated, meat trucks burnt out, and fur and butcher shops smashed up. One attack in May caused over $180,000 in damages. The **DBF** and the **Djurens Hamnars** are the responsible groups....

Germany has also seen a big increase in actions, with several big lab raids and hundreds of animals liberated. A favorite German action is chopping down scores of hunting platforms...

In **Canada**, the **ALF** attacked fur stores and a meat wholesaler in Vancouver in August.

In Finland, A

fur wholesale trader was trashed in July in Lahti, nine meat trucks were damaged in August in Lahti, and there have been numerous hits on the 30 fur stores in Helsinki. The **ALF** has claimed the attacks.

Spain, **Holland**, **Switzerland**, **Australia**, **Poland**, **Norway**, **Italy**, and **Northern Ireland** have all seen action as well in 1994.

United States

Dates Unknown-Beverly Hills, CA-Somper's Furs was hit twice with glued locks and painted slogans. *ALF Southland Unit*

Studio City, CA-Red Lobster was hit twice with glued locks and painted slogans. *ALF Southland Unit*

Woodland Hills, CA-Woodland Hills Furriers and Fashion Furs were hit nine times, once making local tv news. *ALF Southland Unit*

Calabasas, CA-Honeybaked Hams had its front windows blown out with explosives as well as its locks glued. *ALF Southland Unit*

Van Nuys, CA-The Leather Factory was hit twice with glued locks and painted slogans. *ALF Southland Unit*

Sherman Oaks, CA-Winnicks Furs was hit three times. *ALF Southland Unit*

Reseda, CA-Burger King got glued locks and painted slogans. *ALF Southland Unit*

Chatsworth, CA-Vitello's Italian Restaurant was hit twice with glued locks and painted slogans. *ALF Southland Unit*

Encino, CA-Angelo's Italian Restaurant was hit with glued locks and painted slogans. *ALF Southland Unit*

Reseda, CA-Tandy Leather was hit with glued locks and painted slogans. ALF Southland Unit

Sherman Oaks, CA-Mr. Kosher Meats was hit three times with glued locks and painted slogans. *ALF Southland Unit*

Tarzana, CA-Taco Bell was hit with glued locks and painted slogans. ALF Southland Unit

CA-A veal restaurant had its windows smashed. *ALF Southland Unit*

Santa Monica, CA-Cafe Reni's, which serves veal, was hit twice with glued locks and painted slogans. *ALF Southland Unit*

CA-A building owned by Procter & Gamble was spraypainted with slogans and had its locks glued. *ALF Southland Unit*

CA-A Burger King was hit with glued locks and painted slogans. *ALF Southland Unit*

CA-A "B" dealer had his walls, gates, and driveway spraypainted. *ALF Southland Unit*

Reseda, CA-A store selling hunting equipment was hit twice with glued locks and painted slogans. *ALF Southland Unit*

Woodland Hills, CA-A Sheepskin store was hit twice with glued locks. *ALF Southland Unit*

Santa Cruz, CA-A McDonald's billboard was altered to read "Over One Billion Slaughtered" and "ALF." *ALF Southland Unit*

New York, NY-A fur store had its windows smashed by a brick. *ALF Southland Unit*

January-OH-Unspecified action against animal abusers.

January 5-San Jose, CA-Tarlow's Furs had several windows smeared with etching fluid. *ALF*

January 7-Stockton, CA-Mansoor Furs, the only furrier in the city, had its lock glued and slogans spray-painted. A Chuck E. Cheese restaurant received similar treatment. *ALF*

January 8- Seattle, WA-In the second such incident, and Eddie Bauer store received $5,000 damage from slashed merchandise after refusing to stop selling clothing with fur trim.

January 13-Tillamook County, OR-Survey stakes were pulled up at a clear-cut site in an action to sabotage those who destroy wildlife habitat. *ALF*

January 15-Beverly Hills, CA-Display window of American Express smashed to protest promotion of fur. *ALF Nov. 26 Cell*

January 16-San Francisco, CA-Activists not part of ALF threw red paint on Robert's Furs.

January 17-Oakland, CA-Middent's Furs had its windows etched, locks glued, and canvas awning torn to shreds. *ALF*

January 22-San Francisco, CA-Kane's Furs had a lock glued, slogans painted, and holes put in the windows. *ALF*

January 27-Beverly Hills and Santa Monica, CA-Display

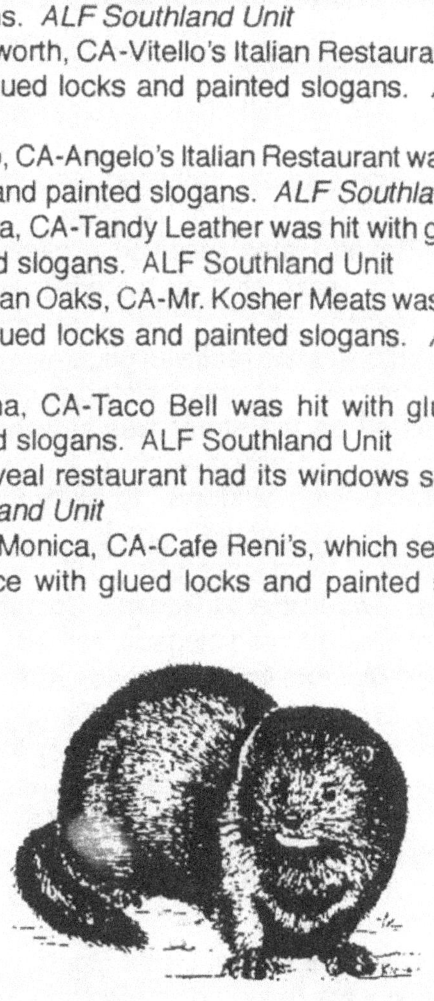

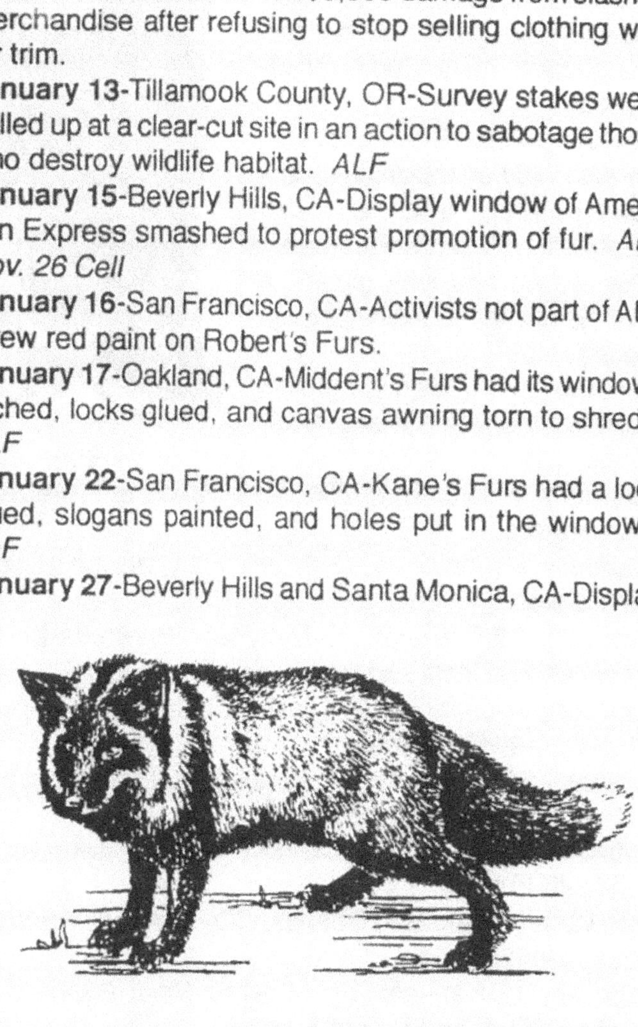

window of Somper Furs smashed. Display window of Adrienne (furs) smashed. An escalation if planned for the succeeding months. *ALF Nov. 26 Cell*

January 27-San Francisco, CA-Nagano Furs had its windows etched. *ALF*

January 28-San Diego, CA-Two vans belonging to the San Diego Meat Company were set on fire. *Farm Animal Revenge Militia*

January 29-San Francisco, CA-Kane's Furs had holes put through its windows. *ALF*

January 30-San Diego, CA-The *Farm Animal Revenge Militia* broke into the San Diego Meat Company through a boarded-over window and set the building on fire. Damages were $75,000 and "F.A.R.M." and "Meat is Murder" were spraypainted on the walls.

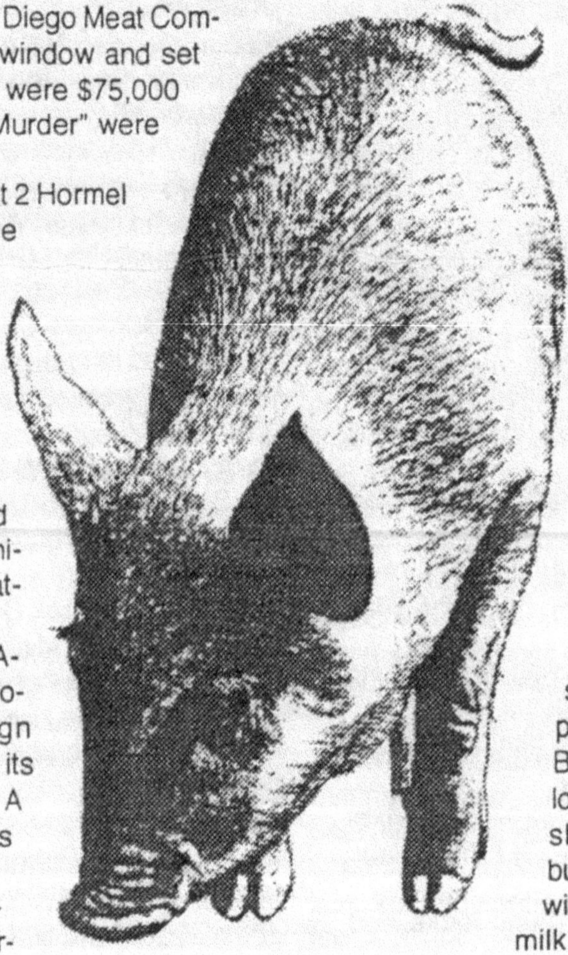

February-Oakland, CA-At least 2 Hormel meat chili billboards were spraypainted with slogans like "Go Vegan."

February-Detroit area, MI-Locks are glued at fur stores week after week.

February-Philadelphia area, PA-Paint filled ornaments were thrown at Ham Sweet Ham and the lock was glued. Other animal abusers have also been attacked.

February 5-San Francisco, CA-Kane's Furs had locks glued, slogans painted, and neon sign smashed. Herbert's Furs had its door etched and lock glued. A veal restaurant had its windows etched. *ALF*

February 8-Pittsburgh, PA-*Paint Panthers* hit Abraville Furriers.

February 9-Columbus, OH-*Paint Panthers* hit at least one fur store.

February 9-Cincinnati, OH-*Paint Panthers* hit at least one fur store.

February 10-Chicago, IL-*The Paint Panthers* hit the American Fur Mart and the Chicago Fur Outlet.

February 11-Omaha, NE-The Julia Talent Fur Store was hit by the *Paint Panthers*.

February 12-Syracuse, NY-A bucket of paint was thrown on the front of a fur store.

February 14-Denver, CO-*The Paint Panthers* hit Koslough Furs.

February 14-Colorado Springs, CO-*The Paint Panthers* hit Lay Limited Furs.

February 15-Kansas City, MO-*The Paint Panthers* hit Genhardt Furs and Sident Furs.

February 16-St. Louis, MO-The St. Louis Fur and Leather Gallery was hit by the *Paint Panthers*.

February 19-Pleasant Hill, CA-The ALF liberated 6 rabbits from Diablo Valley College. Students told the ALF of a professor who killed a rabbit by snapping its neck and then bragged about it. The animals were taken from the Horticulture garden and were placed in a caring, permanent home to guarantee that they will live out their lives in safety. *ALF*

February 20-Oakland and Walnut Creek, CA-Middent's Furs had locks glued, windows smashed, and paint bombs thrown inside. J.E. Harl Furs had locks glued and exterior painted. *ALF*

February 21-New York, NY-*Paint Panthers* hit Elizabeth Arden Furs and Fendi Furs.

Late February-Louisville, KY-At a bowhunting trade show, an elaborate fake bomb was left that contained a note saying that a real bomb was hidden in the building. Five thousand convention goers had to be evacuated for hours.

March-New Jersey-Unspecified actions against animal abusers.

March?-Woodbridge, NJ-A fur billboard was splattered with red paint three times.

March-San Francisco Bay Area, CA-Kanes Furs received glued locks, a sign partially smashed, and slogans painted in front of the store. A Honey Baked Hams received a glued front lock, glass etch on the windows, and slogans all over the store front. A butcher shop received glass etch on the windows and spraypainted slogans. A milk ad on the street was smashed. A McDonald's received a smashed window. A sheep skin store received two broken windows. Robert's Furs received a glued lock and painted slogans. The Harris Steak House received glued locks, painted slogans, and etched windows. Two trucks at Robert's Corned Beef received slashed tires, painted slogans, etched or broken windows, and one had its locks glued. *ALF*

March 7-Atlanta, GA-At the Capitol City Carriage Co. five horse-drawn carriages were destroyed by incendiary devices after the guard dogs were distracted. Years of peaceful protest accomplished nothing, but the blaze put the company out of business.

April-Pueblo, CO-Animal abuse billboards were spraypainted.

April 4-Parma, OH-State Meats, Geiler Meats, and another butcher shop were heavily damaged and had slogans like "ALF" and "Meat is Murder" spray painted on walls and equipment. Despite security camera footag of the masked activists and police questionings of area animal liberation supporters. no arrests were made. *ALF*

April 5-San Francisco, CA-A McDonald's had slogans spraypainted on its walls and smeared onto its windows with etching cream. *ALF*

April 23? (Earth Day)-San Jose and San Francisco, CA-Durham's Meat in and Columbus Sausage and Meat were hit in an effort to radicalize Earth Day. Four trucks were severely damaged at Durham's. *ALF*

April 25-Tempe, AZ-At Arizona State University, the doors of the psychology building were padlocked, the front gate of the Animal Care Program had its lock glued, and slogans were painted at both locations.

April 28-San Francisco, CA-A restaurant is hit because it serves live lobster. Windows etched, locks glued. *Crustacean Liberation Front*

May 1-West Hollywood, CA-Display window of Contemporary Hides smashed. *ALF Nov. 26 Cell*

May-Oakland, CA-Butchers and fish shops were attacked. *ALF*

May-Newtown, PA-Ham Sweet Ham had its windows shot out. *ALF*

May-Southampton, PA-A fur store had its windows shot out. *ALF*

May-Washington, D.C.-A fur store had a ball bearing shot through their display window. *ALF U.S. Congressional Cell*

May-Silver Spring, MD-A Gillette billboard was spraypainted with "Gillette Kills Animals" for their continued use of animals in product testing. *ALF U.S. Congressional Cell*

May 25-Santa Cruz, CA-Buildings were vivisection takes place on the UC campus were spraypainted with slogans including "ALF." *ALF*

May 31-Fond Du Lac, WI-A McDonald's had six windows shattered and "Meat is Murder" spraypainted on a wall. The local paper reported that there was a $700 reward offered for the attackers. *ALF*

June-Kensington, MD-A Roy Rogers/Hardees fast food restaurant had "Meat if Murder" spraypainted on their wall and a brick delivered through their window. "More to Come..." *ALF U.S. Congressional Cell*

June-Oakland, CA-A butcher shop had 'ALF" etched on its windows in very large letters. The shop, located in a crowded shopping district, has visible damage from previous attacks. *ALF*

???July-Miami, FL-33 primates were taken from a lab dealer. Was it a liberation raid???

July-MN-Outside the Twin Cities area, the meeting house for a pro-hunting group called "Hides for Habitat" was burned down in an arson attack.

July-South Dakota-3 teenage girls were arrested for splattering an anti-animal rights billboard with red paint, but soon afterwards two of the signs were cut down with a chainsaw. Unfortunately we have no more details, as this news came from a fur farmer who unknowingly spoke to an animal liberation infiltrator.

July 10-Memphis, TN-Especially Leather Furniture Shop and the Southern

Meat Market had their locks glued.

July 10-Little Rock, AR-Honey Baked Hams received a smashed window. *ALF*

July 11-Little Rock, AR-Specter Furs was paint bombed. *ALF*

August-Berkeley, CA-An animal abuse billboard was altered with animal liberation and vegan slogans.

August-Cleveland, OH-Animal abuse billboards were defaced with animal liberation slogans.

August-Pittsburgh, PA-Fur stores were attacked.

August-Indianapolis, IN-A fur store was attacked and a McDonald's billboard was defaced.

August-Eirie. PA-A local newspaper reported that numerous fur coats in a shop were vandalized.

Autumn months-Minneapolis/St. Paul, MN-We have unconfirmed rumors that fur stores have been attacked several times.

September-Washington, D.C.-Miller's Furs had slogans etched into the windows.

September-Syracuse, NY-A fur store was attacked with glued locks, etched windows, and spraypainted slogans on the sidewalks in front. *ALF*

September-Memphis, TN-Goldsmith's, which sells fur, had windows smashed, truck windshields smashed, slashed truck tires, and glued locks. $6,000 in damages. *ALF*

September 9-Syracuse, NY-A fur store was hit for the second time in a week; this time it was paintbombed and had more slogans spraypainted. *ALF*

September 17-New York, NY-Four stores received glued locks-Billy Martin Leather, Bally's Limited (fur,) and Elizabeth Arden (fur) had locks glued, and the front window at Rubin Furs was defaced with a glass cutter. *ALF*

September 27-Santa Cruz, CA-Several fast food restaurants had their locks glued and slogans spraypainted.

November 7-Memphis, TN-Before Jean Benham Furs moved, their new location was firebombed. The owner may now drop fur.

November 17-San Francisco, CA-Robert's Furs paintbombed and windows broken, other unspecified actions. Berkeley's Milk Board office paintbombed.

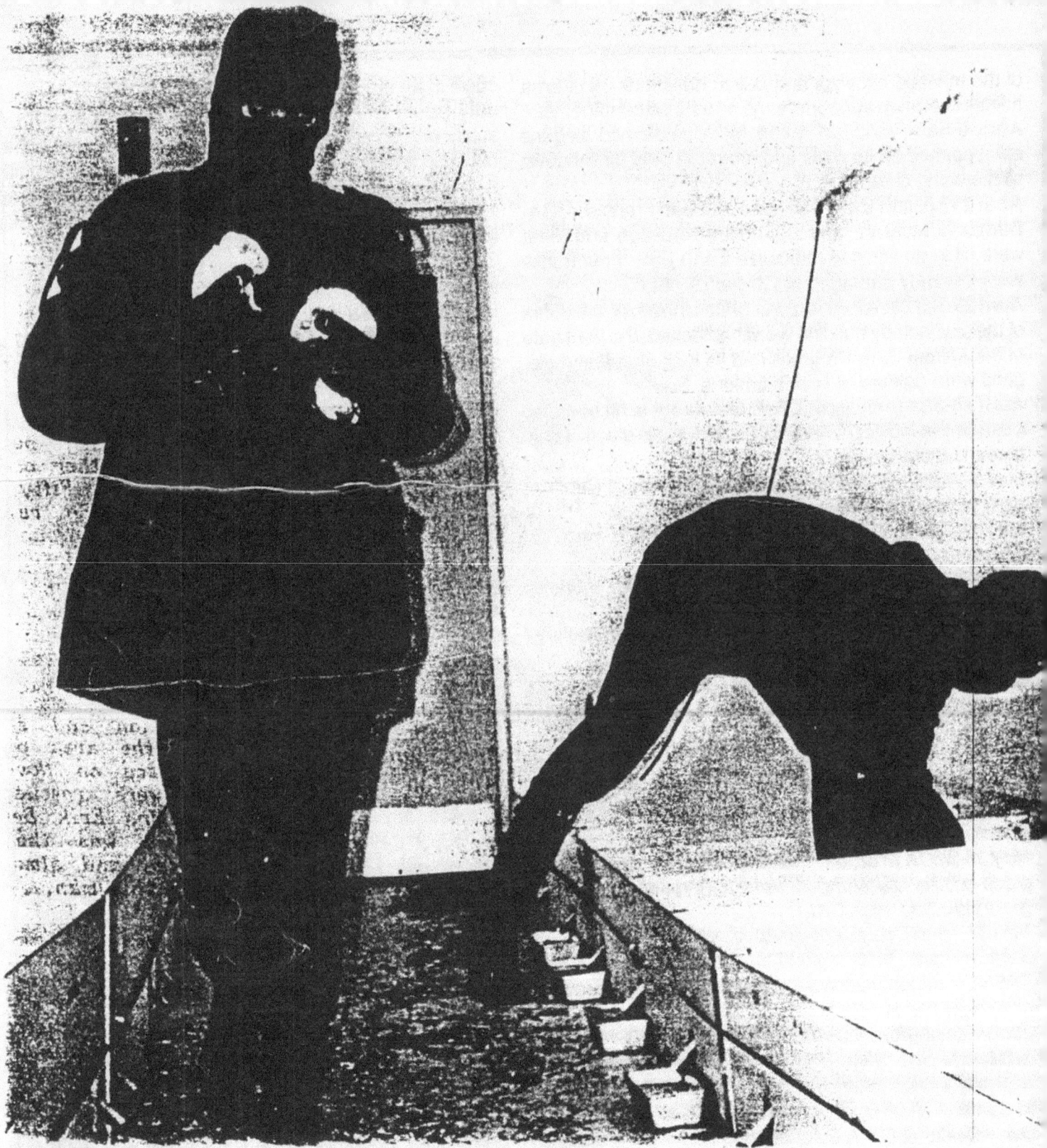

THE MILITANT VEGAN–Next issue out soon

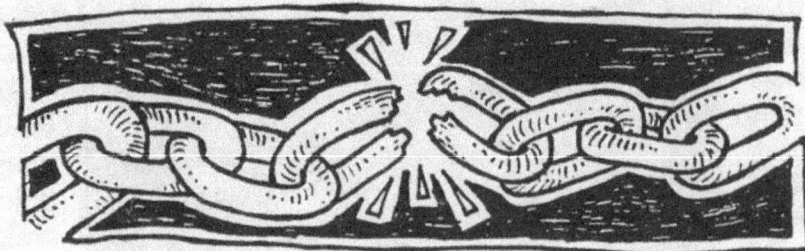

The Militant VEGAN

March 1995

#8

in this issue...

The End of Militant Vegan?

1994 Summary of Actions

A Letter from Rod Coronado

THE MILITANT
VEGAN
AND MORE

THE MILITANT
VEGAN

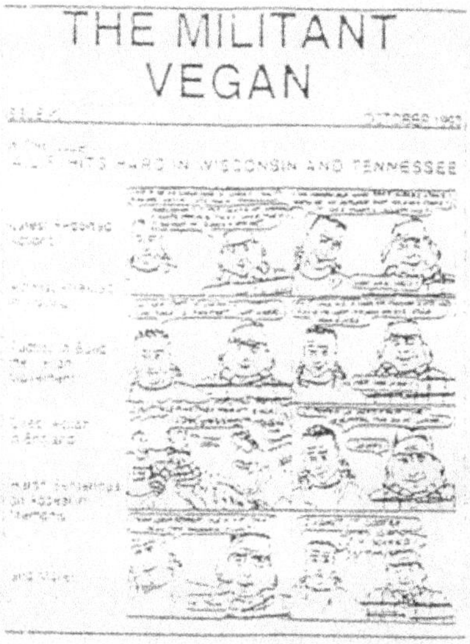
THE MILITANT
VEGAN

THE MILITANT
VEGAN
FURRIERS ATTACKED IN CHICAGO

THE MILITANT
VEGAN
FUR STORE TORCHED IN WISCONSIN
ACTION FOR ANIMALS ACROSS THE COUNTRY

The Militant
Vegan
#6
August 1994

the militant
november
1994
issue# 7
OPEN SEASON ON THE FUR TRADE

The Militant Vegan - Issue Eight

March 1995

Welcome to the Militant Vegan #8, our second anniversary issue. If you are new to vegan ideas and want to find out more, we suggest reading Diet for a New America by John Robbins and contacting PETA at PO Box 42516, Washington D.C. 90015 for information and recipes. You can easily copy recipes from cookbooks in libraries and bookstores, and you can get several well-done cookzines from Vegan Action at PO Box 4353, Berkeley, CA 94704-0353. Shop at Asian and Indian groceries to avoid the rip-off prices at health food stores.

The Militant Vegan is not an ALF support group, so we make no contact with illegal units. This is to guarantee that we can continue to publish the good news of animal liberation. Since many ALF units do not claim their actions, it can be difficult to get a complete picture of all the action out there. The North American ALF Support Group exists to publicize ALF actions and support activists arrested for protecting animals. If you see articles about direct action or are a member of an ALF cell, send the clippings or an anonymous report of your actions to the North American ALFSG at PO Box 8673, Victoria, BC, CANADA V8W 3S2. Their e-mail is un028@freenet.victoria. bc.ca The ALFSG is in need of large donations for prisoner support, and sell their magazine Underground for $4; they need all the money they can get. The Coalition to Abolish the Fur Trade also accepts action reports at PO Box 40641, Memphis, TN 38174.

Note: The Militant Vegan is a news magazine that reports the known facts about direct action for animals. We do not intend to encourage crime against animal torturers and killers. This magazine is for information only.

The English ALFSG is at BCM 1160, London, WC1N 3XX, ENGLAND, and they print a quarterly magazine for prisoner support ($20 a year), sell t-shirts and other items, and take donations for ALF prisoners. A separate ALF Press Office takes action reports and acts as a media spokesperson after raids. They can be contacted at BM 4400, London WC1N 3XX, ENGLAND. The Swedish ALFSG is at DBF-Dujurens Hamnars, PO Box 2051, S-26502, Astorp 2, SWEDEN. The Spanish ALFSG is at APDO, 50390, 28080 Madrid, SPAIN. The Israeli ALFSG is at PO Box 6023, Tel Aviv 6 1060, ISRAEL. Another European organization worth contacting is Vegan Resistance at PO Box 1, 00691, Helsinki, FINLAND.

A good way to keep up with the movement is to subscribe to Arkangel, the best animal liberation magazine around, at BCM 9240, London, WC1N 3XX, ENGLAND. It's $15 for four big issues and they take US cash.

Enjoy this issue, and pass it on to friends! This magazine is not intended to encourage crime, it's a newsmagazine only.

One last thing, we'd like to say than you to all our readers over the past two years, everyone who has distributed this magazine, and everyone who makes an effort for the animals. We're putting what would have been issue #8 over the internet, and this may well be the last one...

News and Comment

More than anything else, the story of the animal liberation movement over the past year has been the phenomenal growth of radicalism among young people across the country. New grassroots groups barely a year old like **Vegan Action, Coalition to Abolish the Fur Trade**, and **SOAR** set the pace of the movement and have inspired a level of activity not seen since the mid '80s, if ever. Now the second wave of this new activism has begun with the formation of even newer groups like the **Animal Defense League** in New York and **SEAL** in Ohio. The interest in animal protection among college students and teenagers is skyrocketing, promising a brighter future for animals in the years to come. Far from the media-created stereotypes of young people as "slackers" and apathetic potheads, these new activists are among the best and brightest of our generation. And believe it, we've only just begun!

It's not our intention here at the Militant Vegan to cut down anyone who works for animals. But it has to be said that grassroots activism for animals declined in the early '90s, even as interest in animal rights increased. Why? because groups which led the movement in the '80s, like **Last Chance for Animals** and **IDA**, lost their sense of urgency and direction, sunk into ritual protests, spent too much time on costly lawsuits and neither-here-no-there issues like pet theft, and therefore ceased to attract and inspire the huge numbers of people who became concerned about animals. We can all learn from this, and keep our activism stylish, innovative, ever-creative, and committed to increasing the number of vegans and the number of activists.

We encourage everyone out there to write to and donate to these new groups, and learn from them how easy it is to set up an active group in your city or state. We've made a lot of progress, but many states will have no regular groups, protests, or actions. You and your friends can accomplish so much, so give it a try!

Fur Free Friday on November 25 saw the most radical day of protest against the fur trade yet, bringing new energy to a ritualistic event which has accomplished little in the past few years. Groups of people blocking store entrances and occupying fur salons were met with riot police, helicopters, and paddy wagons as around 50 people were arrested in about 25 actions in the U.S. and Canada.

The arrests included 5 in San Francisco, 5 in Memphis, 4 in Atlanta, 7 in Minneapolis, 8

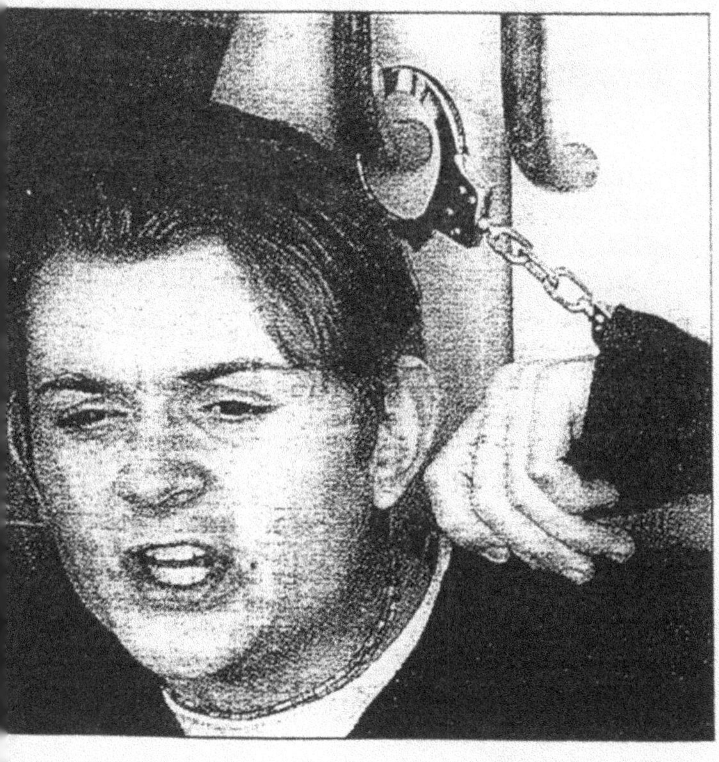

ANTI-FUR PROTESTERS BLOCK DEPARTMENT STORE ENTRANCE

An unidentified customer (above) outside Jacobson's at Keystone at the Crossing asks protesters why they're blocking the store's outside entrance. About 30 young people chanted and held signs Sunday to protest Jacobson's fur sales. Officers with the Marion County Sheriff's Department helped disperse the protesters after an hour-long demonstration. Sheriff's officials said there were no arrests, but that might not be the case next time. One protester, Seth Stevens (left), handcuffed himself to the front entrance of the store, forcing Washington Township firefighters to cut the handcuffs off with bolt cutters. Shannon Dakin, a spokeswoman for the Coalition to Abolish the Fur Trade, said the group plans more protests.

MONDAY, MARCH 13, 1995

in Washington, D.C., 3 in Virginia Beach (although they were not charged afterwards), 12 in Albany, NY, 1 in Columbus, OH, and 1 in New Orleans. Perhaps the most effective action was in Newport Beach, CA, where 48 people sat down in the fur salon of Nieman Marcus and blocked it for 30 minutes before the police arrived. Media coverage was heavy, including CNN. The event was sponsored by **CAFT** (see address on inside cover), the **National Activist Network** (PO Box 19515/ Sacramento/ Ca 95919), **Animal Defense League** (address below,) **SOAR** (235 CMU/ 300 Washington AVE. SE/ Minneapolis, MN 55455), **Orange County People for Animals**, and several others.

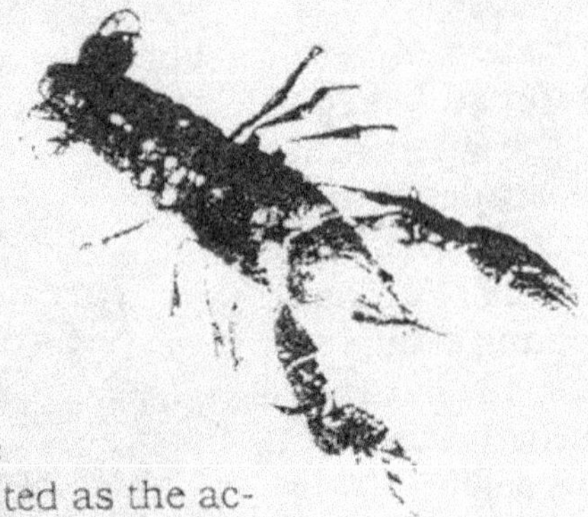

Three days later, activists in Minneapolis dumped animal carcasses outside Dayton's, which sells fur, to highlight the brutality of the fur trade. Two activists were arrested as the action brought shocked reactions from passerby and heavy media coverage.

A similar action was done by the **Coalition to Abolish the Fur Trade** in Memphis on January 8 after **CAFT** members obtained skinned fox carcasses from an Arkansas fox farmer who went out of business. When activists arrived at Goldsmith's, a department store which sells fur, police were waiting in force. Three women who ran up and dumped foxes in front of the store were tackled by the police and arrested. Two others were cited, and protesters on the sidewalk showed two dead foxes to tv crews.

Activists from across the Midwest raided the International Mink Farmers' Convention in Madison, WI, on January 7. As a large crowd demonstrated outside, 30-40 activists stormed into the room where 60 fur farmers were meeting. The fur farmers attacked the crowd, and the two sides chanted back and forth at each other during the scuffling. Three activists who chained themselves to a stairwell were arrested, and one of them had her wrist fractured by the police, who violently dispersed the crowd. The disruption of the convention, which is the main yearly event for the fur farm industry, was sponsored by **Alliance for Animals**, **CAFT**, and **SOAR**.

Two hunt sabs from the **Fund for Animals** may be charged under the new federal "hunter harassment" law after a protest at the Cape Cod National Seashore in Massachusetts in November. Mike Markarian and Todd MacDonald tried to convince hunters killing Chinese pheasants to stop, and Markarian was hit with a rifle butt and threatened. The activists will try to file charges against the hunter while they wait to see what they themselves will be charged under. Contact: Fund for Animals/ 850 Sligo Ave./ Silver Spring, MD 20910.

In a blatant protection of animal abuse, on January 9 the Supreme Court let the ruling of a Montana court stand in defense of that state's "hunter harassment" law, even though it bans speech on public lands by those who protest against hunting. With legal ways of protest shut off, activists may now find no other way to stop the killing than to sabotage hunting vehicles, shops, and equipment.

After months of work, **Vegan Action** in Berkeley, CA, got UC Berkeley to agree to serve vegan food at every dormitory meal. Berkeley is the first large university to adopt a vegan policy, and the victory reflects the enormous interest that young people have in animal issues and veganism. The campaign received heavy local news coverage last fall, and **Vegan Action** looks set to become the leading vegan issues group in North America. For information on running a campus campaign, information on going vegan, or a mail-order of diverse titles, send a SASE + 2 stamps to Vegan Action/ PO Box 4353/ Berkeley, CA 94704-0353. Yearly membership is $15, and we highly recommend donations to one of the best animal rights groups around.

Indiana and Ohio activists have been busy putting pressure on the fur and meat industries, with several militant protests a month. Contact: SEAL/ PO Box 2611/ Dayton, OH 45401, and Animal Defense League/ PO Box 30214/ Indianapolis, IN 46230.

On December 10, 6 members of the **Animal Defense League** were arrested while blocking the entrance to the Bonwit Teller department store, which sells fur. 24 people blocked the door until the police arrived. The **Animal Defense League** is one of the best up-and-coming groups, so contact them at PO Box 6845/ Syracuse, NY 13217 or at PO Box 66302/ Albany, NY 12206. Their excellent 'zine, Dressed in Black, is available from the Syracuse address for $1.50.

How did the Militant Vegan start?

In 1991-92 the Animal Liberation Front had done a series of raids on the fur trade, and they got little to no coverage in the movement or mainstream press. Also, those years were kind of a lull for the movement in general, and we wanted to help get things going again. Other movement magazines were doing a good job of trying to reach new people but there was no publication made for activists. The first one came out right after New Year's in 1993. It was a big success right away, so we've kept it up since then.

Why has every issue been so short?

Most of the distribution is done not by us, but by grassroots activists all over. The 12 page limit keeps xeroxing costs down. We do pack a lot of info in each one...

How do you manage that distribution?

We mail it out to groups and people who xerox copies and sell them to raise money for their groups, events, etc. It's gotten all over North America and into Europe as well.

So is this the last issue of the Militant Vegan?

It might be. The group of us that has done it are all leaving town, going to new places, so it would be hard to work together in the future. We'll all continue to be active in the movement, of course, but this may be the last issue. We feel pretty satisfied with what we've done; when we started, a "militant vegan" was unheard of but now radical veganism is the driving force behind all the new energy out there. A group called the "Militant Vegans' blew up 8 milk trucks in Sweden recently - that was pretty flattering.

Hopefully, new activists can publish a grassroots magazine to inform and unify the movement nationally. To get our news, we just call groups and talk to them and then print it all up. It's pretty easy.

What should the movement concentrate on in 1995?

The fur trade must be confronted with more force, it's a battle that has gone on far too long and it's time to put a stop to their killings once and for all. More generally, the meat and dairy industries are responsible for most of the animal suffering in the U.S., so the pressure against those industries must continue to increase.

Internally, we're seeing the big groups from the '80s like PETA go mainstream, with huge memberships and increasing influence. We should all support that necessary aspect of the fight to save animals, but the real task for all of us is to strengthen the growing grassroots movement. Ideally, vegans in every city should set up a group that maintains contacts and coordinates campaigns with others around the country. Aggressive campaigns and stylish, innovative approaches can win over young activists and set the stage for more to come. The Coalition to Abolish the Fur Trade, Vegan Action, and SOAR are all good examples of radical groups started in the past year.

Won't the government crack down on activists, like they did with Earth First!?

It is inevitable that the FBI, local police, and private security agencies will spy on, and in some cases seek to disrupt the movement. People should read books on the subject and be prepared. That said, most people will never be bothered and fear of the government must not be a damper on our actions to stop cruelty to animals.

Since you mentioned Earth First! as an example, we'd like to add our opinion that they sort of boxed themselves in for a crackdown and an internal collapse by a combination of infighting, irresponsible rhetoric, and an attitude that cut them off from the majority of people. If the animal liberation movement continues to support different levels of activity, and maintains its image as highly ethical, responsible, and positive, then we will have the numbers and public support to prevent or lessen the effects of FBI activity. The critical difference between positive radicalism that is inclusive and constructive and the anti-social nihilism of some movements is the difference between whether we remain in the fringes, like Earth First!, or succeed in making our radical message accepted, like the gay/lesbian movement has done over the past decade.

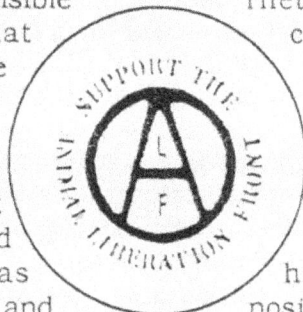

What about direct action and the ALF?

We can't encourage crime in this magazine, but it's possible that daily attacks on furriers along with well-directed strikes against key points in the industry could put the fur trade under, like the British ALF did in the late '80s. Actions against the meat trade increase awareness of the barbaric conditions farm animals suffer under and are a warning to the butchers of what will come in the future...

Prisoner Support

Rod Coronado was bailed out in December, and returned to the Yaqui reservation in Tucson. His trial will start in the spring for the February 1992 ALF raid at Michigan State, so send donations and write him at Rod Coronado Support Committee/ PO Box 1891/ Tucson, AZ 85702.

Lise Olsen has been moved to a new address. Write her at Lise Olsen B48426/ 2600 N. Brinton/ PO box 1200/ Dixon, IL 61021.

Darren Thurston was released from jail in Canada in January.

International prisoners would love to hear from you; two stamps will cover air mail.

Keith Mann was sentenced to 14 years in jail, the longest ever sentence for an ALF activist. See his statement later this issue and write him at Keith Mann EE3588/ HMP Wandsworth/ PO Box 757/ 23 Heathfield Road/ Wandsworth, London SW18 ENGLAND.

Angie Hamp was recently sentenced to 4 years for ALF actions, write to her at Angie Hamp TW1687/ HMP Holloway/ Parkhurst Road/ Holloway/ London N7 ONU ENGLAND.

Gurjeet Aujla is awaiting trial for "conspiracy to cause explosions," write him at Gurjeet Aujla HV 2047/ HMP Birmingham/ Winson Green Road/ Birmingham/ B18 4AS ENGLAND.

Allison McKeon RE2370/ HMP Askham Grange/ Askham Richard/ York/ Y02 3PT ENGLAND.

Max Watson BJ2477/ HMP Haverigg/ Haverigg Camp/ Millom/ Cumbria/ LA18 4NA ENGLAND

Dave Callender HV3314/ HMP Birmingham/ Winson Green Road/ Birmingham/ B18 4AS ENGLAND.

Greg Avery HV3313/ HMP Birmingham/ Winson Green Road/ Birmingham/ B18 4AS ENGLAND.

The above two are new prisoners awaiting charged of conspiracy to cause criminal damage. Two others, Colin Chatfield and Annette Tibbles, will be near release by the time you read this.

Restaurateurs at wit's end over veal protesters' tactics

Frank and Leslie Worth recall the social activism of the '60s, the positive things that came out of it, and the occasional folly that sometimes accompanied the protest movement.

So they sat back and took it when anti-veal protesters thrice spray painted their protests on the windows of Leslie's Italian Villa, the downtown restaurant they co-own.

The latest act of vandalism has both restaurateurs at wit's end, however. Instead of spray painting the windows, someone used what appears to be an acid compound to etch the word, "veal," into the glass.

Eight door-sized windows across the front of the restaurant were damaged, apparently beyond repair. One window also was cracked. One estimate places the damage at more

MIKE LEONARD
H-T Columnist

"It's a real shame they feel they have to deface a landmark building," Frank complained this week. "Four of those windows were turn-of-the-century glass from the original Princess Theater."

"And the thing is, if we replace them, what's going to stop them from coming back and doing it again?" added Leslie. "Apparently, they have no interest in negotiating whatsoever."

The ironic aspect of it all is that Leslie agrees with the protesters' disdain for veal. "I think it is raised in an

that reason and I haven't eaten veal for 12 years," she said.

"But veal is indigenous to an Italian menu and I'm not going to sit in judgment of people who do want to eat it," she said. "It's something our customers want."

As social protests go, the anti-veal protesters do seem to be childish and vindictive. "Their only contact with us was one phone call in which a woman (unidentified) asked me if we served veal," Leslie recalled. "I said yes. She gave me a quick spiel on how the animals are raised and then she asked me if I would consider taking veal off the menu.

"I said no and that was it," Leslie said. "Nobody came in to speak with us. Nothing. It seems like they're more into hassling people than trying to educate anyone."

The basic rap against veal is this: The calves used in veal production are milk fed in confined quarters under low light conditions. These conditions help limit the development of tough muscle fibers and that tends to make the animals' meat more tender and therefore more desirable to consumers.

Veal defenders say that virtually all consumer meat comes from animals raised for slaughter, and the youth of veal doesn't make it significantly different from other meat. In addition, confined feeding — tethering animals to limit their movement — is widely used in modern beef and pork production.

Protesters are striking out at other business interests as well. "We've been seeing 'Meat is murder' written at various locations," Bloomington Police Dept. Sgt. Joe Qualters noted. "A while back I know they hit Sam's Poultry pretty hard with graffiti. They even unplugged some of the refrigeration trucks.

"If you want to pick on veal, fine, at least I understand the argument," Qualters said. "But chicken to me is a

going to become complete vegetarians."

Plus, Qualters said there is a clear legal distinction between protest and vandalism. "There's a right way to go about protesting something and there's a wrong way. Any time you damage property you've crossed the line of decency and gone from a civil protest to a criminal act," he said.

Police admit that it's difficult to catch people who commit such vandalism because the acts usually occur in the wee hours of the morning when few people are on the streets. They do, however, have some leads.

Frank Worth has decided to install surveillance cameras monitoring the outside of his restaurant. And he says that the nature of the anti-veal protest has only caused him to dig his heels in deeper. "I will never surrender to terrorism, and that's exactly what this is," he said.

"These people have not had a dialog with us. They've not tried the political process. They can't even claim they represent a majority opinion," he said. "As far as I know, there are five people out there who don't like veal. Well, they don't have to eat

DIARY OF ACTIONS

Please Note: The Diary of Actions is intended to report the news of direct action to save animals, not to encourage crime. All reports come from other publications, the internet, or communiqués sent to animal rights groups.

As we reported in the last issue, it seems that the Animal Liberation Front, which made headlines in the 1980s with scores of lab break-ins in California and the east coast, has changed tactics and spread to many other areas of the U.S.

Since around the middle of 1993, a flood of small actions concentrated against the meat and fur trades have taken place at the rate of 8-15 a month. A state/province breakdown for 1994 alone from reported actions is as follows:

Arizona: At least 1 actions. Unclaimed.
Arkansas: 2+. *Animal Liberation Front* active.
British Columbia: 6+. *ALF, Animal Rights Militia* active.
California: 77+. *ALF, ALF Stockton Unit, ALF Golden Gate Unit, ALF Southland Unit, ALF November 26 Cell, Crustacean Liberation Front, Farm Animal Revenge Militia* active.
Colorado: 3+. *Paint Panthers* active.
District of Columbia: 5+. *ALF* active.
Georgia: 1+. Unclaimed.
Illinois: 1+. *Paint Panthers* active.
Indiana: 3+. *ALF* active.
Kentucky: 1+. Unclaimed.
Maryland: 9+. *ALF* active.
Michigan: 1+. Unclaimed.
Minnesota: 7+. *ALF* active.
Missouri: 2+. *Paint Panthers* active.
Nebraska: 1+. *Paint Panthers* active.
New Jersey: 2+. Unclaimed.
New York: 10+. *ALF, Paint Panthers* active.
Ohio: 6+. *ALF, Paint Panthers* active.
Oregon: 1+. *ALF* active.
Pennsylvania: 6+. *ALF* active.
South Dakota: 2+. Unclaimed.
Tennessee: 11+. *ALF* active.
Utah: 3+. *Vegan Revolution* active.
Washington: 3+. *Paint Panthers* active.
Wisconsin: 5+. *ALF* active.
location unspecified: 2.
Totals: At least 171 actions in 23 states, D.C., and 1 province.

BEING BOILED HURTS!
LOBSTER LIBERATION

This increase in actions since mid 1993 corresponds to an increase in actions across Europe, which has seen numerous arsons, break-ins, and smaller attacks across the continent, and in England, where the already high levels of actions increased with tens of millions of pounds of damages and scores of bombings and arson attacks in 1994.

The following are actions we missed last issue when we listed over 80 actions from January to September 1994. Undoubtedly, this issue's list for October through December is also incomplete and we'll find out much more later.

February - Madison, Wisconsin - Herschlender's Furs "Fur Her" billboard paint bombed. Local papers reported $11,000 damage (!) and the sign was permanently removed. Savidusky's Furs had windows smashed. *ALF*
February 12 - Memphis, Tennessee - Hattaway Taxidermy: truck engine damaged. *ALF*
March - Rochester, New York - Rodeo trucks were damaged with smashed windows and paint. *ALF*
March 5 - Memphis, Tennessee - Jack Lewis Furs: paint bombed, locks glued. *ALF*
March 30 - Memphis, Tennessee - Jack Lewis Furs: locks glued. *ALF*
April - Madison, Wisconsin - A taxidermist was hit three times, with windows smashed. *ALF*
May 1 - Rochester, New York - Windows were smashed at a hunting store, and the display window of Lipsitz Furs was smashed. *ALF*
May 2 - Rochester, New York - Federal Meats had locks glued, windows smashed, and the building and sidewalk was spray painted. *ALF*
May 4 - Rochester, New York - Red paint was

1-800-LAB RATS

World Lab Animal Week is coming up this April 24-April 28. Sitting in my room late one night I had some wonderful ideas. What would happen if hundreds of activists from around the country decided to call 1-800-LAB RATS in celebration of world lab animal week? Would it be possible for them to not sell a single animal the entire week because dedicated animal rights activists called them from 8 to 5 and jammed their phone lines? Would Lab Rats have to permanently change their phone number because they could not deal with the constant harassment?

Maybe it's time we got answers to these questions.

Calling is easy. Just run down to your local pay phone (DO NOT CALL FROM HOME) and dial them up. Bang the phone or simply hang up after one of their ever friendly operators answers. Repeat this process until your finger gets tired from dialing or they lock out all calls from your area code. If they lock you out, don't be discouraged, it's usually only for a day or so and you have a whole week to make them sick and tired of selling animals for profit. Keep trying.

If you call after 5, you can abuse their voice mail. *32 will access the main menu and then you can play around and record as long a message as you want (NOT YOUR VOICE)

Some points of caution:

1) They have caller I.D. and this nasty program that dials you back and when you answer and hang up it calls you again and again and again. Don't call from your house / dorm / apartment / igloo. If they ring you back, pick it up and hang up again. If you get tired of this little game just leave the phone off the hook and walk away.

2) Do not leave your name or even your voice. These calls may be recorded. If you want to leave a message you could hum them verse after verse of that song you have had stuck in your head all day or pick a rude and/or disgusting noise to annoy them with and stick with it. Be creative.

3) This is most likely illegal so memorize the number (it's not *that* difficult) and pass on or destroy this flier.

The entire goal of this campain is to give the animal abusers a glimpse of the hell that they cause the animals. Begin on Monday, April 24 and don't ever let up. Spread the word to your friends and copy and distribute this all over the US. This is an very easy action that could easily make a difference to the millions of animals they sell to research each year. Have fun.

---

thrown on the sidewalk and front windows of Federal Meats. *ALF* (Note - we also have rumors of activity in Buffalo, NY, in 1994).

June - San Francisco, California - The *Crustacean Liberation Front* hit several businesses which sell live lobster.

July - San Francisco, California - The *Crustacean Liberation Front* continued their campaign, getting coverage in three newspapers and local radio.

Summer - Minneapolis, Minnesota - A McDonald's was spray painted with slogans like "McDeath" and had its locks glued. A KFC had its walls sprayed with slogans like "ALF" and "Meat is Murder" and had its locks glued. A fish restaurant was spray painted with "stop raping the oceans," and its locks were glued and a screen door was ripped off. A butcher shop had its locks glued and had "veal is child abuse" and "Meat is murder" spray painted. *ALF*

Summer - Fond du Lac, Wisconsin - Many downtown restaurants were spray painted with vegan slogans. *ALF*

July - Olney, Maryland - Boston Chicken: "Meat is Murder" spray painted on a wall, brick thrown through a window. *ALF U.S. Congressional Cell*

July - Olney, Maryland - KFC: rock thrown through a window. *ALF U.S. Congressional Cell*

July - Washington, D.C. - Jennifer Leather ad displayed in the metro subway station destroyed. *ALF U.S. Congressional Cell*

July 29 - Madison, Wisconsin - ALFSG reports that three people were arrested after two pro-animal abuse billboards were cut down. We've been unable to confirm this with activists in Madison, so we await further details from the *ALFSG*.

August - Washington, D.C. - Another Jennifer Leather subway ad destroyed. *ALF U.S. Congressional Cell*

August - Washington, D.C. - DC 101 Annual Championship Barbeque ad "with two happy dancing pigs" in the subway was destroyed. *ALF U.S. Congressional Cell*

August - Southern California - A starving, emaciated goat was liberated from a county fair and "is now happily and healthily living on a spacious farm." Farm Animal Revenge Militia

August - Memphis, Tennessee - Goldsmith's, which sells fur, had windows smashed four times. *ALF*

August 6 - Memphis, Tennessee - Jack Lewis Furs: paint bombed, locks glued. *ALF*

August 8 - Vancouver, British Columbia - Western Freezer Meats: locks glued, van windows smashed, tires slashed. *ALF*

August 9 - Vancouver, British Columbia - Capilano Furs: tires slashed, paint bombed. Speiser Furs: locks glued, all windows etched. *ALF*

August 10 - Vancouver, British Columbia - Western Freezer Meats: locks glued, windows etched, truck tires slashed and windows etched, paint bombed. *ALF*

August 25 - Memphis, Tennessee - Jack Lewis Furs: paint bombed. *ALF*

August 31 - Memphis, Tennessee - Factory farm: pigs liberated. *ALF*

September 4 - Memphis, Tennessee - On the same night as the attack on Goldsmith's we listed last issue, a McDonald's and a KFC has their windows smashed and Fur Fashions of Memphis had their locks glued. *ALF*

September 18 - Beverly Hills, California - Beverly Hills Fur Company: display windows smashed. "Every fur store in the area has now had some action performed against them. More to come." *ALF November 26 Cell*

OCTOBER-DECEMBER 1994: U.S. AND CANADA

mid-October - Pleasant View, Tennessee - At the McEllis fur farm, cages holding 20-25 foxes were opened so the animals could escape. *ALF*

October 17 - Salt Lake County, Utah - Three windows worth $500 were smashed at a Honey Baked Hams. *Vegan Revolution*

October 18 - Sebastopol, California - Jose LaCalle, a chinchilla fur farmer facing cruelty charges for killing chinchillas with genital electrocution, had his office spray painted with anti-fur slogans.

October 26 - Salt Lake County, Utah - Honey Baked Hams was hit again and a window was smashed at Meier's Meat Market. *Vegan Revolution* activists left a note at Meier's saying "Murderers. Next time it won't be windows..."

October / November? - West Valley City, Utah - A pipe bomb was thrown through the window of Jordan Meat Co., causing about $1,500 in damages. *Vegan Revolution*

November - Spokane, Washington - Exclusifurs II was spray painted by the *Paint Panthers*.

November - Seattle, Washington - A Kentucky Fried Chicken was attacked. No details at this point.

November - Maryland - Thousands of dollars of fur coats had fake blood thrown on them at Best Kept Secrets. *ALF*

November - Olney, Maryland - A KFC was spray painted and had its windows smashed out. *ALF*

November - New York, New York - A large steel garbage can was thrown through the front picture window of a fur salon. *ALF*

November 7 - Memphis, Tennessee - The new location of Jean Benham Furs was firebombed before it opened. The BATF investigated, questioning nearby shop owners and trying to question at least one local activist, who refused to speak to them. It appears that the investigation has gone nowhere, but the fur store is now open for business. *ALF*

November 17 - San Francisco, California - Robert's Furs was hit, other actions. Berkeley's Milk Board was paint bombed. *ALF*

November 29 - Dayton, Ohio - A Lazarus Department Store, which sells fur, had a van spray painted with slogans. *ALF*

Late November - Mankato, Minnesota - A fur store had "Fur is Dead" spray painted on it. *ALF*

Nov./Dec. - location unspecified - Local grocery store continually has rodent glue traps thrown away and UPC reorder tags for them removed with the result that the store no longer sells them. *ALF*

December 2 - Bloomington and Indianapolis, Indiana - In an apparently coordinated attack, Lazarus Department Stores had windows smashed and were spray painted. *ALF*

December 6 - Madison, Wisconsin - McDonald's was paint bombed. *ALF*

December - Gaithersburg, Maryland - A McDonald's was extensively spray painted with a number of slogans and had its windows smashed out. *ALF*

December - Maryland - Hundreds of dollars worth of fur coats were splattered with fake blood at Best Kept Secrets. *ALF*

December - Maryland - Fur coats spray painted at a used clothing store. *ALF*

December - location unspecified - "Giant" grocery chain has a large number of semi-trucks with meat advertisements on them spray painted with "Meat Kills," "Meat is Murder," etc. *ALF*

December - Berkeley, California - A store had gum stuck in fur trim coats on display and fur trim hats were torn, smeared with red paint, and had slogans written on them. *ALF Golden Gate Unit*

December 16 - Berkeley, California - The Northwest Animal Facility at UC Berkeley was hit with six large Christmas ornaments filled with red paint. *ALF*

December 22 - 23 - Vancouver, British Columbia - After receiving letters saying that turkeys had been injected with rat poison, Safeway and Save-On-Foods chains pulled turkeys from the shelves of all their stores and offered refunds to customers. Tests showed no poison, and the action seems to follow on the often-used British tactic of a contamination hoax. The action caused over one million dollars in damages. *Animal Rights Militia*

December 23 - San Francisco, California - Locks were glued at Robert's Furs and Home Fine Sausage had locks glued and was paint bombed. *ALF Stockton Unit*

December 24 - Memphis, Tennessee - Two windows were smashed at Tandy Leather. *ALF*

December 25 - Oakland, California - Barney's Gourmet Hamburgers: front lock glued. *ALF Golden Gate Unit*

late 1994 or early 1995 - San Francisco, California - Herbert's Furs had "Fur Scum" burnt into their glass front door with acid during their going out of business sale. *ALF*

January 16 - Syracuse, New York - Georgios Furs was paint bombed. *ALF*

Spread Your Love Through Action

An open letter from Rod Coronado

On March 3, 1995, I pled guilty to aiding and abetting a fire at Michigan State University (MSU) that destroyed 32 years of research intended to benefit the fur farm industry. The Animal Liberation Front (ALF) claimed responsibility for the raid, the seventh in a series of actions dubbed "Operation Bite Back" which targeted fur farms and universities engaged in tax-payer supported research jointly funded by the fur trade. I also pled guilty to one count of theft of US Government property; in particular, a journal belonging to a 7th Cavalry Officer killed at the Little Bighorn near Crow Agency, Montana in 1876. This negotiated plea agreement is the result of a seven year investigation by the FBI into my activities, and the federal government's continued targeting of indigenous activists who assert their sovereignty and continue their fight for cultural survival. It is also the culmination of nine federal grand juries that have lasted over three years, subpoenaed over sixty political activists, jailed four for six months each, and harassed and intimidated countless others in the hunt for members of the ALF.

editors' note:
although rod's letter was not a part of the original material for mv8, we thought it was important enough to be included. take the time to read it and be inspired...

In return for the guilty pleas, the US government promises not to seek further prosecution of me in the remaining districts investigating the ALF, nor subpoena me to testify against others suspected of ALF activity. The price I pay for not testifying against my compatriots is a three to four year prison sentence.

Prior to the plea agreement, I was the sole defendant in a seven court indictment alleging that I was responsible for a nationwide coordinated effort to cripple fur farm research and development. With a lifetime commitment to protect the earth behind me and in front of me, I must choose carefully the battles in which I fight, and the arenas in which I fight them. Like most indigenous people, I am unable to match the limitless of the US government in their efforts to incarcerate me, nor am I able to adequately defend myself amidst laws that criminalize the preservation of our sacred earth mother.

This is only the latest attempt by the US Government to make an example of those who break free from the confines of legitimate protest. At a time when ecological and cultural destruction is common place and within the perimeter of the law, it sometimes becomes necessary to adhere to the highest laws of nature and morality rather than stand mute witness to the destruction of our land and people. I believe it to be the obligation of the earth warrior never to be ashamed of one's own actions to honor the sacred tradition of indigenous resistance. Therefore, I accept full responsibility for my actions and remain grateful to have had the honor of serving as a member of the ALF as their spokesperson and supporter.

With a record of over 300 animal liberation actions and rescues in the US without injury or loss of life, yet thousands of lives spared from the horrors of vivisection and fur farming, the women and men of the ALF remain to me some of the most respected of non-violent warriors in the struggle to save our planet. MY role in the MSU raid was a non-participant, acting as a conduit for the truth hidden behind locked laboratory doors. While in Ann Arbor, Michigan, awaiting instructions, I received a phone call from an anonymous ALF member detailing the raid for inclusion into a press release. Later, I received research materials and evidence seized during the raid. These documents would have exposed taxpayer sponsored research benefitting the fur farm industry, and experiments where mink and otters are force-fed toxins and other contaminates until they convulse and bleed to death. Accompanying these documents was a video tape of the cramped and unsanitary conditions mink and otter endure at MSU's research laboratories. My desire to release this information to the public was greater than my desire to protect myself from rabid investigations by the FBI and the ATF. Seventeen months later, I was indicted by the Michigan grand jury based on this evidence.

Earlier in the month of February, 1992 I was at the Little Bighorn River in Montana. I went to the sight of the infamous battle and was shocked at this, the only monument I know of that glorifies the loser. In further disgrace to the warriors who lost their lives defending their families and homelands, the monument paints a one-sided story of the conquest of the indigenous peoples of the Great Plains by the US military. The truth remains that George Armstrong Custer and his 7th Cavalry were an illegal occupational force trespassing in clear violation of the Fort Laramie treaty of 1868 to attack peaceful encampments of noncambatants in the heart of the Lakota Nation. The theft of the Cavalryman's journal is a reminder of indigenous discontent with the treatment of our heritage and culture by the US Government.

Over the last ten years I have placed myself between the hunter and the hunted, the vivisector and the victim, the furrier and the fur bearer, and the whaler and the whale. These are my people, my constituency. It is them that I owe my life. I have chosen to continue the time honored tradition of resistance to the invading forces that are ravaging our homes and people. Many people have been tortured, murdered and imprisoned on this warrior's path, yet we must continue to stand tall against the tyranny that has befallen this continent in the last 503 years. As warriors we must accept that prison awaits those who are unwilling to compromise the earth and her people when we choose to remain allegiant to fellow warriors whose identiy remains unknown. We are all Subcommandante Marcos, Crazy Horse and the ALF. Never, ever, should we forget that in order to achieve the peace and liberation we strive for some sacrifice is necessary. This will not be the first time an indigenous person has gone to prison while upholding the obligation to protect our culture, homelands and people, and it most definitely will not be the last. It is with total love that I say good-bye to my earth mother for a little while to enter the concrete and steel prisons of US Government reserves for its discontent citizens. Such rewards await those who must give their lives and freedom to prevent destruction of the most beautiful planet in the universe, our life-support system our beloved mother earth.

To those who have fought besides me, you will always be my friends and familes and for you I will give up that which I love the most, my freedom. I will face prison rather than speak one word against those on the frontlines of the battle to protect earth. Our relationship is a sacred one, and in your freedom I pray that you spread your love through action that continues to rescue all that remains wild. Never surrender!

Though we may never see each other again in the trenches of the struggle for animal and earth liberation through illegal direct action, in my heart I will always hold you closest. Be patient my friends. I have not forgotten those already behind bars, those in the traps and in the rifle sights of man's ignorance and greed. It is time for me to hand over my role as a "hero" to the animal and environmental movement to others whose faces are not yet known.

To you I give the responsibility to preserve and protect what is left of the splintered nations of others we call animals. In your hands lie the future of this centuries-old struggle, in yourselves you must find heroes. Now you must take the risks rather than cheer on those who have walked before you. Carry her spirit well, and shower yourselves in her beauty when in need of true power. I have been brought back home to my people, the Yaqui Nation and it is to them that I now return to satisfy the restless spirits of my great grandmothers whose cries I must answer.

Sometimes we are forced to do things we do not like when we are warriors. On this land that I now live, where my ancestors are buried, the great warrior Geronimo sometimes found it necessary to surrender to the enemy in order to recruit young warriors for future battles. We are a patient people. Never forget the beauty, magic, love and life we fight so hard to protect and that others have given so much to defend. Our pain and sadness is very real but so is our happiness and joy as we witness the coming Spring. I will always be beside you and you may always find shelter in my home. I love you all, and in you I place the hopes for a rebirth and a rekindling of our sacred relations to all animal people and creation.

Forever in Your Honor and in Her Service,
Rod Coronado-Wiiko Yau Ura
Pascua Yaqui Tribe

Pork, please.
It's an important part of a well-balanced diet.

LEAN PORK

www.ingramcontent.com/pod-product-compliance
Lightning Source LLC
Chambersburg PA
CBHW080550030426
42337CB00024B/4826
* 9 7 8 1 7 3 2 7 0 9 6 7 6 *